Music Lesson Plans for Social Justice

Music Lesson Plans for Social Justice

A Contemporary Approach for Secondary School Teachers

LISA C. DELORENZO AND MARISSA SILVERMAN

OXFORD
UNIVERSITY PRESS

OXFORD
UNIVERSITY PRESS

Oxford University Press is a department of the University of Oxford. It furthers the University's objective of excellence in research, scholarship, and education by publishing worldwide. Oxford is a registered trade mark of Oxford University Press in the UK and certain other countries.

Published in the United States of America by Oxford University Press
198 Madison Avenue, New York, NY 10016, United States of America.

Library of Congress Cataloging-in-Publication Data
Names: DeLorenzo, Lisa C. (Lisa Carey) author. | Silverman, Marissa, author.
Title: Music lesson plans for social justice : a contemporary approach for secondary school teachers / Lisa C. DeLorenzo and Marissa Silverman.
Description: New York, NY : Oxford University Press, 2022. |
Includes bibliographical references and index.
Identifiers: LCCN 2021060878 (print) | LCCN 2021060879 (ebook) |
ISBN 9780197581476 (hardcover) | ISBN 9780197581483 (paperback) |
ISBN 9780197581490 (epub)
Subjects: LCSH: Music—Instruction and study—Outlines, syllabi, etc. |
Social justice—Study and teaching. | Education, Secondary. | LCGFT: Lesson plans.
Classification: LCC MT10 .D387 2022 (print) | LCC MT10 (ebook) | DDC 780.71—dc23
LC record available at https://lccn.loc.gov/2021060878
LC ebook record available at https://lccn.loc.gov/2021060879

DOI: 10.1093/oso/9780197581476.001.0001

1 3 5 7 9 8 6 4 2

Paperback printed by Marquis, Canada
Hardback printed by Bridgeport National Bindery, Inc., United States of America

To Don and Mali
This book is dedicated to my remarkable siblings who have enriched my life
with their acumen, insight, and uncanny sense of humor.
—Lisa

To all my students, past and present.
You have been my greatest teachers.
—Marissa

Contents

Acknowledgments

We have written this book because we care about public school music education: its contexts, contents, peoples, and potentials. However, we could not have succeeded were it not for the support and assistance of a number of people. First and foremost, thank you to the following "tradition bearers"; each one of you supplied knowledge and understandings of musics, cultures, and peoples, without which we could not have responsibly and ethically provided the content that follows: Nani Agbeli, Shelley Axelson, Paul Berliner, Faith Conant, Jennifer Kyker, Robert Levin, David Locke, Thomas McCauley, Moyo Rainos Mutamba, Oscar Perez, and Roshnie Rupnarain.

To the students and Cali School of Music alumni who volunteered to participate and "try out" some lesson plans, we are moved by your energy and enthusiasm: Zach Clements, Pete Diamantis, Megan Falco, Jessica Finkelstein, Konstantina Kioskas, Julia Marra, Daniel Mitchell, Aaron Noriega, Julia Pennello, Kayli Roderick, and Sam Tobias.

To our editor at Oxford University Press, Norm Hirschy, our appreciation for your kindness, generosity, patience, and thoughtful reflections on the content, design, and production of this book. To the copyeditors, especially Ponneelan Moorthy, our thanks for your keen eye and attention to details. And to the anonymous reviewers of our volume—the content of our book is better because of you.

Many of our professors, teachers, and colleagues played key roles in our development as music educators and thinkers in music education. We are grateful to all of you.

Importantly, to the teachers and students who will consider the content of this book: we appreciate you.

1

Introduction

Secondary general music educators often spend a lot of time teaching students how to familiarize themselves with Western genres of music, develop skills in music reading, and learn the rudiments of "popular" or "traditional" instruments. The root of this teaching comes from a perception about the following questions: "What is important to teach?" and "What music is considered valid?" These questions provide the grounding for this book as well. It is understandable, though, that often teachers teach the way they were taught—music institutions tend to emphasize Western classical music and the theoretical structures of music, including standard notation. Consequently, many music teachers believe that these areas of study are integral for general music students.

In this book, however, we strip away such assumptions and begin with the foundation that students learn more fully when they are engaged in music making that has contextual relevance to them. In brief, we posit that music lessons are valuable when they connect with students' lives and experiences in the local or global community. Essentially, we ask: "How does one engage adolescents in active music making that not only advances musical understanding, but also relates directly to the sociopolitical worlds in which students live?" With this in mind, we state unequivocally that all musics, whether from diverse cultures, classical, popular, jazz, and beyond, are valid and deserve prominence in the music curriculum.

What Are the Key Ingredients of Lessons for Social Justice?

We write this book for music teachers who search for meaningful ways to involve students in creating, performing, and listening experiences within a context that challenges students' thinking about fairness, equity, and justice. To do so, we encourage lesson planning and curricular decision-making according to the following points:

1. *Relevance* is key. For this reason, we stress the importance of adjusting and shaping material in this book to fit your students' worlds.
2. *Music of all genres*, especially popular music, establishes a sense of time and place. Social issues always have a "past," while also remaining in the present.
3. *American education is a political enterprise* that involves decisions about curriculum, teaching, and democratic engagement. Likewise, music educators in public

Music Lesson Plans for Social Justice. Lisa C. Delorenzo and Marissa Silverman, Oxford University Press. © Oxford University Press 2022.
DOI: 10.1093/oso/9780197581476.003.0001

schools bear responsibility for teaching music from its social, cultural, and political perspectives.

4. *Active music making*, as reflected in composing, arranging, improvising, listening analysis, and performance, is integral to helping students think critically about the meaning of music within a sociopolitical framework. Lectures, worksheets, and textbooks, however, diminish the joy of music making in the classroom.

Please note: If and when the musical contexts and content explored in these lessons feel somehow beyond reach—for the teacher and students—feel free to "learn" alongside your students. Additionally, invite "tradition bearers" and experts from the locales and places and spaces that make such musics (whether via technology—through video conferencing—or in person). Teaching social justice through music is as much about pointing out and attempting to right inequities as it is about honoring and recognizing the voices of others and one another.

About This Book

This book is written for secondary school general music teachers. Why focus on adolescents? Unfortunately, active classroom music making often ends for students at the elementary school. In fact, many students are shepherded into courses, such as music appreciation or fundamentals of music, when they enter secondary schools. Music instruction, then, shifts from exploration and play at the elementary school level to textbooks, lectures, and worksheets at the secondary level. Imaginative and creative music experiences give way to learning music "literacy" that some music teachers perceive as reading and writing standard notation.

In this book, we hope to help music educators make music class more relevant by designing lessons that revolve around active music making. Relatedly, this book provides the materials and ideas for connecting social justice with music instruction. Neither social justice issues nor music making take precedence over one another, but instead are balanced in such a way as to create significant music experiences while also developing thoughtful citizens who reflect on important issues within a musical context.

Our book is divided into six large units that start with an introduction to the topic and related notes for the teacher. A graphic organizer follows, along with concrete lesson plans, complete with URL references, and other needed materials (see our book's website: https://socialjusticemusics.com). Some graphic organizers contain "essential questions" that guide the teacher and the unit as a whole; some units do not. Also, these units are not presented in any specific order—instead, they can be used intermittently throughout the academic year. Lessons in the "American Protest Movements Unit," for example, have four sections ranging from Introduction to Protest, Rise of the Labor Unions and Woodstock, to the Civil Rights Movement and Black Lives Matter, to School Shootings. Each section includes a cluster of two or three 45–50-minute lessons. Additionally, a unit or a cluster of lessons ends with a culminating project. This provides students with the opportunity to create their own music based on the social justice issues and musical ideas presented in the lessons.

We well understand the challenges that face music teachers today: assessment demands, concert preparation, lack of sufficient instruments, and time constraints. We also know that lesson plans can be prescriptive and include activities that may not fit all students. For this reason, it is vital that teachers adjust or add activities in ways that may work better for specific classroom settings. The lessons are flexible enough to use alternate music listening sources or discussions.

From our communication with undergraduate students who have gone on to professional teaching jobs, lessons that focus on teaching social justice through music have been highly successful. Secondary school students are much more interested in the world around them than we sometimes give credit. In middle school and into high school, adolescents begin to question their identity and place in the world. Consequently, lessons that promote a social justice perspective often speak directly to the heart of what students want to know. It is our hope that these units serve as a model for creating your own units about social justice issues for students, regardless of the school's context and teaching-learning settings. In fact, the epilogue at the end of this book provides information and tips for creating your own socially just music lessons.

What Do We Mean by "Social Justice"?

Social justice is a form of active engagement and thoughtful inquiry about inequities in the world. In essence, social justice serves to uncover injustices, imbalances, and untruths in order to support and promote a more equitable social order. Several of the following questions serve as guidelines for understanding the nature of social justice and engaging with social justice through musical action:

- What are issues and concerns that marginalized peoples speak of with excitement, anger, fear, or hope?
- How might I enter a dialogue so I will learn from specific communities about issues and concerns they face?
- What experiences do people possess that potentially yield solutions for their own issues and concerns?
- What is missing from the "official story" that will make the issues and concerns of the oppressed more understandable?
- What current or proposed policies serve the privileged and the powerful, and how are they made to appear inevitable?
- How can the public space for discussion, problem posing, and problem solving be examined?[1]

For the past 25 years, discussions of social justice, as both a concept and a practice, have blossomed across the domains of music, music education, and community music (e.g., Woodstock, "We Are the World," or Civil Rights and Apartheid protest songs). Despite this, we still do not have a consensus on what we mean when we say "social justice." Why? For one thing, social justice is an extraordinarily complex concept given that "social" and "justice" have no universally agreed-upon definitions. Putting these two individual concepts together does not make things any easier. In fact, it complicates matters. So, if we want to conceptualize, understand, and then actualize social justice, we need to think in multidimensional terms. For example, one crucial dimension of social justice that is frequently overlooked in the practice of music education is *love* or *peace*.

Author bell hooks argues that there can be no social justice without love, and no love without justice.[2] Brazilian educator and activist Paulo Freire[3] also saw love as a vital force in the fight for social justice.[3] Like hooks, Freire asks us to take notice of those around us, for "no matter where the oppressed are found, the act of love is commitment to their cause—the cause of liberation."[4] And hooks explains: "Until we live in a culture that not only respects but also upholds basic civil rights for children, most children will not know love."[5] As Martin Luther King, Jr., confirms: "Love that does not satisfy justice is no love at all."[6]

When we use the concept of "social justice" throughout this book, we do so willingly, knowing the difficulties inherent in enacting social change. Foundationally, it is important to acknowledge that, in order to consider affecting social change for equity and justice, we must, on some level, engage in acts of love for ourselves and those around us. Additionally, without encouraging students' questioning of their worlds and guiding students to think through the potentials and pitfalls for social change through music, we cannot, in good conscience, say we are music educators educating the needs of the students we serve.

Why Music Teachers Avoid Provocative Issues

Music teachers are often skeptical about teaching that involves a focus on social issues. One big fear is backlash from administration or parents who often have very firm ideas about what a music class should look like and ultimately "be." Moreover, many feel that sociopolitical discussions do not belong in the schools, especially in music classrooms. Some parents contend that "teachers have no right to teach my child beliefs that I do not espouse. Schools are neutral places that should stick to teaching content, not stirring up the kids to revolt."

Part of the problem is the term "political," which some connect directly to governmental structure (e.g., political parties, government officials, voting). Given this narrow definition, parents and administrators worry that teachers will impose their beliefs and ideologies on students without considering family-held beliefs and political positions. We do not support this kind of teaching, but at the same time, we believe that teachers cannot remain completely neutral. On one hand, the role of the teacher is to challenge students with different points of view. On the other hand, teachers cannot prepare students for a democratic society without bringing social dilemmas to the table. Consequently, issues with a sociopolitical dimension can range anywhere from advocating for safe drinking water, to one's identity in the community, to factors that advantage some people over others.

What Does This Have to Do with *Music* Teaching?

It all depends on how teachers define music education. If one believes that performance is the ultimate goal of music education, then chances are the curriculum will lean heavily on reading standard notation, acquiring the technical skills for playing instruments or singing, and using repertoire-based/textbook-based music material. If one believes that Western classical music is "real" music while, say, popular musics such as rap and rock are interesting diversions but not worthy of "serious" examination, then chances are that classical music will dominate music instruction, along with the tacit message that some musics are more valid than others. And so on and so on.

All musics and the various methodologies to teach them have something to offer, and we are not suggesting that social justice issues supplant the skills needed to advance musical understanding. On the contrary, critical listening, performing, and composing, all of which require music knowledge and skills, allow students to more accurately express their musical ideas. Take, for example, writing a protest song. Such an activity involves an understanding of song form, singing/instrumental skills to share the music with others, a knowledge base of other protest songs, a sense of stylistic differences between a protest song and other types of songs, the ability to write lyrics that support the rhythmic structure of a song, and a historical framework. In fact, throughout a lesson based on social justice, *music* should remain the primary vehicle for responding. Although discussions are critical for teasing out different points of view and establishing a culture/historical framework, they are not an end in themselves, but rather an avenue for cultivating meanings in music.

Dimensions of an Active Music Class

Individual and group compositions play an essential role in the lessons throughout this book (see Appendix A). Because issues of social justice challenge students to think about themselves in relationship to the school, local community, or worldwide community, much of the critical thinking should come from the students themselves. Likewise, much of the critical thinking in music is reflected through student compositions. We espouse the philosophy of constructivism—that is, the most meaningful learning comes from that which students construct themselves, based on questions and prompts from the teacher or other students. When composition/improvisation activities involve creating, performing, and reflecting, then these activities also involve some of the highest levels of thinking-and-doing in music.

Other forms of active music making involve analyzing recorded selections from a piece that relate to the lesson, as well as creating soundscapes through vocal, percussion, melodic, or digital formats, singing, music technology, arranging, or movement choreography. Music listening is prominent throughout the book, where students listen for the purpose of research (e.g., creating a playlist), analysis (e.g., comparing the mood of two songs), and making comparisons with music from different cultures or genres (e.g., African rhythms indigenous to jazz).

Active music making *needs* to be present in every lesson. Most important, active music making should form the basis of a culminating project, whether composing a song or formatting an original piece using *GarageBand*. Interestingly, the wide expanse of music literature includes many examples of music composed in response to social issues. From Beethoven's *Eroica Symphony* to Bob Marley's "One Love," much of music literature was inspired by issues of social justice. The arts have always been a driving force in expressing truths beyond words.

Wonderful possibilities abound across secondary school general music classrooms when instruments like guitars, ukuleles, electronic keyboards, and drums from around the globe are available. These instruments generally appeal to teenagers and allow teachers to involve students in music making with adolescent-friendly musical instruments. The inclusion of technology provides other important tools for adolescents whose, say, level of musical thinking is higher than their skills on other instruments.

Although these instruments have the potential for increasing—among other dispositions and skills—music skill development in an age-appropriate setting, much of today's current practices with these instruments emphasizes music reading, performing pre-composed songs, and instrumental/vocal technique. Improvisation and composition usually take a back seat to such skill-based lessons. Yet, students can actually improvise the first day they get their instruments. Subsequently, learning chords and melodies not only advances musical understanding, but gives students more tools to use in composing their own music.

Critical Discussions and Reflection in the Classroom

Adolescents are sometimes reticent to express their thoughts, beliefs, and opinions, partly because of the following: (a) peer pressure can quickly shut down a conversation; (b) students may not be used to free-flowing discussions in their other classes; (c) English may be a second language; and (d) music teachers have not been trained to facilitate student-centered discussion. Discussions that go beyond one-word answers, however, are essential for developing the critical thinking skills necessary for connecting music to social justice (see Appendix B). Discussions and reflection need not last more than 5–10 minutes, but should *not* be viewed as poor music teaching if students are highly involved in talking about the issue at hand.

What is the role of the teacher? Teachers provide the prompts for encouraging students to speak honestly and in "full sentences." To do this, teachers should plan beforehand the kinds of questions that will stimulate response. A "Do Now" activity is a good way to have students work out their thoughts through writing before sharing in a large-group conversation. Other ideas involve "pair-share" strategies where students first talk about their ideas with a partner and then share with the class. For another starter idea, the teacher could, without any pre-explanation, play an instrument relevant to the lesson and use this as a basis for asking a critical thinking question such as: "Where might you find this instrument?"; "Can you think of another instrument that works like this one?"; or "What type of environment would produce the materials needed to construct this instrument?" Along with this, a teacher can bring in visual artworks or objects that provoke discussions related to the social justice issue. For an ecology unit, bring in a clear flask of water and ask: "What does this have to do with issues in ecology? How could music play a role in sensitizing people about water pollution?"

Questions that begin with "Why, How, Imagine, What, Where, Compare, Contrast, and Which," are good places to start. And students should do *most* of the talking. Teachers who over-explain or express their own views imply that they have a "right answer" in mind and that students should try to figure out what the teacher wants to hear, instead of creating spaces where students do their own thinking. As mentioned earlier, discussions need not last a long time; still, the teacher's role is to prompt rather than over-explain. The ultimate goal is a "ping-pong" effect. This means that students become so engaged, they take ownership of the discussion themselves, asking questions to the class, responding productively to another student's response, or back-and-forth conversation among the students. Here the teacher takes a back seat, interceding only when clarification is necessary or to offer a question that helps students think about another point of view.

Dynamic discussions will take time and trust to cultivate. Teachers need to create a safe learning environment by teaching students how to respond without criticizing someone else, dominating the conversation, or interrupting a student. These are not automatic behaviors. It is as much a skill to listen actively as it is to monitor oneself to avoid constant talking. Sometimes, building a community of learning takes a month or more; this is worth the effort. Clearly, these behaviors require conscientious teaching and modeling if students are going to trust the process.

How Do I Meet the Core Music Standards and Assessment Requirements?

Core music standards and assessment practices and procedures differ from state to state and school district to school district. Because of this, we cannot speak to individual teacher/curricular needs and assessment demands in a meaningful way. However, we do refer to the *National Core Standards for Music Education* in each lesson.

According to the National Association for Music Education (or NAfME), the standards—which are not enforced, and, therefore, should be seen as guidelines— are as general as they are all-encompassing. Namely, if music teachers are teaching music well through active engagement in, with, and through music—the students will meet the standards, regardless of whether teachers aim to do so explicitly.

For example, the *National Core Standards for Music Education* (National Standards, for short) suggest that teachers should design activities in which students "create, perform, and respond" to music in developmentally appropriate ways. Notably, each of the unit plans, activities, and questions/prompts explored throughout this book invite music students to actively engage within these domains of music. These include performing, composing, improvising, arranging, leading/ conducting, dancing, and active listening. Thus, students' engagement with music is aligned with the standards both implicitly and explicitly. However, because teachers typically must show that they are, in fact, teaching toward "standards," we include the National Standards for middle school (which can be adapted for high school) that are appropriately aligned with each plan for all classroom activities. Please note: When reading these lesson plans, you may find additional standards to be more "in line" with the ways you adapt and reshape activities and musical engagement. Feel free to choose different standards. You will know what will work best given the specific contexts and circumstances of your teaching.

Regarding assessment practices, these, too, differ from state to state and district to district. Some schools require that students take and pass "standardized tests" in music, whether in general music, instrumental music, or music technology classes. Other schools do not. Because of this, the assessment demands placed upon teachers may need to be weighed alongside the teaching and learning episodes proposed in this book, despite our belief that standardized tests in music are neither "standard- ized" nor actual "tests" of legitimate knowledge and deep understanding of music. Nor can such tests ever truly evaluate whether students embody and understand the values of musical engagement for social justice.

Still, please note that we believe assessment and evaluation are not identical terms, and do not reflect the same practice. Accordingly, assessment in music teaching and learning aims to give formative and summative assistance to students for developing musical understanding over time (see Appendix C). Such assessment practices can be seen as giving moment-to-moment feedback, offering students the chance for self-reflection upon their musical experiences, and culminating projects or port- folios that demonstrate the knowledge base that they have acquired throughout any given unit of study. Evaluation, on the other hand, is a "value"—or typically a "grade"—placed upon student work as stipulated by a rubric, set of criteria met, and so forth. Examining the nature and value of assessment processes and procedures, as well as the benefits of evaluative measurements, is beyond the scope of this book.

Still, it is imperative that teachers decide—with the help of their students—how best to assist students' developing musical understanding over time as it aligns with the larger aim of this book: teaching music for social justice and teaching social justice through music.

How to Use This Book

This book serves as a guide for developing lessons that facilitate conversation and music making about social justice. No one, however, knows your students better than you. For this reason, we have tried to ensure that every part of the book is flexible and adaptable rather than a prescriptive, one-size-fits-all unit plan. The following list describes ideas for how music teachers can adapt materials to meet the needs of their students:

- The topics themselves (e.g., war, peace, heroes, and heroisms) are starter ideas. Relevance is key. For example, if the local community is grappling with a particular issue of justice and fairness, music teachers might use this book as a reference (see Epilogue) for developing a unit of lessons that have more urgency and immediacy to the students.
- Each of the lessons incorporates listening examples and music making suggestions. We encourage teachers to substitute music for listening if another piece seems more appropriate for students.
- Music making activities can be redirected from individual work to group work or from large group to small groups.
- Music making activities can be adjusted depending upon the instruments and musical resources that teachers have on hand.
- Culminating projects offer a variety of projects which all meet the same goal. The music teacher might decide to have all students work on the same project, or might give students the choice to select a particular project that plays to their strengths.

Website

To assist your work while utilizing this book with your music classrooms, we've created a companion website. Visit https://socialjusticemusics.com.
   This website provides:

- A blog;
- Individual webpages connected to each unit of study;
- Links, videos, photographs, and audio recordings to utilize in teaching the content of all lesson plans;
- Supplementary readings and links to relevant websites;

- Biographies, photos, and other related media;
- Related literature and resources about social justice and music, as well as related literature and resources showcasing connections between music and social justice.

Because online materials are often "in flux" and somewhat transitory, we will be monitoring the websites and YouTube links included in our book's lesson plans and units. So, if and when a YouTube video is removed, we will provide a replacement on the associated webpage on our site. Because of this, if you enter a URL in your browser and it isn't functioning, visit our website to find, say, an alternative video or audio file.

Elevating Student Work for Social Justice

The many units and lessons in this book have overlapping ideas. For example, themes from the protest unit (e.g., Black Lives Matter) could just as easily fit into the unit on "Heroes and Heroines" or "Love." The units, in effect, are fluid, with porous boundaries. Elevating student work to a social justice level, however, means taking the message to others in the school or surrounding community. In other words, social justice depends on some degree of public awareness.

Teaching music for social justice need not involve all the "bells and whistles" of social activism. One can teach "themes" of social justice for the purpose of sensitizing students to social inequities that have an impact on their lives or the lives of others. On the other hand, teaching for social justice *does* suggest public action. This can be as straightforward as sharing student work with another class or as involved as presenting student work to the community through a fund-raising campaign or concert. In other words, music teachers might choose to teach themes of social justice that remain situated in the class itself, or to teach *for* social justice by helping others become aware of social issues through student-centered musical work.

Making students' work public can take many forms, including short presentations for school staff (e.g., janitorial staff, cafeteria personnel); performing for the school board with an educational narrative about why and how students developed their presentation; podcasts; fund-raising efforts that create opportunities that hope to help rectify inequities; music making at supermarkets, nursing homes, and beyond. Clearly, some of these ideas take place before or after the school day and may involve transportation. Not all schools will support such activities given the cost or policies related to out-of-school experiences. Hopefully, though, there will be enough creative ways to present work through the school system to honor the students' voices and to demonstrate their involvement with social justice issues.

An Invitation

Art plays a dominant role in bringing about change for the public good. As well, youth have historically taken the initiative to propel public awareness and action. It is not too early, then, to help secondary students recognize their right in promoting a just world through the power of music. We hope, with this book, that music teachers will rise to the challenge of incorporating social issues in their music curriculum to advance critical social commentary and growth in musicianship.

Appendix A

Facilitating Critical/Creative Thinking

There are essentially two main ways to facilitate critical thinking in the classroom. The first is through inquiry-based discussions, and the second is through the types of assignments that we give. Inquiry-based discussions are particularly challenging in large classes. One can ask excellent questions but not get a response, or the same few students may participate, rather than a more representative group of the class. Without sustained discussion, however, the teacher has little evidence for assessing the students' critical thinking.

Getting Students to Talk in Upper Grade Levels

Here are a few strategies that have helped us with large groups:

- Start with a challenging prompt and ask students to discuss their responses in pairs before opening up the discussion to the large group. This gives the student psychological safety in "testing" his/her/their idea before speaking in a large group.
- Ask students to write a response before opening up the discussion to the large group.
- Have students write an "exit" question on a small index card. The question should require some analytical thinking on the part of the student. Collect the question cards as students leave and select a few cards as a framework for a next class discussion.
- Set up a forced comparison scenario. For instance, "Which of these two recordings would you purchase?" or "Can you think of some music that is the opposite of this piece?"
- Set up a hypothesis scenario. For instance, "Given the background of this piece, what would you expect to hear?" "If you were the composer, what would be the overall mood of the piece and how would you achieve that musically?"

- Create a perplexing situation. For example, several movements of Shostakovich's Symphony #10 employ his name as a musical code (DSCH). Have students figure out the code by giving them clues about the origin of the code. "Why would Shostakovich use codes in his music?" "How does this practice reflect the life and times of Shostakovich?"

None of these strategies in and of itself is indicative of critical thinking without a lot of "rebound questions" and follow-through. The intent is to prod students into thinking about why and how things occur in music, rather than memorizing facts about the composers or the pieces.

Creating Thoughtful Assignments/Projects

Readings, writing prompts, or projects that require the student to analyze, synthesize, and evaluate information are most likely to promote critical thinking. In the process of creating an assignment or project, ask yourself the following questions:

- Am I asking my students to make reasoned, criteria-based judgments about music?
- Will this assignment raise my students' levels of musical thinking?
- For creative projects: Who is engaged in the higher levels of thinking—the student or the teacher?
- For creative projects: Does the task present a challenge for students of different abilities?

Appendix B

How to Manage a Small Group Composition Project

There are many theories and published articles/books that address the creative process. A detailed overview, however, is beyond the scope of this book. For that reason, this appendix provides information that may be most expedient for the classroom music teacher. In general, the creating process involves two large parts. The first part is characterized by a lot of musical exploration. Students need to find sound materials that best fit their ideas, as well as opportunities to experiment with motivic sound bytes (much like licks in jazz improvisation or "a hook" in a pop song) that form a musical palette for the basis of their piece.

The second part has to do with students selecting and discarding musical ideas in the process of creating as a piece begins to take shape. If students are truly invested in their composition, you will see an increase of intensity as they evaluate the structure, performance skills, and overall intent of the piece. You will notice some debating about how to perform the piece and moments of excitement as the piece takes shape.

Your role is to, first, stand back for a period of time so students have space to get organized. Then visit with different groups, listen to the piece, and offer one or two challenges that the students could think about, such as: "How might a change in dynamics add something special to your music?" or "This part seems really important but I am having trouble hearing it. Can you make some adjustments?" Leave them with these questions rather than telling them what to do. They will work it out on their own.

Expect this exploration to be noisy and seemingly chaotic to someone walking into the classroom who is unaware of the task goals. Despite the sound fall-out, you can always maintain some decorum by establishing a "stop and all eyes on the teacher" signal, as well as habits for working respectfully with instruments and other students. Although there is freedom to create, this freedom does not extend to behavior that intrudes upon other working individuals/groups. Make sure that everyone understands the guidelines before sending them to their work stations.

Often music teachers have deep concerns about "losing control" when students or small groups are working independently rather than as a whole class. Actually, in small groups, you have a wonderful opportunity to become more engaged with your students. This comes from the freedom you have to visit different groups and compliment or issue warnings if needed. Practice the "stop and all eyes on the teacher" signal until you are satisfied that students are responsive to this important classroom habit. In the event that a group of students can't seem to get along, let alone get started, you will need to sit with them and guide them more than you might with other students. Individuals who dominate the group process to the extent that others have no say in the piece need your assistance as well.

Appendix C

Assessing Creative Work

Assessing creative work is a little different from other kinds of performance measures; however, there are a number of tools that you can use to meet the guidelines of your state or school while also giving you an accurate picture of the students' progress. In addition to the sample rubric provided, you might include writing samples of listening logs, tasks that encourage students to write about the decisions they made in the creating process, self-assessments, drafts of iconic notation, and online responses to related prompts such as "How did your piece change from when you first started to the finished composition?" With the advent of school-owned computers for students, or access to online resources, it is much easier to have students maintain an online portfolio for your review.

Sample Rubric for Group or Individual Creating Projects

	Below Standard	Meets Standard	Exceeds Standard
Exploring musical ideas	Student shows little exploration of ideas before developing the final piece.	Student explores some ideas before developing the final piece	Student explores various ideas in depth before developing the final piece.
Creating process	Student makes few or no revisions in creating the piece.	Student makes some revisions in creating the piece.	Student revises continually throughout the process. Shows constant evaluation.
Final product	Student's work lacks coherence and/or is not relevant to the task.	Student's work shows an integration of ideas throughout the piece with a clear beginning, middle, and end.	Student's work meets the intentions of the task and also shows a high level of originality.
Evaluation	Student is unable to explain his/her /their decision-making in creating the piece or to evaluate the piece as a whole.	Student shows reflection in describing decision-making or in evaluating the piece as a whole.	Student shows a high level of insight when describing decision-making or evaluating the piece as a whole.

• This rubric is a generic template and is not meant to be used without adaptations to the specific assessment needs of the teacher.

Notes

1. Ayers, William. [Adapted from] "Trudge Toward Freedom: Educational Research in the Public Interest." In *Education Research in the Public Interest: Social Justice, Action, and Policy*, edited by Gloria Ladson-Billings and William F. Tate, 81–97. New York: Teachers College Press, 2006. 89.
2. hooks, bell. *All about Love: New Visions*. New York: William Morrow, 2000.
3. Freire, Paulo. *Pedagogy of the Oppressed*. New York: Continuum, 1990.
4. Freire, *Pedagogy of The Oppressed*, 81.
5. hooks, *All about Love*, 19–20.
6. King, Martin Luther. *Where Do We Go from Here?: Chaos or Community?* Boston: Beacon Press, 1968.

2

American Protest Unit

Introduction to the *American Protest* Unit

Protest movements are vehicles that allow people to publicly voice concern in an effort to influence political decisions about social participation in wars, governance structures, social inequities, and other issues of social justice. In this sense, protest movements are not "social justice" itself, but, rather, action taken to organize people around an issue of social justice. Peaceful protest movements are characterized, for example, by marches, sit-ins, posters, rallies and demonstrations, and music, rather than assault weapons. Nearly every protest movement involves music of some kind, ranging from percussion accompaniments for street chants to songs that create a sense of solidarity or reflective commentary. Music of the 1960s was particularly prolific in the rise of folk artists and songs that responded to the sociopolitical events at the time.

Although this unit addresses American protest movements, it is important to understand that protest movements were (and are) a global event. For instance, during the time of Civil Rights and the Vietnam War, protest movements were also taking place in China (Cultural Revolution) as well as student uprisings in Europe, Africa, South America, the Eastern Bloc, and Asia. This international cross-current of political protest not only influenced the music in other countries, but also gave rise to festivals—the Humanity Festival in Paris, and the Festival of Committed Song in Chile, and Woodstock—where singer/songwriters gathered to exchange ideas and affirm social and political values.

Youth were, and are, central to protest movements. In fact, student uprisings often provide the impetus for political change. Consider, for example, the student-led protest against the 2018 shooting deaths at Marjory Stoneman Douglas School in Parkland, Florida. Or, the outpouring of anti-war and songs for peace at Woodstock in 1969. Music played a powerful role in unifying youth and expressing raw emotion about current social issues.

Because youth play a key role in propelling protest movements, a unit on American protests hold special relevance for students today. This unit strives to not only advance critical thinking skills, but also model ways in which students can take productive action for social change through music. The series of lessons presented here provides music teachers with a historical timeline rooted in social causes and music development from a historical, evolutionary, performance, and stylistic standpoint. However, even as we write today, there are many more protest movements that merit consideration. The scenario is similar, yet the issues are constantly changing.

Music Lesson Plans for Social Justice. Lisa C. Delorenzo and Marissa Silverman, Oxford University Press. © Oxford University Press 2022.
DOI: 10.1093/oso/9780197581476.003.0002

In terms of this unit, some lessons can stand alone, but we suggest that "From the Rise of Labor Unions to Woodstock" provides historical context and musical grounding for the lessons that follow. It is important that teachers adjust and modify lessons to meet the specific needs and interests of their students. As always, the key to success is facilitating active music making and reflective discussion.

Graphic Organizer: American Protest

AMERICAN PROTEST

School Shootings

LISTENING & MEDIA
- "Shine"
- March for Our Lives
- "Bridge over Troubled Waters"
- "Rise"
- "Imagine"
- "Don't Worry Be Happy"
- "We Are the World"
- "Glory"
- "Columbine, Friend of Mine"
- "Air on the G String"
- "Canon in D Major"
- "Sheep May Safely Graze"

CONTEXT
- Marjorie Stoneman Douglas High School
- Columbine High School
- Sandy Hook Elementary School
- Youth as activists
- Safety at School
- March for Our Lives
- Power of Internet for social change

MUSIC LEARNING
- Analysis of song form.
- Determining the mood of a song through analysis of the musical elements and song lyrics.
- Choosing a song, among several, that is most appropriate as background for a set of poems.

MUSIC LEARNING
- Analysis of song lyrics to enhancing the music and the message of the song.
- Sing "Lift Every Voice and Sing" to describe what musical elements create an expression of hope and joy.

FINAL PROJECTS
- Compose a protest song.
- Create a Freedom Rap.
- Write a poem and set it to music.

From the Rise of Labor Unions to Woodstock

CONTEXT
- Labor Unions
- Safety at work
- Fair wages
- Women in workplace
- Child labor
- Triangle Shirtwaist Fire
- Woodstock Festival
- Peaceful protest
- Civil Rights and Vietnam War

LISTENING & MEDIA
- "Solidarity Forever"
- "Union Maid"
- The Labor Movement in the United States
- "Sometimes I Feel like a Motherless Child"
- Woodstock Documentary
- "Somebody to Love"
- "Freedom"
- "Star Spangled Banner"
- "The Bigger Picture"

MUSIC LEARNING
- Analysis of song form.
- Listening comparison of several songs for form, expression, and other musical devices.
- Role of lyrics in song writing.

VOCABULARY
Labor Unions

Ammendment 1 from *Bill of Rights*

Hippie

Psychedelic Music

Anarchy

Racism

Art as Advocacy

Rally

Social Justice

Peaceful Protest

Song Form

Social Change Through Art

Civil Rights & Black Lives Matter

LISTENING & MEDIA
- "Lift Every Voice and Sing"
- "Better Shop Around"
- "Dancing in the Streets"
- "Rockin' Robin"
- "Yesterme, Yesteryou, Yesterday"
- "Alabama"

CONTEXT
- Martin Luther King
- March on Washington
- Civil Right Act
- Voting Rights
- Fair Housing
- BLM Organization
- March on Washington
- Racism and the early recording industry
- Motown

Introductory Lesson to American Protest

Goal
To introduce protest as an activity which alerts the public to an issue of social justice. This is important because "protest" itself is not an *issue* of social justice but rather a *movement* toward advancing a socially just nation.

National Standards
- MU:Re7.6a: Select or choose music to listen to and explain the connections to specific interest or experiences for a specific purpose.
- MU:Cn10.0.6a: Demonstrate how interests, knowledge, and skills relate to personal choices and intent when creating, performing, and responding to music.

Assessment
- **Formative:** The teacher will assess students' thinking about protest as a form of action by their responses to questions about contemporary social issues. In addition, the teacher will assess students' ability to select a song that calls for protest, whether a rally, march, or peaceful reflective gathering.

YouTube Videos
- Protestors March Nationwide Against Trump Immigration Policies: https://www.youtube.com/watch?v=gkShUw2w0R0
- "Masters of War" (1962–1963): https://www.youtube.com/watch?v=h2mabTnMHe8

Other Materials
- Phones or devices that support internet
- Index cards

Teaching Process

Instruction	Comments/Suggestions
When groups of people experience discrimination or inequitable treatment, the problem becomes a social justice issue. For instance, in some schools, students have computers, music ensembles like band or chorus, hot lunches, and up-to-date textbooks. Other schools, often in the same town, do not provide these resources for students. *Do all students have a right to a quality education?* This is one example of an issue of social justice. *One way that people bring social justice issues to attention is by protesting. There have been many protest movements in this country's history. Some have led to changes in safety in the workplace, civil rights, wars, and laws that protect marginalized peoples, e.g., LGBTQ. Can you think of any social issues today that might lead to a peaceful protest activity? Have you ever participated in a protest demonstration? What was it like?* Show a video example of a contemporary demonstration: "Protestors March Nationwide."	Setting the context for why protest movements take place. "Social justice" is an important term for students to know. Sometimes it helps to break it down into two words—social and justice. When students understand the meaning of social and justice, they are more likely to use the term "social justice" appropriately.

Instruction	Comments/Suggestions
Discussion Questions: • *What did you notice in this video? Who participated?* • *What role did music play in this particular demonstration? Can you identify any other ways that music might be included to protest a social issue?* • *Identify some other forms of protest (e.g., letters to political figures, marches, sit-ins, walk-outs, petitions, songs).* • *What is the difference between a peaceful protest and anarchy?*	Music examples: Songs at a peaceful rally, concerts to raise funds for a cause, individual compositions, songs for marching. Anarchy is a state of disorder created when the people do not adhere to political authority. Some terms include lawlessness, revolution, rebellion, etc.
Decide whether this song would be appropriate for a march/rally or reflective thought about the social justice issue: "Masters of War" by Bob Dylan *How many leaders did you recognize?*	Dylan was angry when he wrote this song, although he said it was not an anti-war song. His rage was directed at the leaders who sustained wars in, e.g., Cuba and Vietnam. He said, "It is supposed to be a pacifist song about war."
Pair–Share Activity: Using a mobile device, find one or more songs that protest organizers could use as a means to energize or reflect on a protest movement.	These might be contemporary songs or songs from another era. Google is a helpful resource.
Listening Activity • Have some students share their song with the class. • Identify the issue of protest. • Compare the songs and discuss how the music sets the mood for the lyrics.	This is an opportunity to talk about how the music conveys a certain mood. Does it inspire citizens to march and rally, or think and contemplate?
Exit Ticket: On an index card, write down one or two issues that are important in your life which might lend themselves to a demonstration or some other form of peaceful intervention.	Collect cards as students leave the room and use this information as a springboard for subsequent lessons.

From Labor Unions to Woodstock

Introduction

The rise of the labor union in the 1920s is a classic protest movement involving grievances about inhumane working conditions, which included the practice of employing children in the workforce. Woodstock, 1969, on the other hand, was quite the opposite in terms of activism. Sandwiched in between the Civil Rights movement and the Vietnam War, Woodstock did not involve marches against social inequities, but, rather, called for love and peace in a three-day marathon of rock and folk music. If anything, the protest element of Woodstock was a call for justice and unity through songs that served as reflective commentaries on the social events surrounding the concert.

This contrast between the call for worker's rights and a concert for love and peace becomes a teachable moment for examining different forms of activism. Whereas the rise of the labor union involved marches, songs of solidarity, protest signs, rallies, etc., Woodstock was a single event on a farm in New York State, with the intention of building community through musical messages of peace. The rise of the labor union was a protest movement that began in the late 1800s, with its peak in the 1920s. Woodstock was not a movement but an empowering event that represented the voice of youth for a better world.

It seems fitting, in this unit, to demonstrate that protest activity can take many forms. It is also important to recognize the vital role that music plays in galvanizing the public. One can look at the songs of both eras as living gems of history that continue to inspire generations to come.

Labor Unions and Woodstock: What We Take for Granted

Lesson 1

Goal
To describe working conditions in the early part of the 1900s and the void of labor unions to protect workers as the impetus for action and music.

National Standards
- MU:Re8.1.7a: Describe a personal interpretation of contrasting works and explain how creators' and performers' application of the elements of music and expressive qualities, within genres, cultures, and historical periods, conveys expressive intent.

- MU:Pr4.2.7c: Identify how cultural and historical contexts inform performance and results in different music interpretations.

Assessment

- **Formative:** Teacher will assess students' ability to describe the working conditions that have changed as a result of labor unions. In addition, the teacher will assess students' ability to analyze two union songs for the meaning of the lyrics, the form, and their role in a protest rally.

YouTube Videos

- The Labor Movement in the United States: https://www.youtube.com/watch?v=ewu-v36szlE&t=22s
- "Union Maid": https://www.youtube.com/watch?v=Rs5_gB582IM
- "Solidarity Forever": https://www.youtube.com/watch?v=Ly5ZKjjxMNM

Other Materials

- Lyric sheets for "Union Maid" and "Solidarity Forever (Appendix A and Appendix B)
- Percussion instruments: drums, tambourines, guiro

Teaching Process

Instruction	Comments/Suggestions
Start with a story about the Triangle Shirtwaist fire: *On a Saturday in 1911, there was a horrific fire in New York City. A fire broke out in the Triangle Shirtwaist Company that was located on the top three floors of a 10-story building. The fire spread fast because of the waste containers from the day's work. Although the workers from the eighth and tenth floors were able to escape, the ninth-floor workers (mostly women) tried to get out of the doors that were illegally locked. Many of the doors were blocked with machinery and there was only one elevator in the building. When the fire became too intense many women jumped out of the buildings, killing themselves instantly. Over a hundred people died in the fire.*	It is more effective when the teacher tells this as a story, rather than reading from a script or having the students read it silently.

Instruction	Comments/Suggestions
This fire changed the course of labor laws and reforms in working conditions, including worker's safety and health. *Can you identify some of the problems that made this fire so deadly?* List on the board. *What safety measures do we now have in place to keep people safe not only in factories but also places where people congregate like malls or movie theaters?*	Some answers might include well-marked exits, sprinkler systems, upgraded fire equipment, etc.
Context of work conditions: Women worked in hot, stuffy rooms but could not open the windows. They lived in boarding houses. They worked 12-hour days and earned about $15 a month—enough to pay room and board. Children were often working in the factory for long hours during the day. The machines were dangerous and workers often lost fingers or limbs. Men worked under similar conditions. There were no labor unions to protect the workers. *What is a labor union?* **Video:** "The Labor Movement in the United States." *What did you learn that you didn't know before?*	
Labor unions had a tough fight and workers often had to hold rallies to get their message heard. In the last class we saw a video about chants and songs in protest marches. Create a chant that might be heard at a rally for worker's rights in the early 1900s. As a class, repeat the following chant: "Safety first, or we can't work." In groups of 5, choose a topic from the list on the board (see step #2) and create a short, rhythmic chant. Each group is given one or two instruments to add to the chant. Each group share their chant. Then conduct a mock rally by bringing in each group until all are responding. It should sound chaotic, like a rally.	Practice the chant with an angry voice. You can use crescendo and decrescendo gestures or cut some groups out, then bring them in again, to create a musical sound piece.

Instruction	Comments/Suggestions
Analyzing Union Songs Pass out lyrics for "Union Maid" (**Appendix A**) to half the class and "Solidarity Forever" (**Appendix B**) to the other half. Analyze the text for its meaning and identify the messages. *What would you expect the music to sound like?* **Video:** "Union Maid" **Video:** "Solidarity Forever," unofficial anthem of the labor movement *What do these protest songs have in common? What function does music play in these political events? Do protest songs have to be loud and assertive?*	Sing along with the chorus of "Union Maid" or/and "Solidarity Forever." Try to sing without looking at the lyrics. Catchy, short chorus: repeating text: easy to sing on first listening: AB form.
Exit Ticket: *What other forms of political nonviolent action can people take to raise consciousness?* e.g., picket, letter-writing campaigns, meetings with people in power, petitions, fund-raising music events, composing songs for the movement.	

Labor Unions and Woodstock: Woodstock—Never Forgotten

Lesson 2

Goal
To consider that protest movements can take many forms and often include music as an important part of the event.

National Standards
- MU:Re7.2.6a: Describe how the elements of music and expressive qualities relate to the structure of the pieces.
- MU:Pr4.2.7c: Identify how cultural and historical contexts inform performance and results in different music interpretations.

Assessment
- **Formative:** The teacher will assess the students' music listening acuity through their verbal responses in comparing and contrasting different styles of protest

songs. In addition, the teacher will assess the students' understanding about the importance of context in songs through listening and discussing headliner performances at Woodstock.

YouTube Videos
- Woodstock Documentary: https://www.youtube.com/watch?v=czFr_kJCdKQ
- "Somebody to Love" (Jefferson Airplane): https://www.youtube.com/watch?v=2EdLasOrG6c
- "Freedom" (Richie Havens) https://www.youtube.com/watch?v=rynxqdNMry4
- "Star Spangled Banner" (Jimi Hendrix): https://www.youtube.com/watch?v=TKAwPA14Ni4

Other Materials
- "Sometimes I Feel like a Motherless Child," African-American slave song (Appendix C)
- Protest Song Project (handouts for students) (Appendix D)

Teaching Process

Instruction	Comments/Suggestions
Do Now: *Let's say that the Board of Education decided to make some changes. The school day is extended to 5:00 pm, lunch is shortened to a half hour with no recess, bathrooms are restricted to lunch time only, and four hours of homework are assigned every night.* *From your point of view, what is fair and what is unfair? If unfair, would you join a protest movement? What would be an effective protest activity?* *What gives you the right to protest?*	Use ideas from exit cards in Lesson 1 to think of different ways to protest. Bill of Rights—First Amendment: *Freedom of Religion, Speech, and the Press* ". . . Citizens have the right to peaceably assemble and petition the government for a redress of grievances."

Instruction	Comments/Suggestions
When we think about protest movements, what are some of the images that come to mind? How could you make a statement through music?	e.g., marches, posters, speeches
In 1969, young people in their teens and twenties had a different idea of protest. Instead of angry signs and marches, a group of people planned a three-day music event. The name of the event was Woodstock and it turned out to be one of the most memorable music events in history.	This was a time marked by the Civil Rights movement and the Vietnam War.
Here are some words and ideas that you should know before you watch the Woodstock video: • Hippie • Folk music • Psychedelic music • Psychedelic drugs • Tie-dye • Peace and love	One way to make this interesting is to put these words all over the board under the heading: "Woodstock—1969."
Show the **video**: "Woodstock Documentary" to establish a context for the music.	*What do you notice? What did you notice about the music?*
I am going to play some of the headliner performances. These were artists and bands that were at the top of the billboard. Every song has a story and sometimes the lyrics are a code for something other than what you first think. In the first song, it is important that you know its origins. Teach or sing as a solo, "Sometimes I Feel like a Motherless Child" (**Appendix C**). *This is a song from the slave era. What are the coded words? What does the song really mean?*	Note to teacher: This song has many other verses but we have chosen a lead sheet that seems most applicable for the purposes of this lesson. The last verse, however, does include "freedom" in the lyrics (not shown here).

Instruction	Comments/Suggestions
Video: "Freedom," Richie Havens. *How did Richie Havens make the song his own? How is it different from ours? Why do you think he called this song "Freedom?"* *Here are some other headliner performances. As you listen, think about what these performances have in common.*	Remind students about the Civil Rights movement happening about the same time.
Video: "Somebody to Love," Jefferson Airplane *This music was performed on the last day of the event. It is a song you know, but listen to how Jimi Hendrix makes the song different from what we usually hear.* **Video:** "Star Spangled Banner," Jimi Hendrix *What did Hendrix do to create a memorable performance of the Star-Spangled Banner?*	Facilitate discussion about the use of electronic instruments, iconic clothes, singing voice, etc. Analyze the form of the song in terms of verse and chorus.
How do these songs sound different from those that we heard in the last class ("Union Maid"; "Solidarity Forever")?	This question prompts thinking about different styles of music.
In all of our lessons, songs have played an important role in the protest movement. Some songs, like "Solidarity Forever," are appropriate for a march or rally in order to unite people for a cause. Other songs, like "Somebody to Love," are more like personal commentaries about the times or a specific issue.	
To write a protest song, you need a topic that you feel strongly about. For instance, you might think about a topic that needs action for justice, such as climate change or extinction of animals. Students brainstorm some ideas as a preparation for the Protest Song Project.	Try to suggest ideas that are relevant to the students' lives.

Instruction	Comments/Suggestions
Give an overview of the project (Appendix D). In small groups, students should decide on a topic and start to write down words or phrases that are central to the issue.	We suggest that friends work with friends. Some adolescents feel vulnerable about singing. It helps to have the support of those with whom you feel safe.

Labor Unions and Woodstock: Protest Song Project

Lessons 3–4

Goal
To use ideas and listening examples presented in this unit as a basis for composing/ arranging a new protest song.

National Standards
- MU:Re7.7a: Classify and explain how the elements of music and expressive qualities relate to the structure of contrasting pieces.
- MU:Cr2.1.6a: Select organize, construct, and document personal musical ideas for arrangements, and compositions within AB, ABA, or theme and variation forms that demonstrate an effective beginning, middle, and ending, and convey expressive intent.

Assessment
- **Formative:** The teacher will assess students' readiness for the song project through a discussion about the musical/lyrical elements that characterize a good protest song.
- **Summative:** The teacher will assess students' songs with a teacher-designed rubric.

YouTube Videos
- "Solidarity Forever," "Union Maid," "Freedom" (see Lesson 2)

Other Materials
- Protest Song Project (Appendix D)

Teaching Process: This project may take 2 classes to complete.

Instruction	Comments/Suggestions
The goal, today, is to write or finish writing a protest song. Go over the project guidelines again (**Appendix D**).	
Play part of "Solidarity Forever," audio only. *What is the original melody of this song? What is the benefit of using a song that most people know already?* *What makes a protest song good for getting everyone excited and unified?* *What makes a protest song reflective?* Play a part of "Freedom" without the video.	e.g., easy repetitive chorus, lyrics that focus on the issue, melody that is easy to sing. Upbeat tempo. Less focus on rallying the troops and more focus on what this all means.
Modeling Activity for the Project Several years ago, a state governor implemented a ban on selling sugary soft drinks more than 16 fl. oz. That means restaurants, fast food places, movie theaters, etc., were banned from selling more than 16 oz. of soda per customer. *What do you think about that? Is this fair? What is the bottom line: Does government have the right to regulate what we eat or drink?* *How would you set this to music? What words or phrases might you use for a song?*	Save the bulk of the class for students to work on their own. State's reasoning: Curb obesity and diabetes, thus saving the state large amounts of money on related healthcare.
You can go about your project in two ways: Find a song and change the lyrics, or compose your own melody and lyrics. Hand out project sheets and have students collaborate in their groups.	

Instruction	Comments/Suggestions
Encourage students to add percussion or pitched instruments (e.g., xylophone, guitar, ukulele, piano).	Note to Teacher: It is often very hard for students to sing in front of their peers, especially if boys are experiencing a change of voice. Here are some ways to involve everyone: • One or two students sing for the group. • The timid singers can serve as backup (either spoken or sung). • Have some students play an instrument. • Record the song on GarageBand and play it for the class.
When everyone is satisfied, each group will explain their topic and some of the ideas that were important for their song. Perform the song.	Whenever students are going to perform, it is critical that you first lay the groundwork for supportive listening and applause.
Reflection: *What did you like about this song? Where would this song fit in a protest movement (e.g., march, picket line, rally, gathering like Woodstock). Why?*	DO NOT SKIP THIS STEP. It is important that performers (who are putting themselves on the line) get positive peer feedback. They need to feel that their efforts were appreciated.

Civil Rights and Black Lives Matter

Introduction

Although nearly four decades apart, the Civil Rights movement and the Black Lives Matter movement share many commonalities. They both focus on the unequal treatment of Black people in our society, they were both precipitated by racially charged events within a social culture of systemic discrimination, and they both advocated for peaceful protest activities such as marches, town meetings, writing, songs, demonstrations, and media coverage.

Racial inequality is a well-covered topic in schools from elementary through high school. Students study the horrors of slavery in literature and history classes as a precursor to the Civil Rights movement. In music class, teachers often design lessons for Black History month that feature the music of black artists and composers. These lessons, whether in the arts or other disciplines, tend to concentrate on factual evidence and first-person stories, rather than tangibly addressing the social justice dimension of human rights.

Race is a sensitive area. Terms like "anti-racism" and "critical race theory" have become contentious language that is often more misunderstood than not. Anti-racism and critical race theory (CRT) scholars define these terms as social constructs that examine the intersection of race, class, economy, identity, and what it means to be fully human.[1] In essence, the core of CRT and anti-racism focuses on the systemic nature of racism which, in turn, maintains a stratified society.

At the time of this writing, CRT had created a political maelstrom across the nation. Many states banned or are in the process of preparing legislation to stop teaching, textbooks, and other curricular materials associated with matters of race. Those most vocal about such sweeping changes regard race-based discussions as anti-patriotic—that students will begin to question the moral and ethical roots of America's development from small colonies to a "more perfect union." This is most unfortunate, because avoiding discussions about racial inequality keeps students from interrogating the substantive issues about discrimination and oppression that lead to respect and dignity for all human beings. In addition, it subverts action to change social systems that have maintained unfair treatment of Blacks from their arrival in America to contemporary times.[2]

For this reason, the unit on the Civil Rights movement and the Black Lives Matter movement concentrates on themes of social justice that question what it means to be unfairly judged based on skin color. This provides the grounding for countless songs, musical compositions, artworks, dances, and multimedia aesthetic responses. It is in this framework that we help students analyze the lyrics of related songs and respond to ideas/images through music activities that involve composition, singing, and instrument performance.

Calling for change and advocacy is not beyond the ability of secondary school students. Indeed, there are several instances in this unit that introduce ways that teens have responded to inequity. Learning constructive strategies for peacefully alerting others to the systems and practices that maintain or escalate racial inequality cultivates empowerment among young adolescents who are struggling to make sense of the world. Subsequently, music activities reflect an important means of grappling with these topics.

Civil Rights and Black Lives Matter: Talking about Race

Talking about race is such a sensitive topic that many teachers avoid the conversation altogether. However, when teachers avoid talking about racial inequities, they deny students the opportunity to think about the deeper meaning of racism underlying the Civil Rights movement and the Black Lives Matter organization. These deeper meanings are crucial for developing a platform for social justice.

Entire books have been written about racial topics in the school curriculum. For that reason, what follows cannot hope to achieve more than a surface level of experience for teachers and students. It is an evolving conversation over time in which the teacher builds trust, community, and respect for other viewpoints. On the other hand, one might consider a short discussion as an entry point for thinking about the humanity of all people.

Therefore, please read this document with the understanding that it is but a drop in the bucket for a very important part of students' education. Facilitating a discussion about race requires courage along with certain guidelines (see the following). In addition, teachers must interrogate their own identity and beliefs about a racial society. Here are few tips for facilitating a conversation on race:

DO . . .

1. *Set some parameters* for a productive discussion. Talk about the importance of listening to other students whether in agreement or not. Emphasize that the goal is to converse, not debate.
2. *Teach students how to respond* to a comment with which they disagree without saying something that might hurt a classmate. Put these phrases on the board, "I hear what you are saying but I disagree because . . ." or "I have a different perspective. . . ."
3. *Clarify student responses* when necessary. Putting a student's thoughts into different words helps other students understand the meaning behind the response.
4. *Keep the discussion focused.* It's easy to get off-track when talking about personal examples or saying the same things over and over again.
5. *Keep your cool* when students say offensive or hurtful things. You can respond by asking something like, "Did you mean to say . . . ?" "Can you re-phrase that comment so that it gives you a chance to express your opinion without hurting someone?" Remind students that everyone is entitled to his/her/their opinion but not entitled to accuse or speak disrespectfully.

DO NOT . . .

1. *Make judgmental comments* about a student's response. Avoid saying, "That's not nice," or "That's a mean thing to say," or "Good answer." Model the language you want students to use.
2. *Talk too much.* There is nothing worse than shutting down an open conversation by giving lengthy explanations or information.
3. *Share your opinion.* This makes students feel as if they need to please the teacher by only sharing what they perceive as the "right" answer. There is, however, merit in sharing some of your own thoughts as points for discussion, rather than encouraging students to agree with you.

4. *Show anger or frustration.* This keeps students from speaking honestly. Understand that conversations about race are uncomfortable for almost everyone in the room. Remember that this is a dialogue to help students listen respectfully to one another. Your anger gives them license to respond in a similar way.

Sometimes with even the best intentions, students are unable to sustain a productive dialogue. It may be the first time that a teacher has ever given them permission to talk openly and they are wary of conversations that go beyond a question-answer format. It could also be that the students have not had enough time to trust that music class is a safe place. For those reasons, it is better to continue the discussion at another time when a more supportive learning community is in place. Alternatively, a potentially chaotic situation may be a teachable moment for talking about how the class response is very much like similar conversations throughout history. Race relations can only get better when people listen to one another, and such skills are critical for any conversation about social justice.

Civil Rights and Black Lives Matter: Other Forms of Protest

Lesson 1

Goal
To listen and analyze the lyrics for "Lift Every Voice and Sing" as a springboard for discussing the Civil Rights era and the Black Lives Matter movement.

National Standards
- MU.Pr4.2.6c: Identify how cultural and historical contexts inform performances.
- MU.Re7.7a: Classify and explain how the elements of music and expressive qualities relate to the structure of contrasting pieces.

Assessment
- **Formative:** The teacher will assess students' ability to decipher the meaning of the song, "Lift Every Voice and Sing," by analyzing the lyrics. In addition, the teacher will assess students' comparison of three different song arrangements in a class discussion.

YouTube Videos
- "Lift Every Voice and Sing": https://www.youtube.com/watch?v=-BIjUy_Z19s (a cappella quartet)
- "Lift Every Voice and Sing," Darion Thompson (dance performance): https://www.youtube.com/watch?v=GW16X23WfRU

- "Lift Every Voice and Sing," Beyoncé: https://www.youtube.com/watch?v=
  RBlrgsRD2e8
- Black Lives Matter, NC, 2020 https://www.youtube.com/watch?v=h4Hx0z6-zPI
  Pride Protest in Solidarity with the Black Lives Matter movement

Other Materials
- Lyrics to the song, "Lift Every Voice and Sing" (handout for the class) (Appendix E)
- Poem by James Weldon Johnson (on a screen or have on a board) (Appendix F)

Teaching Process

Instruction	Comments/Suggestions
Do Now: *When we sing the Star-Spangled Banner, some people stand up or put their hand over their heart, or drop to one knee. What is the meaning of these gestures? Here is the Black National Anthem: Please rise to show honor to the Black community:* **Video:** *"Lift Every Voice and Sing," a cappella quartet* *What was the best part about this group? Can you think about how this song relates to the lesson about protest in the last class? (Quick review for students)* On your lyric sheet, notice that verses #1 and #2 are marked. Pair–Share: Choose one and answer the following questions: • *What do you think this verse is about?* • *Think of two adjectives that describe the message of the verse.* Students share responses with others in the class. Explain the reasons for their response.	Background: Identify "Lift Every Voice and Sing" as the Black National Anthem. It was written at the time in history when Jim Crow laws started to come into place. Slavery may have been legally abolished but the Jim Crow laws kept African Americans from having the same privileges as White people. "Lift Every Voice and Sing" was a song that gave African Americans a sense of identity.
Different artists bring their own interpretation to a song. This is a dance performance, and the gestures have symbolic meaning based on the lyrics. Look for these movement symbols and see what you can remember after the video. **Video:** "Lift Every Voice and Sing," Darion Thompson	

Instruction	Comments/Suggestions
Where does this song come from? (**Appendix F**) Read the poem by James Weldon Johnson (**on board**). Ask students to look carefully at the song to find their verse. *How does the beginning of the verse compare to the part that you just read? In what decade do you think this poem was written?* *What clues in the poem tell you that the poem is about the history of African Americans? Why was this written as a celebration for Lincoln's birthday?*	This poem, by James Weldon Johnson, was written in 1900 for a celebration of Abraham Lincoln's birthday. It was set to music by Johnson's brother, John Rosamond Weldon. Both brothers were African American.
This last **video** is Beyoncé's interpretation. After this performance I'm going to ask you which of the three videos (versions) you liked the best. **Video**: Beyoncé	
The Civil Rights movement (1960s) and Black Lives Matter (2013–present) are two movements that focus(ed) on a similar goal: Equal rights for all citizens in the United States of America. *Do you think this song serves as a protest song for the Civil Rights era and the Black Lives Matter movement?*	
Video: "Black Lives Matter," NC Why does this march honor Gay Pride as well?	This step can be eliminated if necessary.
Critical Thinking Prompt: *Why is music such a powerful tool in creating community as well as showing resistance?*	Examples: Every person can sing a song; singing the same song brings people together; when a community of people sing a song to support a protest movement, they show peaceful signs of resistance.

Civil Rights and Black Lives Matter: Racism and Music

Lesson 2

Goal

To investigate racism from a systemic level by exploring songs produced under the first recording label (Motown) to feature Black performers and musicians.

National Standards

- MU:Re8.1.6a: Describe a personal interpretation of how creators' and performers' application of the elements of music and expressive qualities, within genres and cultural and historical contexts, conveys expressive intent.
- MU:Pr4.2.6a: Identify how cultural and historical contexts inform the performances.

Assessment

- **Formative:** The teacher will assess students' perception of systemic racism through a discussion about Motown as the first Black-owned recording label.

YouTube Videos

- "Shop Around," Smokey Robinson and the Miracles: https://www.youtube.com/watch?v=dA5509mcQd8
- "Dancing in the Streets," Martha Reeves and the Vandellas: https://www.youtube.com/watch?v=GuCBXTfoVq8
- "Rockin Robin," The Jackson Five: https://www.youtube.com/watch?v=z-OteAgvINc
- "Yesterme, Yesteryou, Yesterday," Stevie Wonder: https://www.youtube.com/watch?v=2T3m9PWN6B8
- "Alabama," John Coltrane: https://www.youtube.com/watch?v=saN1BwlxJxA

Other Resources

- "What Went On?: The (Pre)History of Motown's Politics at 45 RPM" https://quod.lib.umich.edu/cgi/t/text/text-idx?cc=mqr;c=mqr;c=mqrarchive;idno=act2080.0049.406;g=mqrg;rgn=main;view=text;xc=1
- "American Anthem: Dancing in the Streets," transcription of NPR podcast: https://www.npr.org/2019/01/05/682394160/american-anthem-dancing-in-the-street

Teaching Process

Instruction	Comments/Suggestions
Do Now: *Did you ever witness or experience an act of discrimination based on skin color?* Write about your thoughts when this happened.	Writing is often a good way for students to think through an event on their own before discussing their experiences.
Have students voluntarily share their writing (or verbal overview) from the "Do Now" activity.	This is a sensitive area and must be voluntary. Let students know that they should not mention names or give details that might reference an event known to other students. Keep discussion at a minimum. This is strictly for sharing personal experiences.
What does the word, racism mean to you? *Most people associate racism with individual acts of meanness. Some of your stories described these types of situations. There are, however, much larger forms of racism where people are discriminated against because it is actually part of society, like buying a house in a "white neighborhood."* *In terms of music, it wasn't until the 1960s (around the time of the Civil War) that Black artists were allowed to produce their music on the radio. Before that time, Whites were the primary artists that had access to the recording industry. Blacks were restricted to live performance venues for public performance.*	Brief sharing of personal definitions on racism.
Why is it a good thing for any pop musician to get his/her/their music played on the radio or digitally? Is banning musicians of color from recording their music the same as someone bullying another person?	The last question refers to the difference between bullying (one or several persons) and systemic racism.

Instruction	Comments/Suggestions
Motown (1959) was the first record label for Black artists to share their music with a wide-ranging audience. It was the first Black-owned, Black-centered music that offered White people a chance to experience music which continues to influence popular music today. *Here are some Motown singles that topped the charts:* **Video:** "Shop Around." Snap on beats 2 & 4. Sing the tag line "You better shop around" with the video. Try imitating some of the dance moves along with the video. Watch **videos** from several other songs recorded on the Motown Label. **Videos:** "Dancing in the Streets," "Rockin' Robin," and "Yesterme, Yesteryou, Yesterday."	No need to play the entire video unless students are engaged. No need to play videos in their entirety.
As a class, create a dance segment, to "Dancing in the Streets," using some movements from the video. Students volunteer to create other movement episodes. Perform this segment with the music. Ask if any students want to improvise another move during the music. If time permits, see if the same segment works with a different song.	Most students love to dance but many are uncomfortable in front of their peers. To manage a class dance activity, you or a student can replicate some simple moves from the dances so students have something they can all do. This could lead to a dance improv based on large group and solo (or small group).
One last word about Motown: The artists that recorded on this label created songs that reflected the social context of the time. Many were directly linked to issues of social justice. There are references to racial discrimination which are not always obvious to the uninformed listener. Long story short—Motown was a political enterprise in addition to a company for Black artists.	e.g., "Dancing in the Streets" is a party song with references to racism. There was a time when Blacks were not allowed to hang out on street corners (see Other Resources—"American Anthem").

Instruction	Comments/Suggestions
Motown may have been upbeat and fun to listen to, but it was also a form of protest against a dominant White recording industry. Black artists often composed songs relevant to the turbulent social times of the day. Imagine how different our pop music culture would be without the Black voice.	Time permitting, identify Black artists in pop music who benefited from Motown: e.g., Michael Jackson
We'll close with Coltrane's haunting song "Alabama," which is a sorrowful response to the four little girls who were killed in the bombing of their church (Birmingham, Alabama).	

Civil Rights and Black Lives Matter: The Bigger Picture

Lessons 3–4

Goal
To demonstrate that issues of social justice have also inspired the arts as a form of activism.

National Standards
- MU:Re8.1.6a: Describe a personal interpretation of how creators' and performers' application of the elements of music and expressive qualities, within genre and cultural and historical contexts, conveys expressive intent.
- MU:Cr3.2.7a: Present the final version of their documented personal composition, song, or arrangement, using craftsmanship and originality to demonstrate unity and variety, and convey expressive intent.

Assessment
- **Formative:** The teacher will assess students' understanding of activism through the arts with a discussion of selected readings from the article, "Atlanta Teens Speak: Art as a Tool of Social Change."
- **Summative:** The teacher will assess students' understanding of the connection between politics and the arts by having them compose and perform a rap based on themes of social justice.

YouTube Videos

- "The Bigger Picture," Lil Baby: https://www.youtube.com/watch?v=_VDGysJGNoI
- "12th Grader Shedding the National Anthem": https://www.youtube.com/watch?v=-uPCIuopoPs

Materials

- Handout: Selected excerpts from "Atlanta Teens Speak: Art as a Tool of Social Change": https://voxatl.org/art-social-change/ *Note to teacher—This is a long article. For the handout, we suggest that you cut and paste the opening paragraph and two to three comments by students (scroll down to the pictures).
- Freedom Rap (Appendix F)

Teaching Process

Instruction	Comments/Suggestions
Do Now: Have students respond to excerpts from "Atlanta Teens Speak: Art as a Tool of Social Change."	Share responses in a class discussion.
These last few lessons have been about protest for change. The Black Lives Matter movement, for example, was triggered by the murder of a young unarmed Black teenager (Trayvon Martin) whose killer (George Zimmerman) was not convicted. This single event created many protest actions—some not peaceful—in the country.	
How much do you know about Black Lives Matter? What kinds of peaceful protest actions have they advocated? Can you name some other groups of people who suffer inequality? (e.g., Latinx immigrants, anti-Semitism, LGBTQ)	e.g., human rights, equality, respect and dignity for African American citizens.

Instruction	Comments/Suggestions
The arts have always been an important vehicle for giving oppressed people a voice. So, how do artists in all areas respond to social justice issues? Here's an example: **YouTube**: "The Bigger Picture," Lil Baby, https://www.youtube.com/watch?v=_VDGysJGNoI *Is this a protest rap? From the pictures and the rap, what is this about? What are some words that you remember or associate with the video, e.g., "Stand up and do what is right;"* What is the main issue of social justice here?	Spoken word poems, murals, dance, songs, etc. Unequal treatment of Black citizens.
Music Making Appendix F <u>Preparation</u> Have the words from the handout on the board. Ask students to identify which words are in 2's and which words are in 3's. As someone to create a phrase with all the words in any combination. Talk about how the triplet gives forward movement and the duple gives special emphasis. Hand out **Appendix F** and set some guidelines for working in small groups, including a quiet signal.	If you have a number of Spanish-speaking students, include the Spanish. Some students may want to create the rap in another language with like-speaking students.
Groups create their own raps.	This will be noisy but you can contain the noise to a reasonable level with the quiet signal and talking to individual groups. You can give students the option of using their phone for a beat background.
Groups perform their raps for the class. Reflection: *How did you decide what to do in your rap? What did you like in one or more of the other groups? Identify some composition ideas that worked well.*	Always wait until each group is satisfied before performing for the class. If some students are uncomfortable, have one student do the rap and others do the backup. Make sure every group gets positive feedback.

Instruction	Comments/Suggestions
Conclusion *Music and the arts can be used in many ways to protest and call for change. Throughout history it has been the youth (like you) who have started or participated in the protest activities. Here's an example of a 12th grader using the freedom to play his own interpretation of the National Anthem.* **Video**: "12th Grader Shreds the National Anthem." *It is unclear whether he intended to make a political statement or wanted to pay homage to Jimi Hendrix, However, the fact that music, beyond a traditional performance, is accepted and welcomed says something about how far the arts can take place in in a political climate.*	

School Shootings

Introduction

According to World Population Review,[3] the United States has more mass school shootings than any other country. Of all the protest lessons in this unit, school shootings are probably the most difficult for teachers to address. Tough questions include, "How can I talk about school shootings without offending parents or administration?"; "What do I say to help students talk about these issues without creating fear among those in the class?"; "What if students bring up controversial issues like gun violence in their community?"

There are two online articles, among others, that provide helpful information for initiating a discussion with students. The first is, "How to Talk with Kids about Terrible Things."[4] The second article is, "Nine Ways to Help Students Discuss Guns and Violence."[5] Both offer effective tips on what to expect and how to facilitate such a conversation.

Children and adolescents have emotional responses to school shootings because they identify so strongly with the school context. Some say that these discussions belong in the home; however, many parents avoid talking with their children either because they don't feel comfortable with the issue or they want to protect the child from frightening events. On the other hand, schools have a commitment to preparing students for adulthood in a democracy. For that reason, such conversations not only are helpful in answering probing questions, but also give moral grounding for bringing this discussion into the classroom.

This unit focuses on three tragic events that continue to receive media attention: Columbine High School, Sandy Hook Elementary School, and Marjory Stoneman Douglas High School. What makes these shootings unique?

Columbine High School in Littleton, Colorado (April 20, 1999), was the worst mass school shooting in the US public schools at that time, leaving one teacher and 12 students dead, and scores of wounded students. The two gunmen, Eric Harris and Dylan Klebold, were 12th grade students at the school who committed suicide at the scene. Surviving students held a school rally on the first day of their return to the high school. Two Columbine students, Jonathan and Stephen Cohen, composed the song, "Friend of Mine," which was released as a single with proceeds benefiting parents of the victims.

Sandy Hook Elementary School in Newtown, Connecticut, was a deadly mass shooting at an elementary school (December 14, 2012) that left 6 teachers/staff and 20 children dead. Adam Lanza, the gunman, shot himself at the scene. An outpouring of grief consumed the country following this horrific tragedy. In the aftermath, families of the victims took action by starting charitable foundations, organizing fund-raisers, engaging in political activism, and filing suits with companies that manufactured the assault weapons used in the crime. Remembrances often included the phrases "26 Angels" and "Always Here, Never Forgotten."

Marjory Stoneman Douglas High School in Parkland, Florida, was the first time that surviving students took an active role in protesting gun control on a national level. The shootings took the lives of 17 students and staff. Given that the surviving students launched such a timely and well-orchestrated protest movement, the lessons in this section focus primarily on the shootings at Marjory Stoneman Douglas High School.

When confronted with such horrendous situations, artists turn toward their medium as a way of expressing anger, sorrow, hope, and so forth. Music, art, and poetry have particularly inspired those suffering losses. For that reason, the two lessons in this cluster emphasize music and poetry as powerful mediums for healing and comfort. The point of these lessons is to illustrate how students can take control, through the arts, at a time when they feel most helpless. Consequently, the lessons in this section focus on resilience and remembrance, rather than gun violence or specific details about the tragedy. Regrettably, other situations that occur—a child lost in an accident or from illness, the sudden death of a teacher—also have an impact on the student population. These lessons are adaptable to such experiences other than school shootings. In essence, students need a caring place to talk about their grief. Music class, among other disciplines, can provide the space and the means for helping students cope with profound loss.

School Shootings: The Aftermath

Lesson 1

Goal
To help students use music as a means for responding to tragic events such as a school shooting.

National Standards
- MU:Re8.1.6a: Describe a personal interpretation of how creators' and performers' application of the elements of music and expressive qualities, within genres and cultural and historical contexts, conveys expressive intent.
- MU:Re7.1.6a: Select or choose music to listen to and explain the connections to specific interests or experiences for a specific purpose.

Assessment
- **Formative:** The teacher will assess students' verbal description and use of music terminology to describe the mood of several songs. In addition, the teacher will assess students' ability to place songs in different categories and explain the reasoning for his/her/their choice.

YouTube Videos
- "Stoneman Douglas Drama Club and Student Choir sing 'Shine'": https://www.youtube.com/watch?v=MrZiB2jV7dw
- "Bridge over Troubled Water" (Simon & Garfunkel): https://www.youtube.com/watch?v=xC5gFakHeMk
- "Rise" (Katy Perry): https://www.youtube.com/watch?v=ytMUjBogO1Q
- "Imagine" (John Lennon): https://www.youtube.com/watch?v=v27CEFE02Hs
- "Don't Worry Be Happy" (Bobby McFerrin): https://www.youtube.com/watch?v=Xh4ugYiXF-Q
- "We Are the World" (Michael Jackson & Lionel Richie): https://www.youtube.com/watch?v=9AjkUyX0rVw
- "Glory" (John Legend): https://www.youtube.com/watch?v=yuBPb7Es-2o

Other Materials
- Personal mobile devices such as a smart phone or laptop
- "March for Our Lives" (Washington, DC): www.nytimes.com/2018/03/14/us/school-walkout.html
- Lyricsheetfor"Shine":https://littlehingesusa.com/2018/02/25/lyrics-to-stoneham-douglas-song-shine/

Other Resources
- "The National School Walkout, Explained": https://www.vox.com/policy-and-politics/2018/3/13/17110044/national-school-walkout-day

Teaching Process

Instruction	Comments/Suggestions
Do Now: On February 14th, Nikolas Cruz, a former student, walked into Marjory Stoneman Douglas High School (Parkland, Florida) and, using an assault weapon, killed 17 people including students and teachers. *On your desk are the **lyrics** from a song composed by two students who survived the school shooting in Parkland, Florida. Read the lyrics and respond to the prompt below:* *Which of these words describes the mood of the song?* hope, fear, resilience, terror, peace, anger, sorrow, grief, shock, confusion.	The shooter remains in custody. Handout: Lyrics for "Shine," composed by Sawyer Garrity and Andrea Peña Have the words, "fear, hope, sorrow," etc., on the **board** as a reference.
Video: "Stoneman Douglas Drama Club . . ." *What words did you choose to describe this song? What are some lyrics that support your answer? How does the music enhance the mood of the song?* Play again and sing the chorus of the song. *In what kinds of settings would this song be especially powerful?* (e.g., memorial, school assembly, concert to raise money for victim's families).	
Tragedy doesn't just affect those directly involved but also affects families, friends, and countless unknown persons on a national and international level. *Grieving takes on many forms, from shock and denial to anger, acceptance, and resilience. Resilient people often want to actively respond to the situation by forming organizations or social activist committees ("Never Again MSD" or some type of annual memorial).*	

Instruction	Comments/Suggestions
Activism helps youth and adults feel that they are doing something—that the public will never let this happen again. The surviving students of Marjory Stoneman Douglas High School quickly formed a nationwide gathering of students to meet in Washington, DC, or at their own schools. Out of their grief, they protested gun control while also maintaining a time of silence to honor the dead.	
Protest is powerful when there are a lot of people involved. How did the student survivors inform so many students across the country?	Facebook, Twitter, other digital platforms.
Music Activity Put the following categories in a row at the top of the board: (a) Activism and Change, (b) Loss, (c) Unity, (d) Hope *Under which category would you place "Shine?"* Listen to parts of the following songs and decide in which category they belong. *Besides the lyrics, what about the music helps you place it in a category?* Facilitate use of musical terminology (e.g., dynamics, instrumentation, tempo): • "Bridge over Troubled Water" (Simon & Garfunkel) • "Rise" (Katy Perry) • "Imagine" (John Lennon) • "Don't Worry, Be Happy" (Bobby McFerrin) • "We Are the World" (Michael Jackson) • "Glory" (John Legend)	There are no "right" or "wrong" answers, but students should explain their reasoning. There is no need to reach a consensus. Some songs may be placed under several categories.

Instruction	Comments/Suggestions
In pairs or trios, use a mobile device to find a song appropriate for a memorial setting.	Some students may have a specific song in mind. If not, you can facilitate a search by telling students to Google one of the categories.
Exit Ticket: *If you were to choose a song from this class for a peaceful protest in the aftermath of a school shooting, would it be a song of activism, loss, unity, hope? Give a two-sentence explanation for your answer.*	

School Shootings: In Remembrance*

Lesson 2

Goal
To explore how a peaceful gathering, for the purpose of honoring victims of violence, can also reflect a sign of protest.

National Standards
- MU:Re8.1.7a: Describe a personal interpretation of contrasting works and explain how creators' and performers' application of the elements of music and expressive qualities, within genres, cultures, and historical periods, conveys expressive intent.
- MU:Pr4.1.8a: Apply personally developed criteria for selecting music of contrasting styles for a program with a specific purpose and/or context and explain expressive qualities, technical challenges, and reasons for choices.

Assessment
- **Formative**: The teacher will assess the students' connection between music and the intent of a poem by giving him/her/them a choice of different musical pieces for enhancing the meaning of the poem.
- **Summative**: The teacher will assess the students' ability to collaborate with others in designing a class performance of poems and music that honor those lost.

YouTube Video
- "Columbine, Friend of Mine": https://www.youtube.com/watch?v=i9Seqhcq23M

Other Materials

- Choose three pieces of instrumental music, any genre, that could serve as inspiring background for reading the students' poems. We used "Air on The G String" (J. S. Bach); "Sheep May Safely Graze" (J. S. Bach); "Canon in D Major" (J. Pachelbel). These, however, may not appeal to your students as much as more contemporary instrumental music that you might choose instead. Use exit tickets from last class to get other ideas.
- "Shine" Lyric Sheets (from last class)

Teaching Process

Instruction	Comments/Suggestions
Do Now: Listen to "Friend of Mine" and compare its message to "Shine." *How would you describe the music? What about the music makes it a good fit for the lyrics?*	"Friend of Mine" was composed by two Columbine students.
Review the last session and introduce school shootings at Sandy Hook Elementary School and Columbine High School *Something that survivors and their families fear is that we will forget their trauma. What are ways that our society continue to memorialize a traumatic event even after many years?* (e.g., holding a short memorial each year on the same day; stopping to give a moment of silence; making a piece of art; taking political action to introduce new legislation). *Think about how we remember the Holocaust or 9/11 or Martin Luther King.*	e.g., holding an annual memorial; stopping for a moment of silence; making a piece of art; or taking political action to introduce new legislation.
If you were going to create a poem to honor the victims of a tragedy, what category would you choose? (see right sidebar).	Have these categories on the board: Unity, Call for Change, Resilience, Loss, Hope.
Divide class into groups by category. *Create a three- or four-line poem that demonstrates the intent of your category. The poem need not rhyme. It can be a grouping of three different length phrases.*	If more than four in a group, create two groups for the same category. Example: "I do not understand / Yet I grieve / A life lost"

Instruction	Comments/Suggestions
Have students find a quiet space to work. Ask them to keep their voices soft so as not to disrupt the mood.	
Listen to the poems of each group (one or more readers). *Let's create a read-in where we participate in a meaningful performance of all our poems.* As a class, decide on which poem should begin and which poem should end. Determine the order of the other poems so that everyone knows whom they follow. Ask students to insert pauses for reflection between each poem. This should be felt rather than "conducted."	The teacher becomes a quiet observer.
Play the beginnings of three instrumental pieces. *Which of these pieces would make a good accompaniment for reading all the poems?*	Students reach a consensus on one piece of music.
The Performance To create the mood, lower or turn off the lights and ask each group to turn on the flashlight function on a smartphone when it is their turn to read. Perform the poems in tandem with the music. End with a brief period of silence.	If possible, keep the lights shining for a "candle" effect. Some students, however, may not have enough battery power for that length of time.

* This lesson is more meaningful when students are honoring a loss from an event that recently happened or is part of history (Martin Luther King or Harvey Milk). It could be someone, say, in the school, community, parent, victims of war. Without this human connection, the lesson has little relevance.

Appendix A

"Union Maid"

For lyrics to "Union Maid," please see our book's website:
   https://socialjusticemusics.com/unit-1/.

Appendix B

"Solidarity Forever"

Chorus

Solidarity forever / Solidarity forever / Solidarity forever / For the union makes us strong.[6]

Verse 1

When the union's inspiration / Through the workers' blood shall run / There can be no power greater / Anywhere beneath the sun / Yet what force on earth is weaker / Than the feeble strength of one? / But the union makes us strong.

Chorus
Verse 2

It is we who plowed the prairies / Built the cities where they trade / Dug the mines and built the workshops / Endless miles of railroad laid / Now we stand outcast and starving / Mid the wonders we have made / But the union makes us strong.

Chorus
Verse 3

They have taken untold millions / That they never toiled to earn / But without our brain and muscle / Not a single wheel can turn / We can break their haughty power / Gain our freedom when we learn / That the union makes us strong.

Chorus
Verse 4

In our hands is placed a power / Greater than their hoarded gold / Greater than the might of atoms / Magnified a thousand-fold / We can bring to birth a new world / From the ashes of the old / For the union makes us strong.

Chorus

Appendix C

"Sometimes I Feel like a Motherless Child"

Sometimes I feel like a motherless child
Sometimes I feel like a motherless child
Sometimes I feel like a motherless child
A long way from home
For sheet music, see our book's website: https://socialjusticemusics.com/unit-1/.

Appendix D

Protest Song Project

Here's your chance to write a protest song. You can either write a song that is appropriate for a march/rally or a song that would be appropriate for a public music event.

What to Do: *Choose a topic* for protest and discuss (or write down) different phrases, words, or ideas that are important for people to hear.

Then What? *Create a melody* that supports the lyrics from your brainstorming. OR *Pick out a song* you already know and change the lyrics.

Consider: Writing a song that has a *verse and a chorus*. If you are writing for a march or rally, the chorus should be simple so that everyone can sing along.

Almost Finished: You may add instruments if you want. *Practice the song* so that everyone has a part in the performance. If some of you are uncomfortable singing, you can play an instrument or record the song on a smartphone or other device. It is very important that you sing clearly so that we can understand the words.

The Last Step: *Perform* your song, either live or recorded.

Appendix E

Lyrics for "Lift Every Voice and Sing"

1. Lift every voice and sing / Till earth and heaven ring / Ring with the harmonies of Liberty / Let our rejoicing rise / High as the listening skies / Let it resound loud as the rolling sea.

   Sing a song full of the faith that the dark past has taught us / Sing a song full of the hope that the present has brought us / Facing the rising sun of our new day begun / Let us march on till victory is won.

2. Stony the road we trod / Bitter the chastening rod / Felt in the days when hope unborn had died / Yet with a steady beat / Have not our weary feet / Come to the place for which our fathers sighed?

We have come over a way that with tears has been watered / We have come, treading our path through the blood of the slaughtered / Out from the gloomy past / Till now we stand at last / Where the white gleam of our bright star is cast.

3. God of our weary years / God of our silent tears / Thou who has brought us thus far on the way / Thou who has by Thy might / Led us into the light / Keep us forever in the path, we pray.

Lest our feet stray from the places, our God, where we met Thee / Lest, our hearts drunk with the wine of the world, we forget Thee / Shadowed beneath Thy hand / May we forever stand / True to our God / True to our native land / Our native land.

Appendix F

Original Poem by James Weldon Johnson

Lift ev'ry voice and sing,
Till earth and heaven ring,
Ring with the harmonies of Liberty;
Let our rejoicing rise,
High as the list'ning skies,
Let it resound loud as the rolling sea.
Sing a song full of the faith that the dark past has taught us,
Sing a song full of the hope that the present has brought us;
Facing the rising sun of our new day begun,
Let us march on till victory is won.

Stony the road we trod,
Bitter the chast'ning rod,
Felt in the days when hope unborn had died;
Yet with a steady beat,
Have not our weary feet
Come to the place for which our fathers sighed?
We have come over a way that with tears has been watered.
We have come, treading our path through the blood of the slaughtered,
Out from the gloomy past,
Till now we stand at last
Where the white gleam of our bright star is cast.

God of our weary years,
God of our silent tears,
Thou who hast brought us thus far on the way;
Thou who hast by Thy might,
Led us into the light,
Keep us forever in the path, we pray.
Lest our feet stray from the places, our God, where we met Thee,
Lest our hearts, drunk with the wine of the world, we forget Thee;
Shadowed beneath Thy hand,
May we forever stand,
True to our God,
True to our native land.

Appendix G

Freedom Rap

What should we stand up for? In school? In your community? In America?

Create a rap that begins with any word or words. The rap can be in English or your native language.

	Freedom	Rights	Humanity	Justice	Equality
Spanish Trans.	Libertad	Derechos	Derechos Humanos	Justiciar	Igualdad

Notes

1. See website for more resources on anti-racism and critical race theory.
2. It should be noted that other marginalized people, such as Latinx, American Indians, Asians, and others outside the dominant group, have also experienced much oppression and racial hostility. Because this unit focuses on the Civil Rights movement and Black Lives Matter, however, we decided that the experiences of Black people were more relevant, though not less important, than others.
3. World Population Review, "School Shootings by State." 2020–2021. https://worldpopulationreview. com/state-rankings/school-shootings-by-state
4. Turner, C. "How to Talk With Kids about Terrible Things." *nprEd*, February 18, 2018. https://www. npr.org/sections/ed/2018/02/18/586447438/how-to-talk-with-kids-about-terrible-things
5. Tavares, L. "Nine Ways to Help Students Discuss Guns and Violence." *Greater Good Magazine: Science-Based Insight for a Meaningful Life*, March 7, 2018. https://greatergood.berkeley. edu/article/item/nine_ways_to_help_students_discuss_guns_and_violence
6. Source: LyricFind; Songwriters: Ralph Chaplin; Solidarity Forever lyrics © Public Domain.

3
War Unit

Introduction to the *War* Unit

Civilizations have been plagued with wars of all kinds. From those that are outwardly militaristic—e.g., World War II and the Vietnam War—to those that are insidious and less visible, but still destructive—e.g., the Black Plague and the War on Racism. Notably, and related to the main thrust of this book, wars are complicated sites where we can witness and experience both negative and positive sides: that which works against social justice (e.g., death and devastation), as well as that which seeks social justice (e.g., communities banning together to create change; recognizing and correcting inequities/power imbalances). Relatedly, the lessons in this unit prompt us to better understand how people have engaged in music and music making during and because of war. But first: What counts as a "war" and what might not? So that we're all engaging with the concept similarly, let's think through the nature of "war" together.

There are many, many ways to understand the word "war." The dictionary will say one thing; the United States Constitution will say another. There is a "declaration of war" and there are wars that aren't necessarily "declared" by a governing body. To make the matter more complicated, there are political wars, religious wars, economic wars, cyber wars, and more. So, ask 10 people what counts as a "war" and you'll likely receive 10 very different answers. While all wars possess "conflict" (of one kind or another), not all conflicts are wars. What seems to help distinguish between conflict and war are answers to some critical questions. For example: Is there funding for either side's conflictual activity? Is there political support on either side? Does either side have a hope of winning, or is this just about money? How many lives are at stake? Or, is a war simply not a war if no one "counts" the dead? Importantly, can a war end, yet the conflict still remain? For example, while racial injustice has been going on in the United States since long before the Civil War, some claim this war only lasted from 1861 to 1865. Yet, many of the issues fought during the war between 1861 and 1865 currently exist. Racial injustice persists, slavery—or human trafficking—abounds, and inequality maintains its grasp on cross sections of our country's population. Because of this, can we claim this war actually ended? If so, how so? If not, why not?

Although this unit addresses some of these questions, together we will look at particular contexts and time frames of "wars" of many kinds. Lessons will include examining the contexts of communities plagued by war, including but not limited to the United States and Europe before, during, and after World War II; the United

Music Lesson Plans for Social Justice. Lisa C. Delorenzo and Marissa Silverman, Oxford University Press. © Oxford University Press 2022.
DOI: 10.1093/oso/9780197581476.003.0003

States and Vietnam during and after the Vietnam War. Students will engage with musics that focus their attention on those specific contexts and wars. Those musics will serve as inspiration and models for student-based improvisation and composition projects.

Additionally, and it goes without saying, some of the content found within this unit (as with the content found in others units included in the book) may be difficult for some students. Please be sure to be sensitive to what students may be feeling as they empathize and sympathize with victims and survivors of war.

Notes to Teacher

As noted in this book's Introduction, the units provide for flexibility and alterations. The War unit is no exception. Throughout the unit, there may be lessons that work best over two or more class sessions. Feel free to flexibly negotiate the time it will take to complete the lessons included in this unit.

Although the succeeding lessons seem to follow a particular sequence, they are simply organized this way for ease of use. Feel free to reorganize the lessons depending on what might work best at any given time. Also, some of the lessons from other units in this book—such as those that focus on, for example, creating activities for rap, technology, and listening analysis—may be utilized as "review" or "further refinement," depending on the needs of students.

Here are some specific points for each section to keep in mind when teaching some or all of the War unit:

Introductory Lesson to War

1. You may (or may not) decide this lesson is important. Either way, the pieces briefly explored in this lesson will be showcased in more detail in subsequent lessons. Because of this, it might be helpful to let students have a "taste" (aurally) for what they will examine and explore throughout this unit.
2. You will need to decide how much (or how little) you have students understand about the context of each of the pieces. Again, because you will examine each of the pieces showcased in this lesson in detail at various points throughout this unit, less might be more for now.

World War II

1. It is essential that some discussions and musical engagement focus on how victims maintain their humanity (e.g., protest and other forms of resistance, maintaining identity, self-expression of values/beliefs) despite attempts at dehumanization.

2. Students should contextualize prewar and postwar life to better empathize with stakeholders' choices, issues, and actions.
3. Students should understand that "seeing"—or witnessing and acknowledging— injustices that correspond to war is an aspect of empathizing with/for others.
4. There are various roles to be understood in relation to World War II (and every war, for that matter) including but not limited to bystanders, collaborators, perpetrators, rescuers, heroes, victims, and survivors.

The Vietnam War or the Second Indochina War (known in Vietnam as the Resistance War against America)

1. "Bearing witness" is not only a form of empathy; it can be considered a form of "activism." What bearing witness does is see, hear, and attempt understanding with survivors of victimization. So "activism" during and after the Vietnam War, as is the case with all the "wars" examined throughout this unit, takes on a different form in providing "voice" with/for those who have been silenced. This helps students understand that people can be an "activist" for social justice and reconciliation in many ways.
2. There are so many songs from popular culture, film, and rock, pop, and folk genres of music making history that examine the Vietnam War. Teachers might want to supplement other musics that seem appropriate for class activities.

The Bogside Massacre (or Bloody Sunday)

1. Every effort has been made to highlight the experiences of those who may be somewhat close in age to the students you teach. Because of this, it's important to empathize with the youth of this place in history.
2. The lessons focus on the emotional ethos of conflict. Teachers may find it helpful to provide ways for students to "empathize" with issues beyond their current (political, religious, geographical) landscape in order to teach empathy—for all sides of conflict—through music making.

The War on Racism

1. Unlike "bounded"—geographically and/or time-wise—wars that have been pronounced as such (e.g., the Civil War, World War I, World War II), a "War on Racism" has not been acknowledged "out loud" by all stakeholders across the globe, nor has it been labeled as such. Still, we know that racism is insidious and destructive. Because of this, we are labeling the "calling out" and protesting of racism as a "War on Racism." Thus, the lessons in this unit, like their counterparts

in other units in this book, address ways for students to engage with the emotional content of racism through civil acts of disobedience.

2. Reggae music was chosen specifically here as this music is rooted in acts of civil disobedience and love: two verbs that are powerful tools toward resisting and combating hateful platforms of racism.

Within the graphic organizer of this unit, you will find a list of culminating projects and a rubric that have been designed to engage students in thoughtful music activities. These activities range from creating electro-acoustic compositions to creating soundscapes. The projects are intended to allow students the choice to select a project that best suits their musical interests and skills; or, you could ask the students to complete all projects listed, depending upon how much time your students want/ need to complete creative work. Related to actively creating music is listening—listening to and listening for a variety of components (e.g., emotional/psychological, historical, gendered, political). Because of this, each lesson in this unit begins with a music listening activity related to content/contexts of war.

Pedagogy for Teaching the Human Story

There is no one right way to teach the human story. There are likely only better or worse ways. And the only way to know what will work for you and your students will be to know your students as best as you can. Additionally, there are some considerations that will potentially result in "better," more "refined" practices. First, be sure to define the terms and concepts you will explore *with* students (rather than *for* students). Also, provide enough background information on the content and contexts for the topics that you and your students will be examining. It's important to be operating on the same "page." While connecting people and events to context and content, educators should aim to utilize as many primary source materials as possible, encourage inquiry and critical reflection, foster empathy, and ensure a supportive learning environment.

Helping Students Engage in Empathy Work in the Secondary Schools

Here are a few strategies that might assist to engage large groups. Whenever possible:

- Utilize personal stories, especially when giving statistics;
- Utilize survivor and witness testimony (note: in some cases, and with some wars, survivors' voices may be impossible to locate);
- Examine how victims attempt to maintain their humanity despite attempts at dehumanization (efforts to maintain identity and continuity of life, expression of values/beliefs, forms of resistance);

- Discuss and contextualize the "choiceless choices" of survivors/victims with little or no power to escape;
- Contextualize victims'/survivors' prewar life/return to life; doing so illustrates their choices, dilemmas, and action-plans;
- Examine the mindsets of individuals who had the ability and the opportunity to choose between that which is morally right and morally wrong;
- Include the narratives of bystanders, collaborators, perpetrators, and heroes/heroines.

None of these strategies in and of itself is indicative of empathy work. And critical thinking cannot occur without a lot of "rebound questions" and follow-through. The intent is to help students reflect about why and how things occur in the world. Additionally, this reflection is compounded by the active creation of music, rather than memorizing facts about history, the composers, or the pieces under examination.

Graphic Organizer: WAR

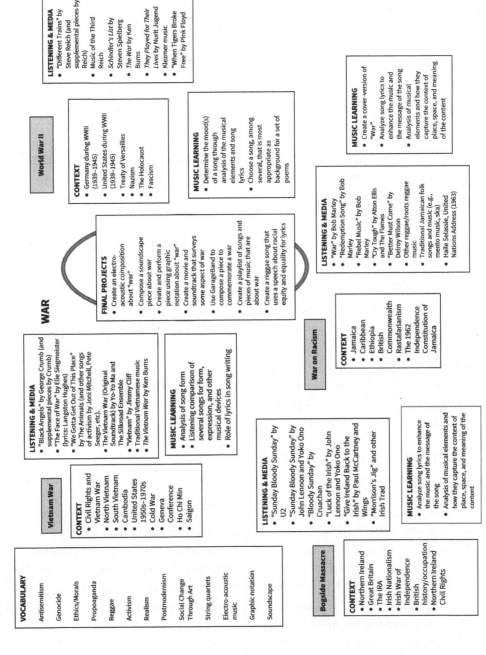

WAR

FINAL PROJECTS
- Create an electro-acoustic composition about "war"
- Compose a soundscape piece about war
- Create and perform a piece using graphic notation about "war"
- Create a movie and soundtrack that surveys some aspect of war
- Use GarageBand to compose a piece to commemorate a war
- Create a playlist of songs and pieces of music that are about war
- Create a reggae song that uses a speech about racial equity and equality for lyrics

---

VOCABULARY
Antisemitism
Genocide
Ethics/Morals
Propoaganda
Reggae
Activism
Realism
Postmodernism
Social Change Through Art
String quartets
Electro-acoustic music
Graphic notation
Soundscape

World War II

LISTENING & MEDIA
- "Different Trains" by Steve Reich (and supplemental pieces by Reich)
- Music of the Third Reich
- *Schindler's List* by Steven Spielberg
- *The War* by Ken Burns
- *They Played for Their Lives* by Nurit Jugend
- Klezmer music
- "When Tigers Broke Free" by Pink Floyd

CONTEXT
- Germany during WWII (1939–1945)
- United States during WWII (1939–1945)
- Treaty of Versailles
- Nazism
- The Holocaust
- Fascism

MUSIC LEARNING
- Determine the mood(s) of a song through analysis of the musical elements and song lyrics
- Choose a song, among several, that is most appropriate as a background for a set of poems

MUSIC LEARNING
- Create a cover version of "War"
- Analyze song lyrics to enhance the music and the message of the song
- Analysis of musical elements and how they capture the context of place, space, and meaning of the content

---

Vietnam War

LISTENING & MEDIA
- "Black Angels" by George Crumb (and supplemental pieces by Crumb)
- "The Face of War" by Elie Siegmeister (lyrics: Langston Hughes)
- "We Gotta Get Out of This Place" by The Animals (and other songs of activism by Joni Mitchell, Pete Seeger, etc).
- The Vietnam War (Original Soundtrack) by Yo-Yo Ma and The Silkroad Ensemble
- "Vietnam" by Jimmy Cliff
- Traditional Vietnamese music
- *The Vietnam War* by Ken Burns

CONTEXT
- Civil Rights and Vietnam War
- North Vietnam
- South Vietnam
- Cambodia
- United States
- 1950s–1970s
- Cold War
- Geneva Conference
- Ho Chi Min
- Saigon

MUSIC LEARNING
- Analysis of song form
- Listening comparison of several songs for form, expression, and other musical devices
- Role of lyrics in song writing

War on Racism

CONTEXT
- Jamaica
- Caribbean
- Ethiopia
- British Commonwealth
- Rastafarianism
- The 1962 Independence Constitution of Jamaica

LISTENING & MEDIA
- "War" by Bob Marley
- "Redemption Song" by Bob Marley
- "Rebel Music" by Bob Marley
- "Cry Tough" by Alton Ellis and The Flames
- "Better Must Come" by Delroy Wilson
- Other reggae/roots reggae music
- Traditional Jamaican folk songs and music (e.g., mento music, ska)
- Haile Selassie, United Nations Address (1963)

Bogside Massacre

CONTEXT
- Northern Ireland
- Great Britain
- The IRA
- Irish Nationalism
- Irish War of Independence
- British history/occupation
- Northern Ireland Civil Rights

LISTENING & MEDIA
- "Sunday Bloody Sunday" by U2
- "Sunday Bloody Sunday" by John Lennon and Yoko Ono
- "Bloody Sunday" by Cruachan
- "Luck of the Irish" by John Lennon and Yoko Ono
- "Give Ireland Back to the Irish" by Paul McCartney and Wings
- "Morrison's Jig" and other Irish Trad

MUSIC LEARNING
- Analyze song lyrics to enhance the music and the message of the song
- Analysis of musical elements and how they capture the context of place, space, and meaning of the content

Introductory Lesson to War

Goal
To introduce connections between feelings and music with various components of "war." Doing so can capitalize on emotional arousal through and emotional feeling in musical experiences. Building such understanding attempts to "move" others to understand the complexities and impact that "war" may have around the world.

National Standards
- MU:Pr4.2.8c: Identify how cultural and historical contexts inform performances and result in different musical effects.
- MU:Cr2.1.8a: Select, organize, and document personal musical ideas for arrangements, songs, and compositions within expanded forms that demonstrate tension and release, unity and variety, balance, and convey expressive intent.
- MU:Re8.1.7a: Support personal interpretation of contrasting programs of music and explain how creators or performers apply the elements of music and expressive qualities, within genres, cultures, and historical periods, to convey expressive intent.

Assessment/Evaluation
- **Formative:** Students will receive feedback throughout the lesson.
- **Summative:** Summative assessment could occur as part of a portfolio process.

Materials
Audio recordings of music: George Crumb, *Black Angels;* Steve Reich, *Different Trains;* U2, "Sunday Bloody Sunday"; and Bob Marley, "War": found on our book's website.

Teaching Process (This may take two class periods)

Instruction	Comments/Suggestions
Do Now: In their notebook, students will think of and write down "sounds" or "noises" (from the environment) that express the following emotions: HATRED; FEAR; HAPPINESS; COMFORT. Students will then go around the room and share their answers (without passing any judgment or critiquing the answers of each other).	Setting the context for "how" sounds and noises create meaning. Help listeners interpret songs and pieces of music that "evoke," "arouse," and "express" particular emotions, feelings, and spaces/places in time.

Instruction	Comments/Suggestions
Procedure and Questions for Discussion: • Play and listen to selections (about 1–2 minutes of each) of instrumental music (see "Materials" section; Crumb and Reich). Do not explain anything about the music or the context. Have students identify what they have in common. • Explore the "program" associated with each piece of instrumental music. • How does the context of each piece/song yield better "understanding" of the piece of music? • How does the music explore the context of each piece?	These are open-ended questions to facilitate a range of responses. Musical "elements": e.g., Crumb's "Departure" from *Black Angels* uses a variety of sounds to express aspects of the Vietnam War and evoke fear, empathy, and sympathy in listeners. Reich's "Before the War" from *Different Trains* highlights the ways in which music can be an aural "documentary" of life; used to reflect different perspectives of people living in the world at the same time (i.e., being Jewish and living in America during WWII versus living in Europe during WWII).
Play and listen to U2's "Sunday Bloody Sunday" and Bob Marley's "War." Pair–Share Activity: Discuss with a partner what U2's "Sunday Bloody Sunday" and Bob Marley's "War" might have in common with the Crumb and Reich.	These songs will help connect students to compositions from other eras and times and places around the world.

Instruction	Comments/Suggestions
Music Creating Activity: Students create their own piece of music (i.e., via "soundscape" composition using "found instruments" and/or music technology) that is indicative of "WAR." Use the same "tactic" as the one used in the Do Now activity. Ask students: Choose a sound that is indicative of "war" and through GarageBand, Protools, or the Digital Audio Workstation (DAW) of your choosing, manipulate the "war sound" so it creates a "war soundscape." The piece should be less than 1 minute in length, contain a climax, and begin the same way it ends.	This is an opportunity for students to examine and explore the possible "sounds" of war and their "emotional arousal." Supply a model "war soundscape"; for example, sample the sound of a person screaming (or take an acoustic sound sample from the internet; like the sound of thunder); input that scream (or other sound sample) into GarageBand, and manipulate the speed, volume, pitch, frequency (etc.) so that this soundscape is less than 1 minute in length, contains a climax, and begins the same way it ends.
Have student volunteers share their creations.	Whenever students are going to share compositions, it is critical that you first lay the groundwork for supportive listening.
Exit Ticket: *Besides the music shown here today, what other songs/pieces emphasize the theme of WAR? Write down one or more pieces that illustrate this social issue. Why do you think the creators created the works they did in relation to WAR? What specific elements can you point out that would confirm this?*	Collect cards as students leave the room and use this information as a springboard for subsequent lessons.

World War II

Introduction

Wars do not emerge out of thin air. Typically, when there is a war, it results from previous unresolved conflict. Case in point: World War II. In many ways, World War II couldn't have happened were it not for the Great War (World War I, 1914–1918) and the subsequent instability in Europe. Unresolved issues, conflict, political turmoil, and more, all served as a catalyst for World War II.

The global conflict of World War II (1939–1945) claimed more than 60 million lives. On September 1, 1939, the German dictator Adolf Hitler invaded Poland.

The aim at the time was to "restore" Germany's "greatness" as a worldwide super-power after the country was defeated in World War I. Hitler's strategy was to expand German territory by first occupying and then claiming countries in Europe. Following the German invasion of Poland, Great Britain and France declared war on Germany. At this point in time, the United States remained neutral. However, under President Franklin Delano Roosevelt, the United States supported the Allies (Great Britain, France, the Soviet Union) by sending food, supplies, and weapons. And in December 1941, following the Japanese attack on Pearl Harbor, the United States officially announced that it opposed the Axis (Germany, Italy, and Japan) and joined the war. On the whole, World War II illustrates and magnifies the numerous ways in which fascism and tyranny work against justice. Importantly, levels of cruelty, persecution, torture, and mass murder—including forced labor camps and concentration camps—reached levels beyond belief.

There are numerous more facets of World War II that could be explored, examined, and discussed, though for our purposes, we'd like to mention the ways in which World War II influenced music and music making, both during and after the war. Prior to the United States entering the war, swing bands (jazz big bands) dominated the radio air waves and were featured prevalently at nightclubs. Typically, a 17-piece "orchestra" (or "big band")—5 saxophones, 4 trumpets, 4 trombones, and a 4-piece rhythm section (piano, drums, guitar, bass)—playing the music of Duke Ellington, Cab Calloway, and Glenn Miller rhythmically kicked into high gear, and offered comfort, solace, and entertainment to soldiers abroad and as well as to families at home. Some of the popular songs and charts listened to then were as vast as they were various: Glenn Miller's "In the Mood" and "Moonlight Serenade"; the Andrews Sisters' "Boogie Woogie Bugle Boy" or "Don't Sit under the Apple Tree"; Dooley Wilson's "As Time Goes By"; Aaron Copland's "Fanfare for the Common Man." During this time, listeners and music makers were graced with patriotic, sentimental, morale-boosting, as well as escapist music.

Given the plethora of music, and given the emotional range of that music, consider sharing additional music listening with students while they are at work on this cluster of lessons. For example, see our book's website for additional music and media (e.g., *Quartet for the End of Time* by Olivier Messiaen); consider watching scenes from *They Played for Their Lives* by Nurit Jugend, *Schindler's List* by Steven Spielberg, and *The War* by Ken Burns. Clearly, music created for various purposes during this time period served those at home and abroad in different, yet similar ways, depending on their own circumstances. Additionally, during World War II, music served as propaganda (see https://holocaustmusic.ort.org/politics-and-pro paganda/third-reich/). For more music, more songs, and more context of music during World War II, see Annegret Fauser's book, *Sounds of War*.

The group of lessons that follow focus primarily on music that was written long after World War II was over. Please note: some music from this time frame (1930s–1940s) could easily be included throughout these lessons. Please see the book's website for additional selected examples of the music of World War II. Integrating such music, its contexts, and stories into your classroom teaching would likely provide valuable resources for students to understand connections between this war and issues of social justice.

World War II

Lesson 1

Goal
To experience some of the social, political, and emotional concerns of World War II through music, including Steve Reich's *Different Trains*.

National Standards
- MU:Re7.2.8a: Compare how the elements of music and expressive qualities relate to the structure within programs of music.
- MU:Re7.2.8b: Identify and compare the context of programs of music from a variety of genres, cultures, and historical periods.

Assessment/Evaluation
- **Formative:** Teacher will determine, primarily through questioning, whether students understand how electro-acoustic music can engage two sonic types—electric/sampled vs. acoustic instruments/voices—and how they can evoke empathy in listeners.
- **Summative:** Summative assessment could occur as part of a portfolio process.

YouTube Video
- "When Tigers Broke Free" from Pink Floyd's *The Wall*: https://www.youtube.com/watch?v=YKfwwlEcowk

Other Materials
- World War II Timeline (Appendix A)
- Photographs of World War II, from Getty Images: https://www.gettyimages.com/photos/world-war-ii
- Steve Reich's program notes for *Different Trains* (Appendix B)
- Audio recording Steve Reich's *Different Trains*: https://www.youtube.com/watch?v=-xKH7t_MXT8

Teaching Process

Instruction	Comments/Suggestions
Do Now: Have "When Tigers Broke Free" playing as students enter the classroom. Write the following on the board: Listening to the song played, answer the following questions in your Listening Log: • What does this music make you think of? What scene or personal experience comes to mind from the musical selection? • What emotions do you hear in the music? • What is happening in the music that makes you think of these emotions or experiences? For example, how does speed play a part in this? How does, say, volume play a part in this? How does, say, instrumentation play a part in this?	The teacher should keep her/his own Listening Log in order to participate with students if/when possible. Allow students to share their responses. Total time for this activity: 5–6 minutes.
Briefly discuss the concept of "electro-acoustic music"; students should then be asked to point out possible electro-acoustic components of Pink Floyd's "When Tigers Broke Free."	An "electro-acoustic" piece of music is any music that combines electronic sound with acoustic sound. Possible answer may be: wind sounds.
Watch video of "When Tigers Broke Free" to provide some context for World War II, by experiencing this through Roger Waters's (songwriter) father's life as expressed through this song. Follow along with the song's lyrics. Think–Pair–Share Activity: Ask students to consider the tone, color, and pace of the lyrics, video, and music: *Why do you believe the tone, color, and pace are created this way? What might be the desired effect?* Also ask: *What might all this tell you about World War II?*	Roger Waters of Pink Floyd wrote this song, in part, to pay tribute to Operation Shingle (Anzio, Italy; liberating Rome from German occupation) during World War II, and to pay tribute to his father, who fought and lost his life at the hands of German soldiers. For more information about this song, see: https://thewallcomplete.com/2016/03/17/when-the-tigers-broke-free/ Model this kind of question-and-answer technique when listening to music (to include the elements, but only as they relate to understanding the content/context of "what" the music is representing).

Instruction	Comments/Suggestions
World War II history is as complex as it is complicated. Hand out World War II timeline of events (**Appendix A**) and share photographs taken from the War. Think–Pair–Share Activity: Ask students to consider which aspects of the World War II timeline seems particularly moving (whether powerful or haunting or tragic).	Make sure students understand that some of the material examined may be difficult to experience. Model the kind of empathy needed from students by sharing your own questions and reactions to photographs and timeline of events. Additionally, if need be, utilize online resources to supplement the many narrative layers of World War II (e.g., https://www.history.com/topics/world-war-ii/world-war-ii-history).
Introduction to Steve Reich's *Different Trains* Pass out Reich's "program notes" (**Appendix B**) to *Different Trains*. Analyze the text for its meaning (look up words you don't know) and identify the main purpose of the composition. *What would you expect the music to sound like? What kind of story is it trying to tell?* Listen to the opening (30 sec) to *Different Trains*, "Before the War." *What are the "acoustic" aspects of the opening to* Different Trains? *What are the "electric" (sampled) aspects of* Different Trains? (e.g., string instruments vs. train whistle). Analysis/Conversation: *What does the "locomotive" sound feel like? What do you feel listening to it, knowing what the piece is about?*	The "analysis" questions might be difficult for students to answer. If so, ask follow-up questions that would allow for empathy (e.g., What might the "safe" Steve Reich be feeling while taking the train across the United States? How might the people riding a train taking them to a concentration camp be feeling? Compare/contrast the two sets of feelings.)

World War II

Lesson 2

Goal

To consider that World War II was an important part of world history and worthy of musical examination by one of America's most celebrated composers.

National Standards

- MU:Re7.2.6a: Describe how the elements of music and expressive qualities relate to the structure of the pieces.
- MU:Pr4.2.7c: Identify how cultural and historical contexts inform performance and results in different music interpretations.

Assessment/Evaluation

- **Formative**: Through questioning and discussion, the teacher will assess students as to their understanding of Steve Reich's musical documentation of World War II. Through reading students' Listening Logs, questioning and discussion (as needed), the teacher will assess students' abilities to assign sounds/noises to important cultural/social events.
- **Summative**: Summative assessment could occur as part of a portfolio process.

YouTube Videos

- "Shalom Alechem," Barcelona Gipsy Orchestra: https://www.youtube.com/watch?v=iSU0UG4VSEI
- On Steve Reich's *Different Trains*: https://www.youtube.com/watch?v=1r-kxJqjrws
- *Different Trains*, "Europe during the War": https://www.youtube.com/watch?v=pZRBfRXJyak

Other Materials

- Steve Reich biographical information (Appendix C)
- Lyrics to *Different Trains* (located on the book's website)
- Steve Reich's *Different Trains*, "Before the War" (audio only)
- Notes to *Different Trains* (Appendix B)

Teaching Process

Instruction	Comments/Suggestions
Do Now: Have video of "Shalom alechem" by the Barcelona Gipsy Klezmer Orchestra playing as students enter the classroom. Write the following on the board: Listening to the song played, answer the following questions in your Listening Log: • What does this music make you think of? What scene or personal experience comes to mind from the musical selection? • What emotions do you hear in the music? • What is happening in the music that makes you think of these emotions or experiences? For example, how does speed play a part in this? How does, say, volume play a part in this? How does, say, instrumentation play a part in this?	The teacher should keep her/his own Listening Log in order to participate with students if/when possible. Allow students to share their responses. Explain to students that "Shalom alechem" mean "Peace be among you." Traditional song usually sung at the start of the sabbath. Total time for this activity: 5–6 minutes.
Klezmer music began because people needed to find ways to manage being "displaced," especially during wartime. Think–Pair–Share Activity: *Thinking about "displacement," what are some of the pictures you think about?* *Why might displaced people want/need to sing songs and/or play instrumental music?*	Try to steer the conversation in such a way that students can begin to "empathize" with displaced peoples.
Let's get to know the composer of *Different Trains*, Steve Reich, by reading his biography (**Appendix** C) and watching **On Steve Reich's** *Different Trains*. While watching, write down any questions you may have about the composer's life and/or his motivations for creating *Different Trains*.	
Listen to *Different Trains*, "Before the War" (audio only). Follow along with the "lyrics." *What do you notice?*	
Put students in small groups and discuss the content of *Different Trains*, "Before the War."	Facilitate discussion about the use of electronic sounds, acoustic instruments, speech etc. Analyze the form of the song. *Is this a typical verse/chorus form?*

Instruction	Comments/Suggestions
Watch Steve Reich's *Different Trains*, "During the War" (video performance). Sometimes, music can document history. On doing so, the experience of musical documentation allows victims and survivors a chance to be seen and heard. We cannot attempt to rectify suffering unless we understand and empathize with the tragedy of others. Still in small groups, ask students to discuss: In what ways does Steve Reich's *Different Trains* make explicit the experiences of victims and survivors? In what ways does *Different Trains* examine World War II?	
We will work toward the creation of our own electro-acoustic composition that "documents" a war of some kind. What are some "wars" that demand our attention and need musical documentation?	List some ideas on the board such as the Vietnam War, War on Drugs, War on Racism, the War in Afghanistan, COVID-19, etc.
In your small groups, consider the following: • What "war" do you think needs a musical examination? Why? • What are some sounds/noises that are symbolic of, representative of, or expressive of the war of your group's choosing? Why?	The teacher will visit with the small groups and assess their conversations. At the end of class, students will write down the war that they wish to document.

World War II

Lesson 3

Goal
To create/compose an electro-acoustic piece based on war.

National Standards

- MU:Re7.7a: Classify and explain how the elements of music and expressive qualities relate to the structure of contrasting pieces.
- MU:Cr2.1.6a: Select, organize, construct, and document personal musical ideas for arrangements, and compositions within AB, ABA, or theme and variation

forms that demonstrate an effective beginning, middle, and ending, and convey expressive intent.

Assessment/Evaluation

- **Formative:** The teacher will gather evidence (through questioning, observation, and students' pieces) of students' understandings of musical/lyrical/rhythmic components of a quality electro-acoustic piece of music. The teacher will monitor and assess students' participation in small group-work to create and share an electro-acoustic piece.
- **Summative:** Summative assessment could occur as part of a portfolio process.

Materials (for review, if needed)

- Lyrics to *Different Trains*
- Steve Reich's *Different Trains*, "Before the War" (audio only)
- Steve Reich's *Different Trains*, "During the War" (video performance)
- Steve Reich's *Different Trains*, "After the War" (audio only)
- Electro-acoustic Composition Guidelines (Appendix D)

Teaching Process (this may take two to three classes to complete)

Instruction	Comments/Suggestions
Today we are going to work in our project groups to create an electro-acoustic piece. *What makes for a quality "musical documentation" of a war?* Play *Different Trains*, "After the War" (audio only). Write the following on the board: Listening to the song played, answer the following questions in your Listening Log: • What does this music make you think of? What scene or personal experience comes to mind from the musical selection? • What emotions do you hear in the music? • What is happening in the music that makes you think of these emotions or experiences? For example, how does speed play a part in this? How does, say, volume, play a part in this? How does, say, instrumentation, play a part in this?	Go over the "Electro-acoustic Piece Handout" (**Appendix D**) Discuss the elements that Steve Reich utilizes to help listeners "feel" the war, e.g., instrumental parts mirroring the text (or text painting), repetitive rhythmic patterns (to symbolize the relentlessness of war), lyrics that place the listener "there" in the war, etc. Discuss the tempo, lyrics, form.

Instruction	Comments/Suggestions
List some of the creative ways in which Steve Reich composed the "content" for *Different Trains*. Questions: *How did he compose* Different Trains? *What is the overall structure of the piece? How did the melodic material arise? What sound-samples were utilized and why?*	Model this kind of score/musical analysis. The goal for this kind of analysis is not just to better understand *Different Trains*. It also will serve the students in starting their own projects.
In small groups, brainstorm and consider the following questions: • What "war" do you think needs a musical examination? Why? • What mode of "transportation" is authentically "linked" to that war? Why? • What speech-sounds would you pre-record that would illustrate those people on the "safe side" of the war AND those people "deep inside" the war of your choosing? • How might you adapt Steve Reich's process for musically representing a current day "war" (of your choosing)?	Teacher should monitor student progress in brainstorming by visiting groups, answering questions, helping stimulate deeper thinking, etc. This activity models how students can potentially utilize sound samples and speech sounds to create melodic and rhythmic materials for an electro-acoustic composition.
Small group work through **Appendix D**, Electro-acoustic Guidelines	Let students know that the pace of group work may differ, and that is just fine.
Sharing with the class. Each group will explain their "war" and some of the ideas that were important for their composition. Share their piece with the class.	Whenever students are going to share compositions, it is critical that you first lay the groundwork for supportive listening and applause.
Reflection: *What did you like about each students' piece? Where would each song fit in understanding social justice as related to war? Why?*	DO NOT SKIP THIS STEP. It is important that performers (who are putting themselves on the line) get constructive peer feedback. They need to feel that their efforts were appreciated.

The Vietnam War or the Second Indochina War (known in Vietnam as the Resistance War against America)

Introduction

It's difficult to escape interpretations of the Vietnam War given the plethora of music and films that depict its essence; for example, *Born on the Fourth of July*, *Platoon*,

Forest Gump, *Full Metal Jacket*, *Da 5 Bloods*, *The Deer Hunter*, and *Apocalypse Now*. Because of this, it's important for students to weigh these popular culture references against more objective illustrations of the Vietnam War. Invariably, and across many popular culture interpretations of this war, Vietnamese citizens are depicted as "passive victims" and/or manipulators (e.g., conniving prostitutes), while Vietnamese soldiers (or Viet Cong) are shown as aggressive, war-hungry villains. Conversely, American soldiers are typically coined as young, innocent men who have been sent to war with no real understanding (or concern) for "why" they are fighting overseas. Perhaps because the Vietnam War was one of the longest and most unpopular wars in this country's history, popular culture has taken numerous attempts at re-envisioning its contexts and content. Across films, visual arts, music, poetry, and other forms of fiction, creators have been asking whether American involvement in this armed conflict was "necessary," "immoral," "idealistic," and/or a "failed attempt to fight against fascism." Whether or not artistic depictions maintain stereotypical interpretations will not be the focus of this unit. Instead, students will engage with the content of the Vietnam War as "objectively" as possible and then as "feelingly" as possible, once they have a clearer understanding of "what" happened from 1955 to 1975, both at home and abroad.

So, by way of a very brief introduction to the Vietnam War—note: consider watching the entirety of Ken Burns's documentary series on the Vietnam War, as well as visiting and reading through the History Channels' depiction of the conflict—we must first recognize that long before the "war" began, in 1887, France colonized Vietnam, calling it French Indochina. Less than 20 years later, Japan invaded French Indochina. And in 1941, Ho Chi Min—a Vietnamese nationalist—and his communist supporters started a movement aimed at resisting French and Japanese occupation, and established the Democratic Republic of Vietnam.

After World War II, between 1945 and 1954, the Vietnamese fought France, and sought its independence. The United States supported this fight, and the French were defeated. In 1954, the country was partitioned between the south and the north. The defeat of French occupation resulted in the Geneva Peace Conference (April 26– July 21, 1954), where representatives from Cambodia, Laos, the Peoples' Republic of China, France, the United States, the Soviet Union, the Viet Minh (North Vietnam), and the State of Vietnam (South Vietnam) created a "road map" to reunify Vietnam. As a result of the accords, Vietnam was officially divided between an anti-communist south (called the State of Vietnam) and pro-communist north (called the Viet-Minh). However, despite best intentions, the major stakeholders did not adhere to these steps toward peace and reconciliation.

There is much more to be said about the "what" that occurred in Vietnam from 1954 to 1965; however, doing so is beyond the scope of this book. For now, though: in 1965 under President Lyndon Johnson, 200,000 American troops landed in South Vietnam. The number of troops increased steadily until 1969, when Ho Chi Min died and President Richard Nixon reduced the number of troops as American opposition to the war steadily increased. In 1973 a cease-fire agreement was drafted in Paris, France, and the United States pulled all troops out in March of that year. In April 1975, South Vietnam surrendered to North Vietnam and the country was reunited. As a result of the Vietnam War, the United States lost nearly 60,000 lives; Vietnam saw around 2,000,000 deaths.

While there is so much pop, rock, and folk music that surrounds the Vietnam War, the twentieth-century classical piece, *Black Angels,* is the "centerpiece" of the unit. Why this piece? As we hope will become clear, part of the thrust of this unit, as a whole, is to help students create electro-acoustic compositions. And *Black Angels* serves as an evocative model. About this piece, George Crumb stated the following:

> Things were turned upside down. There were terrifying things in the air . . . they found their way into *Black Angels.* (George Crumb, 1990)

> *Black Angels* was conceived as a kind of parable on our troubled contemporary world. The work portrays a voyage of the soul. The three stages of this voyage are Departure (fall from grace), Absence (spiritual annihilation) and Return (redemption). (George Crumb, 1986)

> The numerological symbolism of *Black Angels,* while perhaps not immediately percep-tible to the ear, is nonetheless quite faithfully reflected in the musical structure. These "magical" relationships are variously expressed: e.g., in terms of length, groupings of single tones, durations, patterns of repetition, etc. . . . There are several allusions to tonal music: a quotation from Schubert's *Death and the Maiden* quartet; an original *Sarabanda;* the sustained B-major tonality of God-Music; and several references to the Latin sequence *Dies Irae* (Day of Wrath). The work abounds in conventional musical symbolisms such as the *Diabolus in Musica* (the interval of the tritone) and the *Trillo Di Diavolo* (the Devil's Trill, after Tartini). (George Crumb, 1986)

> The underlying structure of *Black Angels* is a huge arch-like design which is suspended from the three "Threnody" pieces. The work portrays a voyage of the soul. The three stages of this voyage are Departure (fall from grace), Absence (spiritual annihilation) and Return (redemption). (George Crumb, preface to the score)[1]

Bearing witness is not beyond the ability of secondary school students. Indeed, there are several instances in this unit that introduce ways that teens have responded with empathy to the survivors and victims of war, particularly the Vietnam War. Learning constructive strategies for "seeing" others cultivates empowerment, an awareness of "self–other" responsibilities, and allows young people to make sense of the world around them. Subsequently, music activities reflect an important means of grappling with these topics.

The Vietnam War

Lesson 1

Goal
To experience some of the social, political, and emotional concerns of the Vietnam War through music, including George Crumb's *Black Angels*.

National Standards
- MU:Re7.2.8a: Compare how the elements of music and expressive qualities relate to the structure within programs of music.
- MU:Re7.2.8b: Identify and compare the context of programs of music from a variety of genres, cultures, and historical periods.
- MU:Pr 4.2.8c: Identify how cultural and historical contexts inform performances and result in different musical effects.

Assessment/Evaluation
- **Formative**: Teacher will determine, primarily through questioning, whether students understand how electro-acoustic music can engage two sonic types—electric/sampled vs. acoustic instruments/voices—and how they can evoke empathy in listeners.
- **Summative**: Summative assessment could occur as part of a portfolio process.

YouTube Videos
- "We Gotta Get Out of This Place": https://www.youtube.com/watch?v=Q3mgapAcVdU
- "Most Terrifying Sounds of the Vietnam War": https://www.youtube.com/watch?v=k3LI0OtCw9o
- "Vietnam's Infinite Cave—National Geographic": https://www.youtube.com/watch?v=6cTIA03cwqE&list=PL58E01ED4FB0BC8F3&index=77
- "Wandering Soul (Ghost Tape No. 10)": https://www.youtube.com/watch?v=4d9H_1ygEv8&feature=emb_logo
- Gong ensemble: https://www.youtube.com/watch?v=c5gxavBLkLI
- "Inside the Album" Kronos Quartet's Black Angels: https://www.youtube.com/watch?v=QGeyiXsaDws (watch start to 3′36″)
- Audio recording George Crumb's *Black Angels*: https://www.youtube.com/watch?v=etHtCVeU4-I

Other Materials
- George Crumb's Biographical Information (Appendix E)
- George Crumb's notes for *Black Angels* (see our book's website)
- Vietnam War Timeline (see our book's website)

Teaching Process

Instruction	Comments/Suggestions
Do Now: Have "We Gotta Get Out of This Place" playing as students enter the classroom. Write the following on the board: Listening to the song played, answer the following questions in your Listening Log: • What does this music make you think of? What scene or personal experience comes to mind from the musical selection? • What emotions do you hear in the music? • What is happening in the music that makes you think of these emotions or experiences? For example, how does speed play a part in this? How does, say, volume play a part in this? How does, say, instrumentation play a part in this?	The teacher should keep her/his own Listening Log in order to participate with students if/when possible. Allow students to share their responses. Total time for this activity: 5–6 minutes.
Briefly discuss the lyrics (found via the internet) and what seems to be the rationale for wanting "to get out of this place." Briefly talk about why this song became an "anthem" for the Vietnam War. *Examined through the lens of the Vietnam War, what might the song be saying now?*	Possible answers may be: "being stuck" in a job or place that yields more problems than good. Wanting a "better life." Possible answers may be: Going home; being free.
Watch videos of "Most terrifying sounds of the Vietnam War," moments from "Vietnam's Infinite Cave—National Geographic," "Wandering Soul (Ghost Tape No. 10)," and the Cambodian Gong Ensemble. Think–Pair–Share Activity: Ask students to consider the tones, colors, and "energy" of the sounds, images, and landscapes. Also ask: *What sounds, images, and landscapes seems to evoke the "sensory" experiences of Vietnam? What might be the desired effect? Also ask: What might all this tell you about the Vietnam War?*	Model this kind of questioning of sounds (to include the elements of music). This will serve your students when they listen to George Crumb's *Black Angels.*

Instruction	Comments/Suggestions
The Vietnam War history is a complex as it is complicated. Consider Vietnam War timeline of events (see the book's website) and share photographs taken from the Vietnam War. Think–Pair–Share Activity: Ask students to consider which aspects of the Vietnam timeline seem particularly moving (whether powerful or haunting or tragic).	Make sure students understand that some of the material examined in this unit may be difficult to experience. Model the kind of empathy needed from students by sharing your own questions and reactions to photographs and timeline of events. Additionally, if need be, utilize online resources to supplement the many narrative layers (e.g., https://www.history.com/topics/vietnam-war/vietnam-war-timeline)
Introduction to George Crumb (see **Appendix** E) and his *Black Angels*. Look at "front matter" from George Crumb's *Black Angels* score (images found on this book's website) and read his program notes (also found on our book's website). *What would you expect the music to sound like? What kind of story is it trying to tell?*	
Listen to the opening minute (or so) to *Black Angels*. *What are the "acoustic" aspects of the opening to* Black Angels? *What are the "electric" aspects of* Black Angels? (e.g., string instruments vs. amplified sounds). Watch "Inside the Album" Kronos Quartet's *Black Angels*. Analysis: *What do the "electric instrument" sounds feel like? What do you feel listening to it, knowing what the piece is about?*	The "analysis" questions might be difficult for students to answer. If so, ask follow-up questions that would allow for "bearing witness" to those experiencing the Vietnam War. Ask them to consider some similarities of sounds between Cambodian gong music and George Crumb's *Black Angels*.
Question (for future creation/composition): What other sounds from nature evoke "terror" and why?	Be sure to ask students to share their thoughts about this question in the next class.

The Vietnam War

Lesson 2

Goal
To understand a "threnody" as created through graphic notation in relation to twentieth-century electro-acoustic composition.

National Standards
- MU:Re7.2.8a: Compare how the elements of music and expressive qualities relate to the structure within programs of music.
- MU:Cn10.0.8a: Demonstrate how interests, knowledge, and skills relate to personal choices and intent when creating, performing, and responding to music.

Assessment/Evaluation
- **Formative:** Teacher will determine, primarily through questioning, whether students understand how sounds can evoke a sense of place/space. Teacher will determine, primarily through questioning, whether students understand how the form/structure of a piece of music can allude to place/space.
- **Summative:** Summative assessment could occur as part of a portfolio process.

YouTube Videos
- "Travelin' Soldier" by The Chicks: https://www.youtube.com/watch?v=AbfgxznPmZM
- Audio recording of George Crumb's *Black Angels*: https://www.youtube.com/watch?v=etHtCVeU4-I

Other Materials
- Selections from George Crumb's *Black Angels* score (found on our book's website)
- For the teacher: Helpful guide to George Crumb's *Black Angels* (analysis and score examples) can be found at: https://mtosmt.org/issues/mto.12.18.2/mto.12.18.2.johnston.html

Teaching Process

Instruction	Comments/Suggestions
Do Now: Have "Travelin' Soldier" playing as students enter the classroom. Write the following on the board: Listening to the song played, answer the following questions in your Listening Log: • What does this music make you think of? What scene or personal experience comes to mind from the musical selection? • What emotions do you hear in the music? • What is happening in the music that makes you think of these emotions or experiences? For example, how does speed play a part in this? How does, say, volume play a part in this? How does, say, instrumentation play a part in this?	The teacher should keep her/his own Listening Log in order to participate with students if/when possible. Allow students to share their responses. Total time for this activity: 5–6 minutes.
Briefly discuss the lyrics (to be located via the internet) and ask, why does this song seem to be a "lament"? Ask: *Who mourns for those who die as a casualty of war?* Explain the word "threnody": "A poem, song, ode, hymn to lament and in memorial to a dead person."	Possible answers may be: "young girl being left behind" while the soldier/boyfriend goes off to war; "soldier's name is among the dead" and only the young high school girl recognizes his name.

Instruction	Comments/Suggestions
Let's examine the "structure" of Black Angels *(as explained by George Crumb in the front matter to his score). What do you notice about the FORM of the piece? How is it organized? Why might this be the case?* Thirteen Images From the Dark Land I. Departure 1. Threnody I: Night of the Electric Insects 2. Sounds of Bones and Flutes 3. Lost Bells 4. Devil-music 5. Danse Macabre II. Absence 6. Pavana Lachrymae 7. Threnody II: Black Angels! 8. Sarabanda de la Muerte Oscura 9. Lost Bells (Echo) III. Return 10. God-music 11. Ancient Voices 12. Ancient Voices (Echo) 13. Threnody III: Night of the Electric Insects Who might these three threnodies be for? How do the "bones," "flutes," and "lost bells" help sonically illustrate the three threnodies? How do such sounds help structure the piece as a whole?	Share George Crumb's thoughts about the quartet (see Introduction to the Vietnam War). Also point out that at the front of the score it reads: *"tempore belli* (in time of war) and Finished on Friday the Thirteenth, March, 1970."
Listen to "The Departure" from George Crumb's *Black Angels.* Have students follow along with the score (as best as they can). Consider projecting the score overhead while they follow along themselves. And periodically show students "where the class is" in the score as they listen/follow along. As they are following along, have them mark the score by pointing out things that seem most interesting/evocative.	While George Crumb's *Black Angels* score may seem like an unlikely score for general music students to "follow along" with, with your help they can. Doing so will help them better understand the "form" and "graphic notation" (and numerological structure) of George Crumb's composition. This will serve them in the next lesson.

Instruction	Comments/Suggestions
Small group discussion: *What "wars" have you and/or members of those closest to you personally experienced?* *Where did this war "take place" (literally or metaphorically)?* *What "sounds" best fit when depicting that war and that space/place?*	Ask students to brainstorm, as the answers to these questions will serve their compositional activity in the next lesson.
In the beginning of class, students thought about "lamentations" (or threnodies) for victims of war. *How should we "memorialize" those who perished during wars? In what ways can music be utilized to "bear witness" to those whose lives that have been taken?* *What songs do you know that "memorialize" the dead? What do such songs make you feel? How? Why?*	This is the critical message of all the lessons on the Vietnam War. Feel free to revisit this as much as needed.

The Vietnam War

Lesson 3

Goal
To understand and utilize "sounds" to evoke and memorialize harrowing times as experienced through wars.

National Standards
- MU:Cr1.1.8a: Generate rhythmic, melodic, and harmonic phrases and harmonic accompaniments within expanded forms (including introductions, transitions, and codas) that convey expressive intent.
- MU:Cr2.1.8b: Use standard and/or iconic notation and/or audio/video recording to document personal rhythmic phrases, melodic phrases, and harmonic sequences.

Assessment/Evaluation
- **Formative:** The teacher will gather evidence (through questioning, observation, and students' pieces) of students' understandings connected to musical/rhythmic components to a graphically notated, electro-acoustic piece of music. The teacher

will monitor and assess students' participation in small group work to create a graphically notated, electro-acoustic piece and share the song for the class.

- **Summative:** Summative assessment could occur as part of a portfolio process.

YouTube Videos

- "What's Going On" by Marvin Gaye: https://www.youtube.com/watch?v=H-kA3UtBj4M
- Audio recording of George Crumb's *Black Angels*: https://www.youtube.com/watch?v=etHtCVeU4-I

Other Materials

- George Crumb's *Black Angels* score (examples found online: https://mtosmt.org/issues/mto.12.18.2/mto.12.18.2.johnston.html)
- Composition Activity (Appendix F)

Teaching Process

Instruction	Comments/ Suggestions
Do Now: Have "What's Going On?" playing as students enter the classroom. Write the following on the board: Listening to the song played, answer the following questions in your Listening Log: • What does this music make you think of? What scene or personal experience comes to mind from the musical selection? • What emotions do you hear in the music? • What is happening in the music that makes you think of these emotions or experiences? For example, how does speed play a part in this? How does, say, volume play a part in this? How does, say, instrumentation play a part in this?	The teacher should keep her/his own Listening Log in order to participate with students if/when possible. Allow students to share their responses. Total time for this activity: 5–6 minutes.

Instruction	Comments/ Suggestions
Share some responses from the "Do Now" prompt. Teacher: *Being a teenager is not too young to have a discussion about the pros and cons of wars, even those wars that are long past. Understanding the past helps us be better in the present and grow toward the future. We need the past—even our mistakes—to help us know how better to live.* *What "wars" were you and your group members (e.g., COVID-19, LGTBQ fight for equal rights, the War in Afghanistan) talking about in our last class?*	Class discussion
Teacher: "Music has been an important vehicle for bearing witness, for memorializing tragic/war experiences, and for healing. That's what we will do, too, in our music making/composing/creating." Small group compositional activity will then commence.	
Composition Activity: Before breaking into groups, revisit what George Crumb's *Black Angels* "looks like" and re-examine the numerological form/structure of the piece. Have students create their own numerological form/structure that somehow incorporates the number "3."	See **Appendix F**. This Composition Activity will take more than one class. Note: This review/examination helps give students some ideas to think about.
Groups work through **Appendix F** on their own, with the teacher assisting as needed.	This will be noisy but you can contain the noise to a reasonable level with the quiet signal and by talking to individual groups.
Sharing with the class. Each group will explain their "war" and some of the ideas that were important for their composition. Share their piece with the class.	Whenever students are going to share compositions, it is critical that you first lay the groundwork for supportive listening and applause.
Reflection: *What did you like about each students' piece? Where would each song fit in understanding social justice as related to war? Why?*	DO NOT SKIP THIS STEP. It is important that performers (who are putting themselves on the line) get constructive peer feedback. They need to feel that their efforts were appreciated.

The Bogside Massacre (or Bloody Sunday)

Introduction

Wars, regardless of the rationale behind them, are difficult in and of themselves. But we compound levels of difficulty when wars are riddled with foundational issues and concepts that are inherently complex and complicated—especially concepts such as race and religion. Because of this, the Bogside Massacre is inherently complex and complicated. Still, because its context is (potentially for some people) far removed (politically, religiously, geographically), understanding its contexts, issues, and concerns are nonetheless important. Additionally, such a "war" gives us cause to pause and consider: Might a similar war—one of religious persecution vs. religious freedom; one of land domination and freedom from oppression—occur, despite the nature of "democracy"? Religiously problematic wars are difficult for teachers to address. Tough questions involve, "How can I talk about religion without offending parents or administration?"; "What do I say to help students talk about these issues without creating an 'us versus them' dichotomy?"; "What if students bring up controversial issues that are interpreted depending upon religious beliefs, like abortion, LGTBQ identity, theism versus atheism, and so forth?" All are challenging questions; all are questions worthy of consideration. Because public schools in the United States serve students—those possessing religious faith and those without religious faith—it's crucial that we support our students—all of them, regardless of ethical difference.

Still, we wish to recognize that social justice is messy work. And unfortunately, assumptions and stereotypes about "difference"—whether religious or racial—can lead toward intolerance and violence. Any students' experience of hostility jeopardizes their ability to learn and to thrive. Expanding students' worldviews about the diversity of world religions—and the intolerance religious groups have experienced—is critical for the health and well-being of students and their communities.

Numerous artists—across a variety of genres—have expressed their thoughts and feelings about Bloody Sunday. For example, the visual artist Robert Ballagh, who long criticized the social unrest that occurred on Bloody Sunday, is—at the time of this book's writing—at work on what will be a new, uncommissioned piece, to be completed in January 2022 (for the fiftieth anniversary of the massacre). Conceptual artist Glenn Kaino investigated connections between the "Bloody Sundays" in Selma, Alabama, in 1965 and Derry, Northern Ireland, in 1972. The exhibit "In the Light of a Shadow," curated and held at the Massachusetts Museum of Contemporary Art through 2022, intersects American stories with Irish stories by juxtaposing moving shadows and soundscapes from diverse religious and racial perspectives alongside sculpture made from metal. As Kaino stated in an interview: "the history is also the present; that the fight for civil rights is still pertinent as always."[2] Because of this, we urge you to share and explore connections across time and place. Additionally, consider introducing your students to the video included in Kaino's project: a version of U2's "Sunday Bloody Sunday" as performed by Deon Jones and featuring Jon Batiste.[3]

The Bogside Massacre

Lesson 1

Goal

To help students use music as a means for responding to tragic events such as a war or massacre.

National Standards

- MU:Re8.1.6a: Describe a personal interpretation of how creators' and performers' application of the elements of music and expressive qualities, within genres and cultural and historical contexts, conveys expressive intent.
- MU:Re7.1.6a: Select or choose music to listen to and explain the connections to specific interests or experiences for a specific purpose.

Assessment/Evaluation

- **Formative:** Teacher will determine, primarily through questioning, whether students understand how sounds can evoke a sense of war and militarism. Teacher will determine, primarily through observation, whether students understand how military music and militaristic sounds are evocative and expressive of social/political contexts.
- **Summative:** Summative assessment could occur as part of a portfolio process.

YouTube Videos

- "6/8 Military Cadence: US Army": https://www.youtube.com/watch?v=Gw359o3gFhc
- "Music for Drum and Fife": https://www.youtube.com/watch?v=yLGzw01R434
- "Traditional Fife and Drum Tunes": https://www.youtube.com/watch?v=NT9x9SBBDaQ

Other Materials

- Military music from the American and European Traditions: https://www.metmuseum.org/toah/hd/ammu/hd_ammu.htm
- "Bloody Sunday: What Happened on Sunday 30 January 1972?" BBC News: https://www.bbc.com/news/uk-northern-ireland-foyle-west-47433319
- Audio recording of U2's "Sunday Bloody Sunday"

Teaching Process

Instruction	Comments/Suggestions
Do Now: Have "Morrison's Jig" playing as students enter the classroom. Write the following on the board: Listening to the song played, answer the following questions in your Listening Log: • What does this music make you think of? What scene or personal experience comes to mind from the musical selection? • What emotions do you hear in the music? • What is happening in the music that makes you think of these emotions or experiences? For example, how does speed play a part in this? How does, say, volume play a part in this? How does, say, instrumentation play a part in this?	The teacher should keep her/his own Listening Log in order to participate with students if/when possible. Allow students to share their responses. Total time for this activity: 5–6 minutes.
Ask students: *Aside from "dancing," what other movement might be used to this beat?* Ask them to interpret "Morrison's Jig" as a "military march/cadence." Explain to students that the "bodhrán"—an Irish traditional frame drum—was used during the Irish rebellion of 1603 as a battle drum. Introduce them to a 6/8 military cadence. Ask students: *What do you notice about this military cadence? How does it feel?*	See if students have a response. If not, ask them to march in place.

Instruction	Comments/Suggestions
What Do We Know about the Bogside Massacre? Give students a sense of this massacre. Teacher: *When bad things happen to innocent bystanders and peaceful protesters, first there is grief. Then there is anger, and out of anger comes resilience. Some resilient people actively respond to such a situation by civilly protesting. Yet when civil protest is met with violence, how can people feel secure in expressing their disapproval?* Think–Pair–Share Activity: Students should read "Bloody Sunday: What Happened on Sunday 30 January 1972?" BBC News and comment on their thoughts.	*Context:* On January 30, 1972, in Londonderry, Northern Ireland, 13 unarmed protesters were shot and killed by British troops. The soldiers indiscriminately shot into a crowd. In addition to those killed, 17 were wounded. This event subsequently is known as "Bloody Sunday." And this wasn't the first "Bloody Sunday" in Irish/British history. In addition to this event, the British and the Irish have a complex and complicated history. Notably, religious violence between Protestants and Catholics—known as the "Northern Ireland conflict" or "the Troubles"—involves a long history of not only religious disagreement, but also land and economic segregation. See, for example, November 21, 1920; warring between the Irish Republican Army and the British Army led to more than 30 deaths, as the Irish fought for Independence. This day, like January 30, 1972, was called "Bloody Sunday"; this helped increase international and national support for Ireland.
Have students listen to music for drum and fife (as played by the US Army Band; or from Northern Ireland, or another such example of military music), found on the internet. Teach students a few military drum cadences (either by ear or through reading notation).	As students are experiencing this music, continue to ask them how it feels; ask them to imagine how it feels on either side of a "military engagement," namely hearing this from afar versus near (playing this rather than hearing it).
Listen to the audio recording of U2's "Sunday Bloody Sunday." *Besides the lyrics, what about the music sounds "militaristic" and expressive of war?* Find ways to facilitate musical terminology (e.g., dynamics, instrumentation, tempo).	Put categories on the board. There are no "right" or "wrong" answers, but students should explain their reasoning. Have students decide in which category to place the song. Students will have different ideas, so do not try to reach a consensus.

Instruction	Comments/Suggestions
In pairs or trios, use mobile devices to find drum cadences, loops, and/or sounds that seem *"militaristic" and expressive of war.*	Some students may have a specific loop or sound in mind. If not, you can facilitate a search by telling students to Google one of the categories.
Exit Ticket: *If you were going to choose a drum—from anywhere around the world—what drum seems to evoke "war" and protest?* Give a two-sentence explanation for your answer.	

The Bogside Massacre

Lesson 2

Goal
To explore how can music empathize and promote/provoke empathy within listeners/music makers.

National Standards
- MU:Re8.1.7a: Describe a personal interpretation of contrasting works and explain how creators' and performers' application of the elements of music and expressive qualities, within genres, cultures, and historical periods, conveys expressive intent.

Assessment/Evaluation
- **Formative:** Teacher will formatively assess—through observation and listening—students' understandings of how to create music inspired by other musical creations. Teacher will determine, primarily through questioning, whether students understand how sounds can illustrate historical events, places, and spaces.
- **Summative:** Summative assessment could occur as part of a portfolio process.

YouTube Videos
- Cruachan's "Bloody Sunday": https://www.youtube.com/watch?v=CYGb2xjqlkM
- U2's "Sunday Bloody Sunday" official music video: https://www.youtube.com/watch?v=EM4vblG6BVQ

Other Materials
- Lyrics for "Sunday Bloody Sunday" (located via the internet)

Teaching Process (this may take two class periods)

Instruction	Comments/Suggestions
Do Now: Have "Bloody Sunday" by Cruachan playing as students enter the classroom. Write the following on the board: Listening to the song played, answer the following questions in your Listening Log: • What does this music make you think of? What scene or personal experience comes to mind from the musical selection? • What emotions do you hear in the music? • What is happening in the music that makes you think of these emotions or experiences? For example, how does speed play a part in this? How does, say, volume play a part in this? How does, say, instrumentation play a part in this?	The teacher should keep her/his own Listening Log in order to participate with students if/when possible. Allow students to share their responses. Total time for this activity: 5–6 minutes.
Review the last class by revisiting drum cadences, drum and fife music, and military music. *What are some musical and emotional results of such sounds/music? Why?*	Discuss the ways that such sounds/music can be employed in songs of "protest."
If you were going to create a drum beat (or motif) to illustrate the Bogside Massacre, how would you go about doing so? What considerations would you need to make in order to be successful?	Explore, through discussion, students' perspectives; write down some of their thoughts on the board. Consider revisiting Irish traditional music (and instruments) to help expand students' horizons.
Play and listen to the live performance of U2's "Sunday Bloody Sunday." In groups of three or four, have students create a drum beat that takes inspiration from U2's "Sunday Bloody Sunday" and pays homage to the Bogside Massacre.	Ask students to comment upon what seemed different/perhaps more evocative than the pre-recorded version. Feel free to have students use Soundtrap, GarageBand, or another DAW of their choosing.

Instruction	Comments/Suggestions
Share the drum beats of each group.	Ask student listeners to comment and answer the following questions for each group's drum beat: *What did you notice?* *What questions do you have?* *What did you learn?*

The War on Racism

Introduction

Of all the lessons about war in this unit, a "war" on racism is probably the most difficult for teachers to address. Tough questions involve, "How can I talk about race without offending someone: parents, administration, students?"; "What if students bring up controversial issues that are difficult to answer?" For these very reasons, among many, many others, this book argues that, even though issues and concepts surrounding race and social justice are difficult to discuss and engage with, music teachers must attempt to musically address them.

There are two online articles, among numerous others, that provide helpful information for initiating a discussion with students about race. The first is, "Creating the Space to Talk about Race in Your School."[4] The second article is, "Three SEL Skills You Need to Discuss Race in Classrooms."[5] Both offer important mindsets, tips, and strategies on what to expect and how to facilitate such conversations.

School-aged children, as young as elementary grades, are already processing and discussing race. Like many of the other concepts examined and explored in this book, some say that discussions about race belong in the home. However, many parents may avoid talking with their children about race for one reason or another. On the other hand, schools have a commitment to preparing students for adulthood in a democracy; part of navigating and negotiating the tenets of democracy is engaging in and enacting equity and equality. For these reasons, such conversations are not only integral to being a part of contributing to a democratic society; such conversations help students develop ethical habits both in the classroom and beyond. Importantly, topics and considerations that involve race and racism are not issues of the past; they are part of our everyday world, and should be treated as such.

Issues concerning "race" influence classrooms—all classrooms, including the music classroom—dramatically. And conversations about race are not only about persons of color, but are about "whiteness," too. Because of this, numerous issues and assumptions will likely be magnified, for example, "white privilege," "color blindness," and more. Notably, it's important for teachers to interrogate their own biases and assumptions prior to doing this work with students. So, we suggest that a "war" on racism can be as direct as confronting stereotypes and challenging assumptions that, unknowingly or not, permeate a classroom and its surrounding community.

We hope that the artistic engagement that emerges from this part of the unit will help students feel empowered to challenge the past and the present. The arts—particularly music and poetry—have always given artists modes of expression that help creators to confront racist inequities and inequalities. The two lessons that follow emphasize music as a powerful tool for reflecting and standing against racism. The point of these lessons is twofold: first, to show students how to musically negotiate their thoughts, feelings, and reactions to racism; second, to teach students about the roots of a particular kind of musical "protest"—namely, reggae—as its ethos is one of brotherhood and love. Because of this, these lessons focus on peaceful resistance to racism through reggae music.

The War on Racism

Lesson 1

Goal
To help students use reggae music as a means for responding to racism.

National Standards
- MU:Re8.1.6a: Describe a personal interpretation of how creators' and performers' application of the elements of music and expressive qualities, within genres and cultural and historical contexts, conveys expressive intent.
- MU:Re7.1.6a: Select or choose music to listen to and explain the connections to specific interests or experiences for a specific purpose.

Assessment/Evaluation
- **Formative:** Teacher will assess—through observation—students' understandings of how music is inspired to provoke action for change. Teacher will determine, primarily through questioning, whether students understand how reggae music embodies agency for change.
- **Summative:** Summative assessment could occur as part of a portfolio process.

YouTube Videos
- "Cry Tough" by Alton Ellis and The Flames: https://www.youtube.com/watch?v=_DgfuLLyyIg
- "Get Up, Stand Up" by Bob Marley: https://www.youtube.com/watch?v=JLYOOezs3DA

Other Materials
- "Racism Alive and Well in Jamaica" by Louise Moyston, *Jamaica Observer*, July 7, 2020 http://www.jamaicaobserver.com/opinion/racism-alive-and-well-in-jamaica_196916
- Appendix G: Reggae: A Brief History and Its Breakdown

Teaching Process

Instruction	Comments/Suggestions
Do Now: Have "Cry Tough" by Alton Ellis and The Flames playing as students enter the classroom. Write the following on the board: Listening to the song played, answer the following questions in your Listening Log: • What does this music make you think of? What scene or personal experience comes to mind from the musical selection? • What emotions do you hear in the music? • What is happening in the music that makes you think of these emotions or experiences? For example, how does speed play a part in this? How does, say, volume play a part in this? How does, say, instrumentation play a part in this?	The teacher should keep her/his own Listening Log in order to participate with students if/when possible. Allow students to share their responses. Total time for this activity: 5–6 minutes.
Racism in Jamaica *How is this similar to or different from racism in other parts of the world?*	Have students read, "Racism Alive and Well in Jamaica" by Louise Moyston, *Jamaica Observer*, July 7, 2020.[6]
History of reggae: Vehicle for social justice; vehicle for protest (**Appendix G**). As stated in a previous lesson, "Activism helps youth and adults feel that they are doing something to send a message to the public that action must be taken so that this does not happen again." *How might reggae be a way to "doing something" about racism? What is it about reggae music that might align with acts of social justice?*	Answers will vary: Likely, though, students will focus on the lyrics; try to steer students to consider the rhythm, melodic lines, and timbre of voice of reggae singers.

Instruction	Comments/Suggestions
Listen to Bob Marley's "Get Up, Stand Up." Ask students to consider and list things that this song hopes people will rise and fight for and against.	Write this list on the board so that students have it for a reference point. Answers will vary: Likely, though, students will notice that Marley suggests that people should make life on earth as good as it can be; in doing so, they should demand fair treatment and equality.
Ask students: *What should we "stand up" for? What unfair treatment of people have you witnessed? Are there certain people who are treated more unfairly than others?* Teach students to sing Bob Marley's "Get Up, Stand Up."	The teacher should accompany the students by either playing along on guitar, using a reggae "backing track," or both. Explain that they are singing this song for all the people in the world who are treated unfairly.

The War on Racism

Lesson 2

Goal
To explore how reggae can be used to "protest" racism in a peaceful way.

National Standards
- MU:Re8.1.7a: Describe a personal interpretation of contrasting works and explain how creators' and performers' application of the elements of music and expressive qualities, within genres, cultures, and historical periods, conveys expressive intent.
- MU:Pr4.1.8a: Apply personally developed criteria for selecting music of contrasting styles for a program with a specific purpose and/or context and explain expressive qualities, technical challenges, and reasons for choices.

Assessment/Evaluation
- **Formative:** Teacher will assess—through observation and listening—students' understandings of how to create music inspired by other musical creations. Teacher will determine, primarily through questioning, whether students understand how sounds can illustrate historical events, places, and spaces.
- **Summative:** Summative assessment could occur as part of a portfolio process.

YouTube Videos/Twitter Audio

- Hailie Selassie's address to the United Nations General Assembly during the Eighteenth Session on October 4, 1963, calling for world peace: https://www.youtube.com/watch?v=MDscnpF4RsI
- Martin Luther King, "I Have a Dream": https://www.youtube.com/watch?v=vP4iY1TtS3s
- Barack Obama Live at Town Hall, "On Policing and Racism": https://www.youtube.com/watch?v=RZevgdbMIB0&feature=emb_logo
- Clara Amfo on the death of George Floyd: https://twitter.com/BBCR1/status/1267808690301739008?s=20
- Urgent Meeting on #Racism at 43rd UN Human Rights Council: https://www.youtube.com/watch?v=nbcehKkOPYI
- John Lewis, "Good Trouble": https://www.youtube.com/watch?v=TCqR9LbT1_w

Other Materials

- "War" by Bob Marley (live https://www.youtube.com/watch?v=loFDn94oZJ0; or audio recorded)

Teaching Process (this may take two class periods)

Instruction	Comments/Suggestions
Do Now: Have "War" by Bob Marley playing as students enter the classroom. Write the following on the board: Listening to the song played, answer the following questions in your Listening Log: • What does this music make you think of? What scene or personal experience comes to mind from the musical selection? • What emotions do you hear in the music? • What is happening in the music that makes you think of these emotions or experiences? For example, how does speed play a part in this? How does, say, volume play a part in this? How does, say, instrumentation play a part in this?	The teacher should keep her/his own Listening Log in order to participate with students if/when possible. Allow students to share their responses. Total time for this activity: 5-6 minutes.

Instruction	Comments/Suggestions
Listen to Hailie Selassie's UN Speech. Consider how these words apply to current issues in the world. Students should make a list of the issues this speech raises that are relevant today.	Remind students that they already have listened to this particular Bob Marley song at the beginning of the Unit on War. This time, though, they will focus more specifically on "why" this song matters so much. Explain that this song's inspiration was Emperor of Ethiopia Hailie Selassie's address to the United Nations General Assembly during the Eighteenth Session on October 4, 1963, calling for world peace. Student answers may vary, though they may likely come up with issues such as oppression, racism, injustice, inequality.
Introduce students to other speeches made by leaders that address racism. Possible speeches include (but are not limited to): Martin Luther King, "I Have A Dream" Barack Obama, "On Policing and Racism" John Lewis, "Good Trouble"	
Divide class into groups of no more than four students per group. Have each group select an anti-racist speech to serve as the lyrics to their reggae song. In their groups, they should listen to their selected speech and choose what lines will serve as the lyrics to their reggae song. In their groups, using GarageBand, Soundtrap, or other DAW, students should find and choose a reggae rhythm track. In their groups, they should decide which members of the group will speak/sing which of their anti-racist speech's lines and in what order.	

Instruction	Comments/Suggestions
Student groups should rehearse their reggae pieces. Then, using GarageBand, Soundtrap, or another DAW, groups should record their reggae song.	
Each group should share their reggae song with the class as a whole. Listeners should be encouraged to engage as active listeners.	Ask student-listeners to comment and answer the following questions for each group's drum beat as it relates to the lyrics/speech chosen: *What did you notice?* *What questions do you have?* *What did you learn?*
Allow for reflective responses about the reggae songs. *How are these songs signs of protest?*	

Appendix A

World War II Timeline

1939
- Adolf Hitler and Josef Stalin sign a German-Soviet non-aggression pact (in order to assure a "safer" invasion of Poland).
- Germany invades Poland.
- Great Britain and France declare war on Germany.
- The Soviet Union invades Poland.
- The Soviet Union invades the Baltic States.
- The Soviet Union invades Finland.

1940
- France surrenders to Germany.
- Germany invades Denmark, Norway, Luxembourg, the Netherlands, and Belgium (known as the Blitzkrieg).
- Italy invades France (after becoming an ally of Germany).
- Germany bombs Great Britain (known as the Blitz).
- Japan becomes an ally of Germany and Italy.

1941
- Hungary, Romania, and Bulgaria join the Axis (with Germany).
- Germany takes over Yugoslavia and Greece.
- Germany invades the Soviet Union.

- Germany attempts the extermination of Jewish people throughout German-occupied Europe (the "Final Solution").
- The Soviet Union becomes an ally to France and Great Britain.
- Japan bombs Pearl Harbor.
- The United States declares war on Japan.
- The United States becomes an ally to France, Great Britain, and the Soviet Union.

1942
- Allies invade North Africa.
- Allies defeat Japan at the Battle of Midway.

1943
- Germans surrender at Stalingrad.
- Allies defeat Japan.

1944
- The United States, Great Britain, and Canada attack German forces in France (known as D-Day).
- Japanese are defeated at Battle at Leyte Gulf.

1945
- Germany surrenders.
- United States drops atomic bomb on Hiroshima, Japan.
- United States drops atomic bomb on Nagasaki, Japan.
- Japan surrenders.

Appendix B

Steve Reich's "Program Notes"

Composer's Notes

Different Trains, for String Quartet and pre-recorded performance tape, begins a new way of composing that has its roots in my early tape pieces *It's Gonna Rain* (1965) and *Come Out* (1966). The basic idea is that carefully chosen speech recordings generate the musical materials for musical instruments.

The idea for the piece came from my childhood. When I was one year old my parents separated. My mother moved to Los Angeles and my father stayed in New York. Since they arranged divided custody, I traveled back and forth by train frequently between New York and Los Angeles from 1939 to 1942, accompanied by my governess. While the trips were exciting and romantic at the time, I now look back and think that, if I had been in Europe during this period, as a Jew I would have had to ride very different trains. With this in mind I wanted to make a piece that would accurately reflect the whole situation. In order to prepare the tape I did the following:

1. Record my governess Virginia, then in her seventies, reminiscing about our train trips together.
2. Record a retired Pullman porter, Lawrence Davis, then in his eighties, who used to ride lines between New York and Los Angeles, reminiscing about his life.
3. Collect recordings of Holocaust survivors Rachella, Paul, and Rachel, all about my age and then living in America—speaking of their experiences.
4. Collect recorded American and European train sounds of the '30s and '40s.

In order to combine the taped speech with the string instruments I selected small speech samples that are more or less clearly pitched and then notated them as accurately as possible in musical notation.

The strings then literally imitate that speech melody. The speech samples as well as the train sounds were transferred to tape with the use of sampling keyboards and a computer. Three separate string quartets are also added to the pre-recorded tape and the final live quartet part is added in performance.

Different Trains is in three movements (played without pause), although that term is stretched here since tempos change frequently in each movement. They are:

1. America—Before the war
2. Europe—During the war
3. After the war

The piece thus presents both a documentary and a musical reality and begins a new musical direction. It is a direction that I expect will lead to a new kind of documentary music video theatre in the not too distant future.

   — Steve Reich[7]

Appendix C

Steve Reich: Biographical Information

American composer Steve Reich (b. 1936) is as much of musical storyteller, as he is a musical provocateur. Reich was born in New York City, and growing up split his time between New York and California (note: this is elaborated and musically explored in his travelogue/composition, *Different Trains*). He received his undergraduate degree in philosophy from Cornell University, then studied composition at Juilliard. He received his graduate degree at Mills College, where he worked under Luciano Berio, Darius Milhaud, and Vincent Persichetti. Reich sought out experiences and training opportunities to learn diverse repertoires of music. He studied drumming at the

Institute for African Studies at the University of Ghana (Accra); he studied Balinese Gamelan Semar Pegulingan and Gamelan Gambang at the American Society for Eastern Arts in Seattle, Washington, and Berkeley, California; he studied Middle Eastern singing, as well as chant and canonical singing of the Hebrew scriptures, in New York and Jerusalem, Israel. Given his diverse training, it should come as no surprise that Reich's compositions embrace a variety of contexts: taped-speech sounds juxtaposed with rhythmic phase creativities, vernacular musics, jazz, and non-Western styles and worldviews.

Selected social-justice inspired pieces:

It's Gonna Rain (1965) for tape
Come Out (1966) for tape
Different Trains (1988) for string quartet and tape
The Cave for four voices, ensemble, and video (1993) with Beryl Korot
Three Tales for video projection, five voices, and ensemble (1998–2002) with Beryl Korot
WTC 9/11 (2011) for string quartet and tape

Appendix D

Electro-Acoustic Composition Activity Guidelines

Brainstorming Activity

What "war" do you think needs a musical examination? Why?

Listen to Steve Reich's *Different Trains* and map out what he seems to be doing.

What mode of "transportation" is authentically "linked" to Steve Reich's war? Why?

What speech-sounds would you pre-record that would illustrate the war of your choosing (see earlier discussion)?

What speech-sounds would represent people on the "safe side" of the war AND those people "deep inside" the war of your choosing?

What mode of transportation would you sonically showcase throughout your electro-acoustic composition that is indicative of the war of your choosing? (Re-listen to Steve Reich's *Different Trains* and map out how Reich includes the sounds of transportation that are representative of his "war.") Why?

Pre-compositional Activity

Audio-record the acoustic speech-sounds (see previous discussion) that could be used to form a narrative dimension for your composition.

Once you decide the speech sounds (see previous discussion), create the order in which they will appear in your composition. For guidance and as a model, look at Steve Reich's transcript of speech recordings for *Different Trains*.

Capture the sounds of your chosen transportation (either sampled from the internet or acoustically record) and import into the software of your choosing.

Compositional Activity

Create a two-bar, melodic hook (or mini-phrase) that can be (and will be) looped. To create this hook, use either a MIDI-keyboard or sing or perform on any other instrument of your choosing.

Using software of your choosing, loop the two bars for a minimum of four times and a maximum of the entirety of the piece.

On top of this loop, intersperse the previously prerecorded (from the **Pre-compositional Activity**) speech-sounds.

On top of this loop, intersperse the sounds of your chosen transportation (from the **Pre-compositional Activity**).

Guidelines

Your melodic hook (or mini-phrase) should emotionally capture, in some way, the war of your choosing.

Your electro-acoustic composition should be at least one minute (and no more than two minutes) in length.

Your electro-acoustic composition should contain a climax.

Your electro-acoustic composition should contain at least three distinct timbres.

Your electro-acoustic composition should be considerate of classmates (no foul language, something that might offend another student).

Appendix E

George Crumb: Biographical Information

American composer George Crumb (b. 1929) defies genre. Writing eclectic compositions—electro-acoustic, avant-garde, art-music that includes Western and non-Western idioms—Crumb's versatility and range is as deep as it is wide. Utilizing a variety of sound sources for compositional possibilities, Crumb's music spans a variety of influences, including the poetry of Federico Garcia Lorca (*Night Music I; Ancient Voices of Children*, a song cycle written in 1970, written for the virtuoso mezzo-soprano Jan DeGaetani; *Spanish Songbook I, II, and III*). For more than 30 years, he taught composition at the University of Pennsylvania. He is a GRAMMY winner, as well as a Pulitzer Prize winner.

Crumb was born in West Virginia. Composing music from an early age, in 1947 he attended the Interlochen National Music Camp (Michigan). He received his undergraduate degree from the University of Charleston, a graduate degree in music from the University of Illinois at Urbana-Champaign, and a doctorate in music from the University of Michigan. Prior to his doctorate work, he received a Fulbright to study composition in Berlin at the Hochschule for Music.

Selected social-justice inspired pieces:

Ancient Voices of Children (1970) for mezzo-soprano, boy soprano, oboe, mandolin, harp, amplified piano (and toy piano), and percussion (three players)

Black Angels (1971) for electric string quartet

Vox Balaenae (*Voice of the Whale*) (1971) for electric flute, electric cello, and amplified piano

Star-Child (1977) for soprano, antiphonal children's voices, male speaking choir, bell ringers, and large orchestra

Quest (1989–1994) for solo guitar, soprano saxophone, harp, contrabass, and percussion (two players)

Appendix F

Graphic Notation Electro-Acoustic Composition Activity Guidelines

Brainstorming Activity

Listen to George Crumb's *Black Angels* and map out (with the help from the score's front matter) what he seems to be doing in terms of form/structure.

What "sounds" are authentically "linked" to Vietnam and the Vietnam War, as chosen by George Crumb? Why?

What "war" do you think needs a musical "bearing of witness" and "memorialization"? Why?

What "sounds" illustrate the place and the war of your choosing (see earlier discussion)? Ultimately, choose three sounds.

What "sounds" would represent your "threnody" for the victims of your chosen war? Ultimately, choose three sounds.

Pre-compositional Activity

Audio-record (or download) the sounds (see previous discussion) that could be used to "bear witness" for the victims in your composition.

Once you decide the sounds (see previous discussion), create the order in which they will appear in your composition. For guidance and as a model, look at George Crumb's numerological format of *Black Angels*.

Audio-record (or download) the sounds (see previous discussion) that would represent your "threnody" and import into the software of your choosing.

Compositional Activity

Create three two-bar, melodic hooks (or mini-phrases) that can be (and will be) looped according to a "numerological format" that you and your group members create. To create each hook, use either a MIDI-keyboard or sing or perform on any other instrument of your choosing.

Using software of your choosing, loop the two bars for a minimum of four times and a maximum of the entirety of the piece.

On top of this loop, intersperse the previously prerecorded (from the **Pre-compositional Activity**) sounds that represent the war of your choosing.

On top of this loop, intersperse the sounds the sounds that represent the "threnody" (from the **Pre-compositional Activity**).

Guidelines

Your melodic hooks (or mini-phrases) should emotionally capture, in some way, the war of your choosing.

Your graphic electro-acoustic composition should be at least two minutes (and no more than three minutes) in length.

Your composition should contain a climax.

Your composition should contain at least three distinct timbres.

Your composition should be considerate of classmates (no foul language, something that might offend another student).

Appendix G

Reggae: A Brief History and Its Breakdown

Reggae—its styles, ethos, and energy—is a synthesis of many worlds of music colliding and coming together (e.g., Mento, Ska, Calypso, R&B, American "Soul," and Rocksteady). Additionally, it emerged in Jamaica at a particular point in history. What follows is a very brief overview of reggae. For more information, consider the following sources: *The Rough Guide to Reggae* by Steve Barrow; *This is Reggae Music: The Story of Jamaica's Music* by Lloyd Bradley; *No Woman, No Cry: My Life with Bob Marley* by Rita Marley; *Solid Foundations: An Oral History of Reggae* by David Katz.

While reggae music is a synthesis of diverse musics from around the world (by people of African ancestry), it emerged and was developed primarily in the late 1960s in Jamaica. It's known most for its rhythmic, percussive drive, strong bass line, and up-stroke guitar rhythmic movement. The context and setting of the music are linked heavily with the Rastafarian movement; so, it's socially/culturally linked to 1930s Jamaican history. Because of this, the artists sing primarily of social justice themes, including but not limited to: anti-slavery, freedom from oppression, spirituality, unity, and love. Perhaps the most popular reggae band, Bob Marley & The Wailers (Bob Marley, singer; Peter Tosh, guitarist; Bunny Wailer, drummer; and Aston Barrett, guitarist), was formed in 1963. They produced a number of hits that topped the popular music charts around the world; their album *Exodus* (1977) was named Best Album of the Twentieth Century by TIME in 1999.

Selected reggae artists:

Bob Marley
Peter Tosh
Jimmy Cliff
Delroy Wilson
Lady Saw
Rita Marley
Ziggy Marley
Winston Grennan
Desmond Dekker
Marcia Griffiths
Lorna Bennett

Notes

1. All quotations, whether those that appeared first in the recording's liner notes, or those that appear at the front of the score, also appear in the following: "George Crumb and Black Angels: A Quartet in Time of War." In *Music in the USA: A Documentary Companion*, edited by Judith Tick and Paul Beaudoin, 658–660. New York: Oxford University Press, 2008. For more information, see this resource.
2. https://www.berkshireeagle.com/arts_and_culture/stories-of-collective-resistance-legacies-of-blo ody-sundays-brought-into-the-light-in-mass-moca/article_29893cb4-8e4a-11eb-8751-f3143dd9b 9e4.html.
3. https://www.youtube.com/watch?v=jQR_0O_Zz6s&t=63s.
4. "Creating the Space to Talk about Race." *National Education Association, in Collaboration with Race Forward*, 2017. https://neaedjustice.org/social-justice-issues/racial-justice/talking-about-race/.

5. Eva, A. L. "Three SEL Skills You Need to Discuss Race in Classrooms." *Greater Good Magazine: Science-Based Insight for a Meaningful Life*, October 31, 2017. https://greatergood. berkeley.edu/article/item/threeselskills_you_need_to_discuss_race_in_classrooms

6. Moyston, L. E. "Racism: Alive and Well in Jamaica." *Jamaica Observer*, July 7, 2020. https://www. jamaicaobserver.com/opinion/racism-alive-and-well-in-jamaica_196916.

7. Notes taken from: https://www.boosey.com/cr/music/Steve-Reich-Different-Trains/2699. Reprinted by kind permission of Boosey & Hawkes.

4

Heroes and Heroines Unit

Introduction to the *Heroes and Heroines* Unit

We often use the terms "hero" or "heroine" loosely in our society to mean anyone who rescues or aids people in trouble. This caused us to question: "Who is a hero/heroine?" and "What separates a hero/heroine from any other person?" Given our curiosity about others' perceptions of heroes/heroines, we took a casual survey among family and friends, asking them to name a hero/heroine and to explain what it means to be a hero/heroine. Many of the heroes/heroines were repeated, which gave us a comfortable sense of casual reliability in our search. We then distilled the list into four categories: (a) Beethoven and Spider-Man, (b) Florence Nightingale, (c) Cesar Chavez, and (d) Malala and Queen Latifah.

Some of these pairings may seem perplexing. What, for example, does Beethoven have to do with Spider-Man? How do Malala and Queen Latifah share similar characteristics as heroines? These questions prompted the second part of our interview: "What makes a hero/heroine different from an ordinary person?" Again, many of the responses were similar, culminating in the following list:

1. Takes selfless action for the betterment of society;
2. Fights for a social cause;
3. Meets danger in the face;
4. Has a moral code of ethics;
5. Has the courage to take risks.

In the first lesson, "Beethoven Meets Spider-Man," students first generate their own list of characteristics that describe heroes/heroines. Then . . . "What DOES Spider-Man have to do with Beethoven and why are they heroes?" The first three lessons interrogate this question.

Simply naming a hero/heroine, however, is not enough for a substantive music class. Music, of course, should play a major role. Consequently, all lessons in this unit focus on parallels between music and eminent persons (including comic book characters!). The range of activities—such as learning a Mexican "corrido," a heroic narrative song that tells the story of a villain, hero, or social issue, or selecting excerpts from Beethoven's music to accompany a class-generated "hero/heroine" comic strip—cover a broad range of musical genres and styles.

Music making and technology blend with important works of each hero/heroine, some more directly than others, but all the lessons are designed to engage students with different aspects of social justice. Although these lessons focus on a limited set

Music Lesson Plans for Social Justice. Lisa C. Delorenzo and Marissa Silverman, Oxford University Press. © Oxford University Press 2022.
DOI: 10.1093/oso/9780197581476.003.0004

of heroes and heroines, care has been taken to represent different cultures, genders, and geographic regions. In addition, Spider-Man, Malala, and Queen Latifah were selected because they are closest in relating to the age or experience of adolescents. As an aside, an interesting follow-up activity might involve a class or individually selected hero/heroine project that involves research about the person(s) and related music.

There are several formats for teachers to consider when deciding what to teach. Teachers could present this entire unit over a series of weeks, choose just one cluster of lessons for a shorter time period, or introduce one set of lessons at different times over the duration of class meetings in a year. It is critical, however, to keep each cluster of lessons intact so that students experience a beginning, middle, and end (with a culminating project). As always, materials and/or projects should be adjusted for your own students and technology resources.

Graphic Organizer: HEROES and HEROINES—MUSIC, ART, and SOCIAL JUSTICE

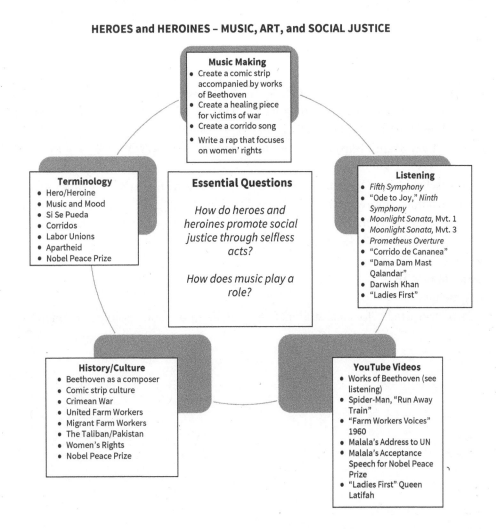

HEROES and HEROINES – MUSIC, ART, and SOCIAL JUSTICE

Music Making
- Create a comic strip accompanied by works of Beethoven
- Create a healing piece for victims of war
- Create a corrido song
- Write a rap that focuses on women' rights

Terminology
- Hero/Heroine
- Music and Mood
- Si Se Pueda
- Corridos
- Labor Unions
- Apartheid
- Nobel Peace Prize

Essential Questions

How do heroes and heroines promote social justice through selfless acts?

How does music play a role?

Listening
- *Fifth Symphony*
- "Ode to Joy," *Ninth Symphony*
- *Moonlight Sonata*, Mvt. 1
- *Moonlight Sonata*, Mvt. 3
- *Prometheus Overture*
- "Corrido de Cananea"
- "Dama Dam Mast Qalandar"
- Darwish Khan
- "Ladies First"

History/Culture
- Beethoven as a composer
- Comic strip culture
- Crimean War
- United Farm Workers
- Migrant Farm Workers
- The Taliban/Pakistan
- Women's Rights
- Nobel Peace Prize

YouTube Videos
- Works of Beethoven (see listening)
- Spider-Man, "Run Away Train"
- "Farm Workers Voices" 1960
- Malala's Address to UN
- Malala's Acceptance Speech for Nobel Peace Prize
- "Ladies First" Queen Latifah

Beethoven Meets Spider-Man

Lesson 1

Goal
To compare Beethoven and Spider-Man, as past and present heroes, who both have (had) extraordinary powers that benefited society.

National Standards
- MU:Re7.1.6a: Select or choose music to listen to and explain the connections to specific interests or experiences for a specific purpose.
- MU:Re7.2.6a: Describe how the elements of music and expressive qualities relate to the structure of the pieces.

Assessment/Evaluation
- **Formative:** Students will be assessed by their verbal participation in a discussion that compares the heroic qualities of Beethoven and Spider-Man.
- **Summative:** N/A

YouTube Videos
- "Ode To Joy" from Symphony No. 9, Beethoven: https://www.youtube.com/watch?v=hdWyYn0E4Ys&list=PL5Z7Tmrflzc4jxWkUZXeMYhZUgTOjgQdj&index=2&t=739s [START 12′20″; STOP 13′42″]
- "Run Away Train": https://www.youtube.com/watch?v=GYOYewO_Veg [START 0′00″; STOP 1′29″]
- "York'scher March." Veteran's Day Parade 2019, NYC Drum and Bugle Corps: https://www.youtube.com/watch?v=XDQ2rAQl03M&t=15s [START 0′28″; STOP 2′26″]
- "York'scher March for Military Music," WoO19: http/www.youtube.com/watch?v=TpAdoxR6Cic&t=7s [START 0′00″; STOP 1′35″]

Other Materials
- Appendix A
- Two "drumsticks" for each student (e.g., pencils, or other accessible implements)

Teaching Process * See Note to Teacher

The teacher will . . .	The students will . . .
Do Now: Think about someone, past or present, who you would call a hero or heroine. Write down three characteristics that you think describe a hero or heroine. List student ideas about characteristics for further reference during the lesson.	Identify characteristics, e.g., • Takes action for the betterment of another person(s) without monetary reward. • Fights for a social cause. • Meets danger in the face. • Has a moral code of ethics. • Overcomes a major challenge in order to do what is best for others. • Has the courage to take risks.
In this lesson I'm going to introduce you to two heroes who seem very different but who actually share similar characteristics. The first is a music composer who had superpowers to write music despite a major challenge in his life.	
Prepare students for the video by asking them to watch silently without comment. Play the excerpt of **"Ode to Joy"** but MUTE the audio. Start at 12′20″ and play just enough to engage students. *What was it like watching the performers without hearing them?* *This is what Beethoven experienced when he conducted the orchestra. Can you guess what his challenge was?* Play excerpt again but with audio. Start at 12′20″ and stop at 13′42″.	Students will watch the performance without hearing the music. Identify the challenge that Beethoven had to overcome.

The teacher will . . .	The students will . . .
Beethoven's superpower was the ability to hear music in his head for an entire orchestra despite being completely deaf. In fact, Beethoven insisted on conducting the premiere performance. At the end, one of the musicians had to turn him around to see the wild applause and cheers of the audience. *How is it possible to compose a great piece of music while not being able to hear anything?*	Students speculate about audiation and hearing music in their mind.
The second video is about a comic book character. As you watch this video, think about what superpowers he has. **Video**: *Spider-Man and the Run Away Train*, Pt. 1 Play the first part of this video and save the rest for the next lesson. Stop at 1'29."	Students will describe Spider-Man's superpowers and explain how he got these powers. [Bitten by a radioactive spider]
Show a cartoon image of Beethoven as a young child at the piano with his father looking on and Peter Parker (aka "Spider-Man") as a high school student being bullied in school (**Appendix A**). Background information: *Beethoven's father was his first piano teacher but beat him regularly and sent him to the cellar when he made mistakes.* *Peter Parker, however, grew up with a loving aunt and uncle but suffered terribly from bullying. For example, students would purposefully bump into him, causing him to fall and drop his books while other students laughed.*	Students will describe what they see and compare the messages of both pictures.
What heroic characteristics do Beethoven and Spider-Man share?	Students refer to the list of heroic characteristics and choose one that Beethoven and Spider-Man both share.
Music Making Activity *What kind of music would we perform to honor Beethoven or Spider-Man if they came to our town for a visit? What does heroic music sound like?*	Students consider characteristics of music or different styles that might be appropriate.

The teacher will . . .	The students will . . .
Sometimes we hold a parade to honor people. **Video:** Show part of a parade with the NYC Drum and Bugle Corps. After a minute ask students to play along and try to imitate some of the rhythms they hear.	Students will play along with the video and try to imitate some of the rhythms they hear.
Marches are one type of music that we often play for heroes/heroines. Here's a march that Beethoven wrote: **Video:** "York'scher March for Military Music"	Students will view the video and discuss the difference between *both* videos.
If you wanted to listen to one of the Beethoven works that we heard today, which would you choose?	Poll students for their choice and ask volunteers to explain why.

* Scripted lessons look much longer than they actually take to teach with engaged students. If, however, students need more time for discussion, it is better to honor that participation than to move ahead too quickly.

Listening to Beethoven for Mood Qualities

Lesson 2

Goal

To choose excerpts from a variety of Beethoven's works and determine how the mood of these pieces might highlight a scene in a movie.

National Standards

- MU:Re7.1.6a: Select or choose music to listen to and explain the connections to specific interests or experiences for a specific purpose.
- MU:Re7.7a: Classify and explain how the elements of music and expressive qualities relate to the structure of contrasting pieces.

Assessment/Evaluation

- **Formative:** Students will be assessed on their ability to verbally analyze the mood of excerpts from Beethoven's works. In addition, students will be assessed on their explanation about how the music creates a particular mood.

YouTube Videos

- "Run Away Train": https://www.youtube.com/watch?v=GYOYewO_Veg [START 1'20" to end]

- Symphony No. 5, First Movement (Gustavo Dudamel): https://www.youtube.com/watch?v=22wEhOdfAfA
- Symphony No. 9, Fourth Movement, "Ode to Joy" (see URL from lesson 1): https://www.youtube.com/watch?v=hdWyYn0E4Ys&list=PL5Z7TmrflzcᴄjxWkUZXeMYhZUgTOjgQdj&index=2&t=739s [START 12′20″; STOP 13′42″]
- Moonlight Sonata, First Movement (Alicia Keys): https://www.youtube.com/watch?v=bT6WmWVYPhI
- Moonlight Sonata, Third Movement: https://www.youtube.com/watch?v=3xyDjgLh-w8
- "York'scher March": https://www.youtube.com/watch?v=TpAdoxR6Cic&t=7s
- *Prometheus* Overture: https://www.youtube.com/watch?v=zS-34-OaKGg&start_radio=1

Other Materials
- Appendix B: Mood Adjectives
- Appendix C: Project Notes for Teachers

Teaching Process

Instruction	Comments/Suggestions
Do Now: Think about a superhero that you would see on an animated film or TV show. Write down the super powers that this hero or heroine has. How did he/she get these powers? *Could this be a female as well as a male? Does gender matter?*	Discuss the different superheroes. Describe a scene where the superhero/heroine comes to the rescue.
In the last class we talked about Spider-Man. Here's the second part of that excerpt. You won't hear any sound, which I'll explain later. Play **"Run Away Train,"** starting at 1′20″; MUTE the audio. *If you only had two pieces of music to choose, which would work the best as an accompaniment to this action video?* Play the first section without repeat of Beethoven's *Fifth Symphony*. Then play part of the *Moonlight Sonata*, **Movement 3**. *What adjectives describe the mood of each piece?* (See **Appendix B**)	Compare the two pieces. Play each with sections of the video. Use as handout or put on the board.

Instruction	Comments/Suggestions
Play an excerpt from each **YouTube video** (except those described in previous step). Ask student to listen to the entire excerpt before choosing appropriate adjectives.	It is important that students listen first and write when the music stops.
Share the selected mood adjectives for some of the pieces. There may be several adjectives for each piece. Avoid suggesting that one of the adjectives is correct.	Students share adjectives for the different musical pieces.
Creating a Story Board Comic Strip *Let's create our own comic strip and we can use Beethoven's music as an accompaniment.* (Note to T: Write down the story as students come up with ideas—the more descriptive, the better.) *Here is a typical superhero story. It goes like this—* (Read each scene. Then go back and have the class create a story line that follows the same sequence.) Scene 1 An ordinary person gets in some kind of trouble. Scene 2 The superhero uses superpowers to try to rescue the person. Scene 3 The superhero encounters unforeseen trouble. It could be an opposing superhero or that the superpowers are not strong enough. Scene 4 Despite these problems, the superhero prevails and rescues the person.	Students should decide: • *Is the superhero a male, female, or gender fluid?* Describe the kind of superhero, including dress, or other features. • *Where does this take place?* • *Who is the ordinary person? Describe that person. What trouble does the person encounter?* • *How does the superhero use superpowers to try and rescue the person?* • *What trouble does the superhero encounter?* • *How does the superhero rescue the person?*
The last piece: Create a title	• Students create a title

Instruction	Comments/Suggestions
Describe the Project (see **Appendix C: Project Notes**) *We're going to make a comic strip movie with the story you created. Some students will be the comic strip artists. Some students will be the music editors and decide which Beethoven pieces work best with the slides. Some students will be the tech crew and combine the comic strip with the music on iMovie.*	
Choose the groups for each task: artists (8 pairs of students), music editors (4–8 students), tech crew (3 students). In other words, every group has artists and music editors. The tech crew are their own group. RECORD STUDENT NAMES FOR NEXT WEEK'S SESSION.	Note to Teacher: Each scene will have four slides (total = 16). You can assign groups or have students choose their own group but stay within the total number of each group. Make sure that tech crew is familiar and capable using iMovie technology. Choose these students first! Music editors should put an excerpt from each Beethoven piece on mobile phone. Tech crew should be comfortable with iMovie.

Culminating Project*

Lesson 3

* This lesson will take two class periods. See **Appendices C, D, and E** for preparation directions.

Goal
To create a superhero/heroine comic strip with excerpts from Beethoven's music on iMovie or related software.

National Standards
- MU:Cn11.0.8a: Demonstrate understanding of relationships between music and the other arts, other disciplines, varied contexts, and daily life.

Assessment/Evaluation
- **Summative:** Students' musical interpretation will be assessed by the choices they make in their roles as artists, music editors, or tech crew.

Handouts
- The Story (Appendix D)
- Culminating Project (Appendix E)

Other Materials
- Two pencils for each artist
- Six blank unlined papers for the artist group
- A spare audio copy of music excerpts (students should already have them on their phone)
- One computer station (capable of integrating pictures and music, e.g., iMovie)
- Digital projector for presenting the finished project

Teaching Process

Instruction	Comments/Suggestions
READ the story on **Appendix C**. Then, on the board, draw a stick figure of the hero and ordinary person with easy-to-draw costumes.	Reading the story helps students focus and is extra assistance for English Language Learners. Why? This does two things. First, it models to the student-artists that even a simplistic drawing will suffice. Second, the hero and ordinary person should be somewhat similar in all the pictures. This maintains consistency throughout the comic strip.
OPTIONAL—Show a slide or two from a comic book. Discuss the style, use of power words, and dialogue (if needed—not required).	
Review the project (**Appendix E**). Establish rules for working as a small group.	
Send students to work stations and hand out materials.	
Allow students to get settled in their groups and begin to work. Go immediately to the computer station and assist tech crew in getting started.	
Visit all the groups and help where needed.	

Instruction	Comments/Suggestions
Share the project in the next class.	The tech crew will need to work in your room during free periods, lunch, or at home. Their job is time intensive. Alternate idea: Put the pictures and music together yourself using whatever the tech crew has finished.

Florence Nightingale: Lady with the Lamp

Lesson 1

Goal

To examine the life of Florence Nightingale as a first responder whose work formed the foundation of nursing as we know it today and to create music that might help the healing process for victims of war.

National Standards

- MU:Cn11.0.8a: Demonstrate understanding of relationships between music and the other arts, other disciplines, varied contexts, and daily life.
- MU:Re9.8a: Apply appropriate personally developed criteria to evaluate musical works or performances.

Assessment/Evaluation

- **Formative:** To assess comprehension, students will verbally participate in a discussion about Florence Nightingale and heroism. In addition, to assess musical decision-making, students will create a sound collage about nurses in a wartime scenario.

YouTube Videos

- Florence Nightingale in the Crimean War: https://www.youtube.com/watch?v=wdL2RgPvSJU
- Big Ocean Waves Crashing on a Rocky Shore: https://www.youtube.com/watch?v=xvNNTc6ZPtQ
- Ocean Waves Lapping the Shore: https://www.youtube.com/watch?v=HdNQQhBKup4

Other Materials

- List of hospital tent "horrors" on the board
- "Sounds for Healing" score (Appendix F)

Teaching Process

Instruction	Comments/Suggestions
Do Now: (background) *Crimea is a peninsula connected to Russia. Because of religious differences and other factors, Russia and Great Britain, along with other allies, went to war with Crimea. This was called the Crimean War (1853–1856).*	It is always helpful to show on a map if one is available.
The following **list** *of "horrors" describes the hospital tents where the wounded soldiers stayed.* *If you were a nurse, as a first responder, what would you change first?* A. Soldiers lying on dirty floors B. Rats running around C. Dirty bandages and dressings D. Toilets overflowing with raw sewage E. Polluted water F. Cold weather but few blankets	Have the list visible to students. Ask students why they chose their example from the list. Compare with a modern hospital today.
The heroine who faced all of these conditions was Florence Nightingale. She is one of the most famous nurses in history and her work is the foundation of modern-day nursing and hospital practice She changed the practice of nursing forever. *Many called her "Lady with the Lamp." See if you can find out how she earned this name.* **Video**: Florence Nightingale in the Crimean War.	Women were typically not allowed in the tents at night. Some of these graphics may be disturbing. Watch it first before showing in class. Discuss what students noticed during the video.
When COVID-19 plagued the world, who were some of the first responders? Would you call Florence Nightingale a first responder? Why?	e.g., firefighters, nurses, doctors, police, paramedics

Instruction	Comments/Suggestions
Music Making Project: *Let's focus on the patients for a minute. Picture rows of beds with victims who suffer from bullet wounds, broken limbs, burns, or nausea. When people are suffering from terrible pain, it is often hardest to fall asleep. However, sleep is a powerful healing agent.* *What does healing music sound like? What kinds of sounds might help a soldier fall asleep?*	Students look around the room for objects that have gentle, soothing sounds.
Put one of the graphics (see **Appendix F**) from the score on the board. *Ask students how they could make a gentle sound that imitated the graphic.*	Repeat with a few other graphics.
Here is a music score that uses gentle sounds separated by silence. Hand out the score (**Appendix F**).	Discuss how to read the score.
Break into groups of 5.	One person in each group will be the time keeper. Students will use objects in their area (change, keys, chair, etc.) to create the sounds. Each group practices with a clock or stop watch, starting at paper wave or "12:00." Sounds can last any duration.
Groups will perform one at a time.	
The hospital tents were probably near the water so that patients could be transported quickly from the ships to the tents. Students close their eyes to imagine the water near the shore line. Play **Video:** Big Ocean Waves Crashing on a Rocky Shore and **Video:** Ocean Waves Lapping the Shore. *Which one do you think might be good background for our piece?*	Have every one put their sound objects down for a listening activity.

Instruction	Comments/Suggestions
Think of a friend or family member who is sick or needs comfort. We will play this healing music for them. Play entire piece with background music. Everyone plays together but teacher will cue the different sound events.	Designate one student as the timekeeper for episodes of silence.
Discussion Prompts: *What did you like about the piece? If you did it again, would you change anything?* *Music can be like medicine. It has the power to help the healing process. What are some of the ways that Florence Nightingale tried to help people heal? Is there a song that you listen to that helps you sleep?*	

Florence Nightingale: Healing Music

Lesson 2

Goal
To use Florence Nightingale's story as the basis for creating healing music.

National Standards
- MU:Cn10.1.8a: Demonstrate how interests, knowledge, and skills are related to personal choices and intent when creating, performing, and responding to music.
- MU:Re9.8a: Apply appropriate personally developed criteria to evaluate musical works or performances.

Assessment/Evaluation
- **Formative**: Given a student-developed set of criteria, the teacher will use the list as a guide for assessing the projects.

YouTube Video
- Ocean Waves Lapping the Shore: https://www.youtube.com/watch?v=HdNQQhBKup4

Other Materials

- Sound sources around the room or classroom instruments
- Battery-powered candle as used to light up windows at Christmas (optional)

Teaching Process

Instruction	Comments/Suggestions
Do Now: *In the last class we talked about the heroine Florence Nightingale who changed the course of nursing forever. Then we shifted our attention to her patients and played a piece of healing music,* *With a partner write down three characteristics that are important when creating healing music.* Discuss as criteria for students to keep in mind when they compose their own music.	e.g., slow tempo, periods of silence, gentle sound production
Music Making Activity Divide class in small groups that are different from the last lesson. Task: Compose a 30-second healing piece that would help a sick person rest. Include at least three different kinds of sounds. You can use sources around the room or classroom instruments.	Students do not need to do a graphic score.
Groups perform their music. After each performance ask the performers to explain the decisions they made in composing the piece.	This activity helps students understand the music and allows the composers to explain their ideas.
Have students <u>ready</u> to play their piece one more time. *If we performed one big piece, what order would you choose for the different pieces? We will have a moment of silence between each piece.* Create a nighttime setting in the classroom, eliminating as much light as possible. Start the audio portion of "Ocean Waves Lapping the Shore." In a quiet voice, tell a fictitious story about a young soldier who was brought to the hospital tent with a serious injury. At night, Florence Nightingale would walk around the beds with her lamp, comforting those who could not sleep. Cue each group to play their piece, allowing silence between the different pieces. During the "silent episodes" students will only hear the lapping of the waves.	You can usually start the discussion by asking whose piece would be a good starting piece . . . ending piece? Embellish the story as much as you want to establish a relevant context and mood for the music. Depending on the safety and darkness of the room, you could have a student play Florence Nightingale by walking to each performance group with a battery-operated candle.

Instruction	Comments/Suggestions
Reflective discussion about the experience. *Do you think we created a healing mood? Did we demonstrate some of the ideas discussed at the beginning of the lesson?*	

Cesar Chavez: Hero for Migrant Farm Workers

Lesson 1

Goal
To introduce Cesar Chavez as a Latin American hero whose leadership took place during the Civil Rights era.

National Standards
- MU:Re7.1.6a: Select or choose music to listen to and explain the connections to specific interests or experiences for a specific purpose.
- MU:Re7.2.7b: Identify and compare the context of music from a variety of genres, cultures, and historical periods.

Assessment
- **Formative**: Students will be assessed by their verbal participation in various discussions throughout the lesson. In addition, given the corrido "Corrido de Cananea," students will be assessed by their ability to analyze the form of this ballad.

YouTube Videos
- Farm Worker's Voices 1960: https://www.youtube.com/watch?v=m_BMMDt40vc https://www.youtube.com/watch?v=m_BMMDt40vc [START 1′15″; STOP 3′09″]
- Rap for Kids: https://www.youtube.com/watch?v=bmdPMEZT3jM
- "Corrido de Cananea" (Linda Ronstadt): https://www.youtube.com/watch?v=MLt4TvNBAxM

Other Materials
- Lyrics for "Corrido de Cananea" (Appendix G)

Teaching Process

Instruction	Comments/Suggestions
Do Now: With a partner, identify three reasons why Martin Luther King was a hero. Share with the class. *Did you know that at the same time that Martin Luther King was protesting for Black American civil rights, there was another powerful leader who was fighting for the civil rights of Latino farm workers? If you lived in California or Mexico, you would know exactly who I am talking about.* *This is a story about a Latino man named Cesar Chavez. He fought for the rights of migrant farm workers who lived in terrible poverty because they could hardly make a living picking the fruits and vegetables that we eat.*	Briefly share responses to the question.
Think about a typical day for yourself. *If your parents were migrant farm workers from the 1950s or earlier, your life would be very different:* • No school; you would work in the fields from 4:00 a.m. to 5:00 p.m. • You'd live in a tiny shack with no running water or indoor plumbing. • Your home might be smaller than this classroom which you would share with 8–14 siblings. • You'd be breathing toxic pesticides which caused illness and sometimes death. • There were no doctors, dentists, or healthcare workers that your family could afford. • With all that work, your family would make $1.00 a day.	

Instruction	Comments/Suggestions
Video: "Farm Worker's Voices" (1′15″ - 3′09″) Prompts for Discussion: *What did you notice in this video?* *Why didn't migrant workers fight for better working conditions?* *What does it take to get better working conditions and better living conditions?* *Think about the ways in which Martin Luther King paved the way for the rights of Black citizens.* *One of the most powerful strategies was to convince people in California and other nearby states to stop buying grapes. This caused a significant loss of money for the growers, so they raised the pay for migrant workers.* *Cesar Chavez used many of the same strategies to fight for migrant farmers from Mexico. His protest call was* "Si se puede" (We can do it!) *He started the United Farm Workers (UFW) in 1962 which allowed farmworkers to help improve their working conditions and wages.*	These prompts are meant to help students learn about the peaceful strategies of protest for social justice. As individuals they had no power against their bosses (growers). They could easily lose their jobs. Plus, they spoke little or no English. e.g., large groups of people, peaceful protest marches, rallies, speeches, meetings with government officials Students say the phrase and repeat several times as if in a rally. The **UFW** embraces nonviolence in its attempt to cultivate awareness of political and social issues.
Video: Rap for Kids	This video is a rap version of the information described previously.
Music was an important part of the movement. Bands played during rallies and strikes to unify people. Songs, like corridos, were sung among the people to give them news since most could not read a newspaper.	
Listen to this corrido sung in Spanish: "Corrido de Cananea." Play two verses without the lyric sheet. *What do you think happened after that? Does the music give you any clue about the mood?* **Appendix G:** Hand out the lyrics. Sing along with the music in Spanish or English.	Cananea is a city near the Mexican border, known for copper mining. Ask if any Spanish-speaking students can translate the story up to that point. It is interesting to hear two languages sung simultaneously.

Instruction	Comments/Suggestions
What is the song about? Does the music fit the mood of the song? Analyze the form and characteristics of the corrido.	The music is generally light and upbeat because the listener is supposed to form his/her/their own interpretation of the story. The song has no repeating refrain—it is a string of verses. *How is this form different from many of the songs you listen to now?*
Listen to the first two verses again. Some students might want to switch the language that they sang before.	Students will need to know the melody for the next class session.

Cesar Chavez: A Corrido as a Fractured Fairy Tale

Lesson 2

Goal
To compose a corrido using the meter and form of "Corrido de Cananea."

National Standards
- MU:CR2.1.6a: Select, organize, construct, and document musical ideas for arrangements and compositions with AB or ABA form that demonstrate an effective beginning, middle, and end.
- MU:Cr3.2.6a: Present the final version of their documented personal composition or arrangement, using craftmanship and originality to demonstrate an effective beginning, middle, and ending, and convey expressive intent.

Assessment
- **Formative**: Students will be assessed on their ability to write a fractured fairy tale. In addition to the created story, the teacher will assess students' ability to write lyrics according to the melody of "Corrido de Cananea."

YouTube Video
- "Corrido de Cananea" (Linda Ronstadt): https://www.youtube.com/watch?v=MLt4TvNBAxM

Materials
- Keyboard or guitar or ukulele
- Note to Teacher: A good video on how to make a corrido can be found on this YouTube location: https://www.youtube.com/watch?v=K45PXkoWboc

Teaching Process

Instruction	Comments/Suggestions
Do Now: Listen to "Corrido de Cananea." Students should hum along.	Retell the story in own words.
Check to make sure that students know the melody by singing on "doo" or humming without the recording.	
Review the term "corrido" as a type of Mexican ballad. The purpose of the song is to tell a story. *Let's say we wanted to write a corrido based on a fractured fairy tale. What is a fractured fairy tale?*	A classic fairy tale with a twist. Changes can be made in the setting, the character(s), the events that take place, etc.
Creating a Corrido Based on a Fractured Fairy Tale *Who can tell me the story of Hansel and Gretel? How could we make this a fractured fairy tale? Could it take place in a different setting? Could Hansel drop something else on the ground to find his way home? What if the witch was some other kind of creature? etc. If we turned this story into a corrido, it might go something like this (sung to the tune of "Corrido de Cananea"): "My name is Hansel Smith I have a sister Gretel (repeat) One day I took the subway To get a brand-new game boy The subway went so fast I missed the stop completely."*	Once students get started, the story will probably evolve on its own without other question prompts.
Divide into groups of 4 or 5. Each should have a different fairy tale: *Cinderella Beauty and the Beast Goldilocks and the Three Bears Jack and the Beanstalk Little Red Riding Hood Three Little Pigs*	Or a group could choose a fairy tale from another culture and write the story/song in the language of that culture.
Groups should spend time writing a brief outline of their fractured fairy tale.	Complete sentences are not necessary.

Instruction	Comments/Suggestions
Using the melody of "Corrido de Cananea," write the lyrics according to the fractured fairy tale.	Review the melody one more time. Sing on a neutral syllable. Groups will be at different stages throughout the process.
Each group shares the song with the class. Teacher accompanies on guitar or keyboard.	A simple ¾ accompaniment is important to support the singing.
What are some of the topics that a songwriter might choose to sing about the conditions of migrant farmworkers?	

Malala, Music, and the Taliban

Lesson 1

Goal
To learn about Malala, an advocate for the educational rights of girls, who began her international activism at the same age as American middle school students.

National Standards
- MU:Re7.2.7b: Identify and compare the context of music from a variety of genres, cultures, and historical periods.
- MU:Pr6.1.6b: Demonstrate performance decorum (such as stage presence, attire, and behavior) and audience etiquette appropriate for venue and purpose.

Assessment
- **Formative:** The teacher will assess students' ability to discuss the power of education and the role that Malala played in advocating for this right. In addition, the teacher will assess students' ability to make connections from "their" music to that of traditional Pakistani music through verbal responses to critical thinking prompts

YouTube Videos
- Malala's Address to the UN (July 2013): https://www.youtube.com/watch?v=5SClmL43dTo
- "Darwish Khan": https://www.youtube.com/watch?v=Gfnoh5ENFx4&list=RDE15V5koHPBA&index=2
- "Dama Dam Mast Qalandar" with singer, Harshdeep Kaur: https://www.youtube.com/watch?v=skQ4GcUiI5k

Teaching Process

Instruction	Comments/Suggestions
Do Now: As students enter to room, have traditional Pakistani music ("Darwish Khan") softly playing in the background. On board, ask students to solve the mystery heroine given the following clues: 1. I lived in Pakistan when the Taliban, a terrorist regime, forbade girls from going to school. 2. I believed that this was terribly unfair and publicly spoke out against the harsh rules of the Taliban. 3. At age 11, I was riding the school bus when angry Taliban soldiers stopped the bus and stepped inside. 4. They shot me in the head.	Although she is a well-known international figure, many students may not be able to identify the heroine as Malala.
The name of our heroine is Malala Yousafzai, who survived the shooting while in the safety of a British hospital. Despite the horrific ordeal, she continued to strongly advocate for the rights of girls to be educated. *Here is a short clip from her speech to the United Nations in July 2013. She was 16 and this day was named "Malala Day."* **Video:** *"Malala's Address to the UN."* Play about five minutes of the speech. *What do you lose when you are denied an education?*	Discussion: *Malala was beginning middle school when she was shot. Can you imagine yourself as a young person who openly defies the orders of a terrorist regime?* Write some words on the board that characterize Malala (e.g., brave, courageous, committed to a cause).
In addition to refusing women an education, the Taliban also took steps to destroy the arts. Instruments were smashed and performing artists punished. *When you came in the room you heard the sound of traditional Pakistani music. This the music that Malala grew up with.*	*Reflection: When you listen to Pakistani traditional music it may seem strange at first. Likewise, if a Pakistani adolescent of your age heard classical American music he/she/they might have the same reaction.* *It's ok to have that response when hearing unfamiliar music. It's not ok to make a judgment that music from one country is not as good as the music you know.*

Instruction	Comments/Suggestions
Play "Darwish Khan" (about 3 minutes) Practice the following hand motion to indicate the beat when the drum begins: tap, tap, tap, wave (flip hand over so palm is facing up). Improvisation: While teacher keeps the beat as in #1, students improvise rhythmic ideas (always tapping two fingers in palm so music will be audible). Break into two groups, switching often so each group gets a chance to improvise. Each instrument has a special role. Play a short clip again and ask different groups of students to be responsible for one of the following questions: 1. *What is the role of the flute?* (e.g., melody/song) 2. *What is the role of the drums? Does the rhythm ever change?* 3. *What is the role of the string instrument? Does the string music ever change? (drone)*	Compare the roles of these instruments to a rock band. e.g., Melody: Singer or lead guitar Backup: Guitars, singers Rhythmic motion: Drum set Harmony/melody: Keyboard
Let's go to a Pakistani concert: "Dama Dam Mast Qalandar" (3 minutes). *It is a spiritual song of the Sufi, about three gods that protect their lives and souls. It begins with three very slow phrases. When the drummers start, watch the audience. Imitate the audience movements or make up your own.*	It is important to prepare students to have patience during the slow phrases. Harshdeep Kaur is a well-loved singer who plays lead roles in Bollywood films and has won awards for her singing.
How would the Taliban respond if they came across a gathering of this sort? *Imagine a country where you could not sing familiar songs, play instruments, or listen to your iPod.* Reflection: *When music is forbidden, does the music die or become extinct like certain animals that lose their habitat?*	When a terrorist group wants to take control of a country, they try to erase the culture of the people and substitute their own values, beliefs, and ideation.

Malala and Queen Latifah

Lesson 2

Goal

To introduce two heroines who advocate for social justice, women's rights, and equity of education.

National Standards

- MU:Pr4.2.6c: Identify how cultural and historical contexts inform the performances.
- MU:Cr3.2.6a: Present the final version of their documented personal composition or arrangement, using craftsmanship and originality to demonstrate an effective beginning, middle, and ending, and convey expressive intent.

Assessment

- **Formative:** The teacher will assess, through discussion, students' ability to compare the lives and advocacy activities of Malala and Queen Latifa. In addition, the teacher will assess creative and critical thinking skills, regarding the significant ideas of Malala and Queen Latifah, through a student-composed rap.

YouTube Videos

- Malala Yousefzai: Nobel Peace Prize, 2014, Oslow, Norway. Malala is 17 years old.
  https://www.bing.com/videos/search?q=Malala+speech+for+Nobel+Prize&view=detail&mid=D6C9F892B3ECA1A58665D6C9F892B3ECA1A586
  65&FORM=VIRE [START 16'56"; STOP 20'00"]
- "Ladies First," Queen Latifah with Monie Love, 1988: https://www.youtube.com/watch?v=8Qimg_q7LbQ

Teaching Process

Instruction	Comments/Suggestions
Do Now: *In our last class we talked about Malala, who spent her childhood in Pakistan. Which of the following statements are true?* 1. Malala was 10 years old when she was shot by the Taliban on her way to school. 2. Malala was shot as a random killing. 3. Malala was shot because she spoke in public about the rights of girls to go to school. 4. Malala's message about the rights of women is still an issue of social justice today.	Statements 1, 3, and 4 are correct; statement 2 is incorrect; however, the last two statements may be the most important to talk about with the students. Other Prompts: *Should boys and girls have access to the same educational opportunities? Why?* *In countries where schooling is forbidden or not offered to girls, who has the power to make laws, lead companies, work in jobs usually held by men?* ** These questions are critical in helping students understand the power differential by gender.
In the United States, there is a particular celebrity who has advocated for the rights of women. Here are some clues to her name: 1. I am one of the first African-American female rappers. 2. I am an actress, a singer, and a celebrity. 3. Some of my hip-hop is meant to empower women. 4. *All Hail the Queen* was my first album.	
Queen Latifah has a very different way of advocating for women's rights. Before you watch this video, you should know that Queen Latifah is addressing women's rights across the world, especially in Africa. You will see a lot of images about apartheid. You will also see pictures of famous Black women who also fought for women's rights. **Video:** "Ladies First." Show this video in stages so students can ask questions or respond to prompts about the content. Watch the entire video a second time. Discussion prompt: *Why do you think Queen Latifah is paired with Malala? Do you see any connections?*	Students may need some extra background about apartheid. Some of the women pictured are: Sojourner Truth, Harriet Tubman, Angela Davis, and Cicely Tyson.

Instruction	Comments/Suggestions
Music Making **Activity: Creating a Rap** Start a word wall. *What are some words or phrases that characterize Malala and Queen Latifah?* Say the words together with a triplet feel to create some rhythmic motion for the rap. *Using the word wall, practice or write a one-line rap.* Volunteers share with the class. Add body rhythm or beat boxing.	e.g., powerful, advocates, empowerment, women's rights. social change . . . If students are reticent to respond, start off with one or two of your own.
Project: Create a four-line rap that honors the heroic work of Queen Latifah or Malala. Or a rap that focuses on the themes that they talked about. Add a rhythmic accompaniment using any of the following: snaps, stomps, claps, rhythmic tapping on the desk or beat boxing.	The rap composition should evolve from student suggestions. It may work better with a recorded beat sequence from YouTube. Alternate Beat Production: It is easy to find free beats for rap on YouTube. You might want to have the class choose between two of three for their rap.
Each group performs their rap, followed by wild applause. After each group has performed, make one long rap using all of their performances: *If we put all of these together in a sequence, what is the order that might work well? Which rap would you start with? Which rap would you end with? Should we use the one-line rap that we composed at the beginning of this activity for a transition between raps?* Record the performance for playback (audio).	
Listen to the playback. *What did you like? Is rap a good medium for sending a message about change? What is one thing that you learned from hearing about Malala and Queen Latifah?*	

Appendix A

Beethoven and Peter Parker as Youths

Link to Beethoven picture:
https://www.lookandlearn.com/history-images/B184752/The-young-Beethoven-was-a-child-prodigy-and-played-the-piano-endlessly

Link to Peter Parker (aka "Spider-Man") picture:
https://www.cbr.com/spider-man-flash-thompson-bully-debate/

Appendix B

Mood Adjectives

Somber	Intense	Peaceful	Rushing	Turbulent	Mellow
Driving	Forceful	Subdued	Serene	Smooth	Energetic
Joyful	Grand	Majestic	Gentle	Startling	Exciting

Directions
Listen to appropriate episodes from each piece. Then write any adjectives that describe the music.

Beethoven	Mood Adjectives
Symphony No. 5, Movement 1	
Symphony No. 9, Movement 4, "Ode to Joy"	
Moonlight Sonata, Movement 1	
Moonlight Sonata, Movement 3	
"York'scher March"	
Prometheus Overture	

Appendix C

The Story

Prepare a handout for the students that details the story, scene by scene. Each student will need this handout. Read the story to students to make sure everything was included.

Appendix D

Project Notes for Teachers—Preparation before Class

This comic strip project may look a little complicated but the students love it and you will find that the preparation is worth the success.

First
Read and adjust, if necessary, Appendices C and F. Make copies for each student.

Second
(Labor intensive—may take 1–2 hours)

Listen to each music piece and select 1 or 2 excerpts for students to use in their movie. The excerpt should run about 20 seconds. For example, if a picture suggests tension and turmoil, students might choose 8–10 seconds of the *Moonlight Sonata*, Movement 3.

Make an audio copy of each excerpt and save in a folder (Example: Excerpt 1, *Symphony 5*, Movement 1). Also include a typed list of the excerpts with titles for reference. Email the folder to each music editor with the directions: "Please put these excerpts on your cell phone."

Third
Become familiar with iMovie and how to add music excerpts as well as pictures. If you need a reference, consult YouTube.

Fourth
Set up *one* computer station for the tech crew. This computer must have movie capabilities and be able to accept pictures via email. Decide where groups of students can work together throughout the room.

** Note: The tech crew will not be able to finish during class. Choose tech-savvy students who are willing to work outside of class or during a free period.

Fifth
Prepare a list of student names and roles (artist, music editor, tech crew) for the credits. Give to the tech crew.

Appendix E

Culminating Project

We are making a comic strip that is accompanied by works of Beethoven. Artists and music editors are listed in the following chart. The tech crew will use iMovie to put pictures and music together.

	Comic Strip Working Groups
Scene 1 (Artists)	(Music Editors)
Scene 2 (Artists)	(Music Editors)
Scene 3 (Artists)	(Music Editors)
Scene 4 (Artists)	(Music Editors)

Tech Crew

Artists: We need a total of four pictures from your group. Each artist needs two graphite pencils and two pieces of unlined paper. Think about adding short bubble quotes or picture words like "ZOOM." Your drawing may not be a work of art but it will be funny . . . just like a comic strip should be. Fill the entire paper.

Music Editors: Put the music excerpts on a listening device (phone, laptop, iPad). As the artists are drawing, choose some excerpts that might go well with the pictures. Each slide needs 8–10 seconds of music. Coordinate with the artists. No need to change the excerpts for each slide.

Note to Artists AND Music Editors: When you are finished, put your pictures in the order they should appear. On the lower left-hand corner, in small print, write "scene ___, picture ___, excerpt and length of time _____" (Example: Scene 1, Picture 1, Excerpt: Moonlight Sonata, 0′00″–0′30″). Scan or send mobile phone picture to your teacher's school email account, (or the students in the tech crew). Make this decision with the teacher first.

Tech Crew: On Google Slides make a title slide, separator slide for each scene of the story, and a credit slide with everyone's name. Here's the order of slides: Title, Scene 1, Scene 2, etc., Credits. You can also write a short caption under the separator slide.

Example: Scene 1
And So, It Begins

When the artists are finished, you will insert their pictures into iMovie. The front of the picture will tell you the scene, picture order, and music excerpt. Drag the music excerpt under the picture. Then place the title, divider slides, and credits.

Appendix F

Sound Score for Healing

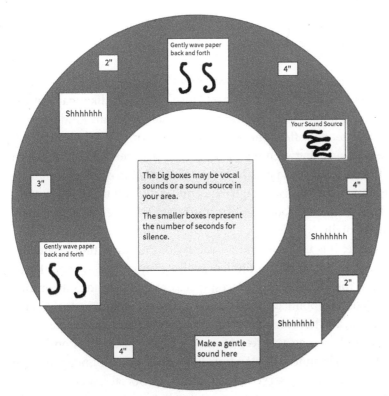

Figure 4.1. Sound Score for Healing.

Appendix G

Corrido de Cananea

For the lyrics and a translation of the lyrics,[1] see our book's website: https://socialjusticemusics.com/unit-3/

Note

1. Source: https://www.musixmatch.com/lyrics/Linda-Ronstadt/Corrido-de-Canenea; songwriter: Rubén Fuentes.

5

Love Unit

Introduction to the *Love* Unit

As we state in the Introduction to this book, we cannot properly engage in any kind of social justice unless we understand and enact "love." However, like many of the concepts explored in this book, "love" is complicated. There are many kinds of love. Love can be passionate, tender, affectionate, benevolent, warm, friendly, and/or full of devotion. There is the love between parent and child; between siblings; between lovers; the love of things; the love of pets; the love of place; and so on. Experientially, then, most people know what love is, though many find it difficult to put into words. All kinds of love, regardless of its "address," are important to adolescents, both personally and developmentally.

Given its significance, this unit examines a variety of musics as they relate, explore, and describe various kinds of love. Students will survey not only various kinds of love, but also love as manifested across places, spaces, and times and as it pertains to particular social/cultural/political issues such as those pertaining to LGBTQ communities, feminism, and home membership. In doing so, students will perform, compose, improvise, and arrange a variety of musics that showcase not only their understanding of the musics under investigation, but moreover their understanding of "love" and its infinite varieties to serve as a foundation for social justice.

The concept of love and its enactment are crucial to living a life well lived. Why? Because our relationships are incredibly important and set the stage for all that matters in our lives. It is through caring about things, people, ideas, places, ideals, and dreams that we infuse our worlds with importance and substance. And it is by receiving care—by receiving love—from people, places, and the outside world that we can understand "why" we matter. We've likely heard the phrase, "love makes the world go 'round." Loving someone or something or some place or some idea/ideal affords us with the reasons for why we live. Still, it would be a mistake to assume that we love someone or something or some place because of some "inherent" value. Instead, love—if it is actually love in the truest sense—engages with people, places, things, ideas/ideals, and so forth without any information about "value." The value resides in the relationship, without any real attention paid to any particular "values" in and of the things (or persons) themselves. The one who gives love shows the importance and/or value in loving.

Relatedly, the concept of love and its enactment are crucial to social justice. And love-as-action allows people to not only feel inequities and injustices of many kinds; it fuels potential action for change. In this sense, love-as-action is not only "social

Music Lesson Plans for Social Justice. Lisa C. Delorenzo and Marissa Silverman, Oxford University Press. © Oxford University Press 2022.
DOI: 10.1093/oso/9780197581476.003.0005

justice" itself, but, rather, action taken to be for others in the pursuit of relationality and social/communal well-being.

Although this unit addresses some of love's varieties, it is important to understand that love is best understood, felt, and enacted locally. And this locality can inspire and fuel more globally felt acts of love. And global love as action has real potency and power. For instance, during the time of the Civil Rights movement, Dr. Martin Luther King, Jr., stated in his address "Where Do We Go from Here?":

> One of the great problems of history is that the concepts of love and power have usually been contrasted as opposites, polar opposites, so that love is identified with a resignation of power, and power with a denial of love. . . .
>
> Now, we got to get this thing right. What is needed is a realization that power without love is reckless and abusive, and that love without power is sentimental and anemic . . . power at its best is love . . . implementing the demands of justice, and justice at its best is love correcting everything that stands against love. . . . And this is what we must see as we move on.[1]

Notes to Teacher

Like some of the other units in this book, this particular theme has an introductory lesson that establishes groundwork for the other lessons. This lesson can be eliminated, however, if it does not meet the needs of the students. Throughout the unit, there may be lessons that work best over two (or more) class sessions. And although the lessons are organized in a particular sequence, you may want to reorganize the sequencing of these lessons; additionally, you may want to insert your own lesson (or lessons) according to the needs of the class. Please note: if and whenever possible, consider inviting—whether via technology or through in-person visitations—culture/tradition bearers for the music-making components found in this unit. This is a good habit across each and every music-making culture, especially those that may seem "beyond reach" for you and your classroom community.

Here are some specific points for each section to keep in mind when teaching some or all of the unit:

Home
1. Love takes on a unique form when understanding it through the lens of "home." This helps students consider that people can find love in many ways and in many "close" places. Moreover, we can feel home and love even through music and music making.
2. There are so many songs to choose from in each of these lessons. Teachers may substitute other relevant songs and/or genres of music that seem more appropriate for the class.

Friendship

1. It is essential that some discussions focus on what "friendship" means, and how true friendship is a conduit for love-as-action.
2. The lessons on "friendship" hope to instill a sense of care, community, and love-as-action while music making. Because of this, consider paying careful attention to the feelings that arise when students are asked to "listen" (and respond) intently to the polyrhythmic materials expressed through the drumming, singing, and dancing from West Africa.

Passion

1. Every effort has been made to highlight the active component of being "passionate" about persons, places, and things. This is why it is crucial that students create music with "love." Doing so is as important for the music making as it is for the teaching of love through music.
2. These lessons lead toward the passion of having and attempting to fulfill a "dream," rather than the more obvious focus on romantic love. Should teachers feel as if this is a missed opportunity, feel free to add to these lessons to serve that need.

Ethics

1. Every effort has been made to highlight the activism inherent in love-as-action.
2. These lessons focus on love-as-action as understood through music, rather than "privately held feeling." We leave it up to the individual teacher to determine how to address this.

Pedagogy for Facilitating Relationality

If we were to think through the nature of relationships, we'd likely all come to the consensus that, at the core of all successful relationships—whether between family members, friends, or romantic partners—is the profound meaning and purpose that comes from relational engagement. In fact, human beings are social beings. This means that our survival, our thriving, depends on the relationships we foster and the ways in which we matter to and with others. Importantly, doing for others not only improves our overall well-being. It also connects us to others in significant ways. And this "connectivity" is paramount for love-as-action and social justice. So, how do we teach for connectivity and relationality?

There are numerous ways to facilitate relationality in the classroom. The first is through *listening*. As we have stated in various ways throughout this book, listening is paramount. If listening—real listening, both in relation to music and in relation to one another—is not being taught, students cannot fully connect with what they are doing or with whom they are attempting to achieve "connection." Additionally, teachers should consistently model active and constructive responses when engaging in conversations and dialogue with students. When students experience their music teacher attentively, actively, and constructively responding to questions and comments by students, they will potentially habituate those ways of engaging with others.

Important Strategies in Relationality

Here are a few strategies that have helped to engage large groups. Some may seem obvious; others may not:

- Greet your students by the door and do something special for each one as s/he/ they enters.
- Model active and constructive responses when having a dialogue with the whole class.
- Ask students to relive important events for you, and if they feel comfortable sharing with the class, then encourage them to do so. Ask them to provide vivid details of their lived experiences, especially when those experiences are positive or potentially opportunities for growth.
- Show genuine interest in not only what students are saying, but how they are feeling.
- Always maintain eye contact when students are speaking.
- Outwardly display positive emotions (e.g., smiling and laughing, when appropriate).
- Model expressing gratitude for the shared experiences of musical engagement.
- Consider instituting "secret acts of kindness" (up to you how to interpret this, given your knowledge of your students).

None of these strategies in and of itself indicates relationality. However, the more you model interest, enthusiasm, and support for students, the more such "micro-instances" of "attachment" are likely to provide students with the comfort needed to open up to you and their peers in class.

Graphic Organizer: LOVE

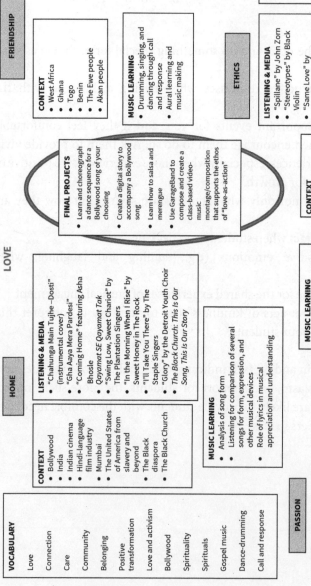

LOVE

VOCABULARY

Love
Connection
Care
Community
Belonging
Positive transformation
Love and activism
Bollywood
Spirituality
Spirituals
Gospel music
Dance-drumming
Call and response

HOME

CONTEXT
- Bollywood
- India
- Indian cinema
- Hindi-language film industry
- Mumbai
- The United States of America from slavery and beyond
- The Black diaspora
- The Black Church

LISTENING & MEDIA
- "Chahunga Main Tujhe –Dosti" (instrumental cover)
- "Gha Aaya Mera Pardesi"
- "Coming Home" featuring Asha Bhosle
- *Qayamat SE Qayamat Tak*
- "Swing Low, Sweet Chariot" by The Plantation Singers
- "In the Morning When I Rise" by Sweet Honey In The Rock
- "I'll Take You There" by The Staple Singers
- "Glory" by the Detroit Youth Choir
- *The Black Church: This Is Our Story, This Is Our Story*

MUSIC LEARNING
- Analysis of song form
- Listening for comparison of several songs for form, expression, and other musical devices
- Role of lyrics in musical appreciation and understanding

PASSION

CONTEXT
- Caribbean
- Puerto Rico
- Dominican Republic
- Washington Heights, New York City, United States
- Latin American Heritage

LISTENING & MEDIA
- Selections from *In the Heights* by Lin-Manuel Miranda
- "Oye mi Guaguanco" by Tito Puente
- "Lejos de ti" by Angel Canales
- "Un verano en Nueva York" by El Gran Combo
- "Que locura enamorarme de ti" by Eddie Santiago
- "Aguanile" by Marc Anthony

MUSIC LEARNING
- Dance and embody salsa and merengue
- Analysis of song lyrics to enhancing the music and the message of the song
- Listening for comparison of several songs for form, expression, and other musical devices

FINAL PROJECTS
- Learn and choreograph a dance sequence for a Bollywood song of your choosing
- Create a digital story to accompany a Bollywood song
- Learn how to salsa and merengue
- Use GarageBand to compose and create a class-based video-music montage/composition that supports the ethos of "love-as-action"

FRIENDSHIP

CONTEXT
- West Africa
- Ghana
- Togo
- Benin
- The Ewe people
- Akan people

MUSIC LEARNING
- Drumming, singing, and dancing through call and response
- Aural learning and music making

ETHICS

LISTENING & MEDIA
- "Spillane" by John Zorn
- "Stereotypes" by Black Violin
- "Same Love" by Macklemore
- "Blackbird" by The Beatles
- "Changes" by 2Pac
- "I Can't Breathe" by H.E.R
- "Society's Child" by Janis Ian
- "Q.U.E.E.N" by Janelle Monáe (featuring Erykah Badu)

CONTEXT
- Gender
- Feminism
- Sexuality
- Ageism
- Racism
- Unconscious bias
- Discrimination

MUSIC LEARNING
- Analysis of song lyrics to enhancing the music and the message of the song
- Analysis of emotional content of melody, harmony, rhythm, timbre, etc.
- Compose music by creating a pastiche of musical melodic, harmonic, rhythmic fragments from other pieces of music, and so forth

Introductory Lesson to Love

Goal
To introduce love as an activity which alerts students to relationality. This is important because "love" is the foundation for any engagement of social justice.

National Standards
- MU:Re7.6a: Select or choose music to listen to and explain the connections to specific interests or experiences for a specific purpose.
- MU:Cn10.0.6a: Demonstrate how interests, knowledge, and skills relate to personal choices and intent when creating, performing, and responding to music.

Assessment/Evaluation
- **Formative:** The teacher will assess students' abilities to reflect on important social issues through music making. The teacher will assess students' musical consideration of foundationally important concepts for embodying social justice.

YouTube Videos
- "Same Love" by Macklemore and Ryan Lewis, featuring Mary Lambert: https://www.youtube.com/watch?v=hlVBg7_08n0
- Macklemore & Ryan Lewis, Same Love (Instrumental): https://www.youtube.com/watch?v=xbNz-il6s80

Teaching Process

Instruction	Comments/Suggestions
Do Now: In their notebook, students will think of and write down "sounds" or "noises" (from the environment) that express the following emotions: HOME; FRIENDSHIP; PASSION; ETHICS. Students will then share their answers (without passing any judgment or critiquing the answers of each other).	Setting the context for "how" sounds and noises create meaning helps student listeners interpret songs and pieces of music that "evoke," "arouse," and "express" particular emotions, feelings, and spaces/places in time.

Instruction	Comments/Suggestions
Watch the video to "Same Love" by Macklemore and Ryan Lewis, featuring Mary Lambert. As students watch, ask them to think about the following questions in relation to the music video: • Consider the words from the Do Now in relation to this music video. What does "home" seem to mean here? What does "friendship" seem to mean here? What does "passion" seem to mean here? What do "ethics" seem to mean here? • What are the struggles faced and experienced in this music video? • In the end, Macklemore states: "No laws are going to change us, we have to change us." What areas of life and love does Macklemore refer to throughout this music video?	These are open-ended questions to facilitate a range of responses. Take time to allow students to think through these questions openly with each other. The teacher should act as facilitator of the discussion, rather than leader.
In small groups, students should create an additional verse to "Same Love" that speaks to their understandings of one or more of the following concepts: home, friendship, passion, and ethics. Once complete, have the students share their verse. Consider using the instrumental track of "Same Love"; or consider playing an accompaniment part on keyboard to support the students' creations/feelings.	
Further sharing with the class. Each group will explain their verse and some of the ideas that were important for their lyrics.	Whenever students perform, it is critical that you first lay the groundwork for supportive listening.
Reflection for student-listeners: *What did you like about this verse? How does this verse fit in potentially seeking change? Why?*	DO NOT SKIP THIS STEP. It is important that performers (who are putting themselves on the line) get positive peer feedback. They need to feel that their efforts were appreciated.

Home

Introduction

No examination about "love"—which, again, is foundational for social justice—could be considered complete without acknowledging "home." Why? Because we learn best about love in the places, communities, and with the people we consider "home." Like the concept of love, "home" is difficult to conceptualize, and even more difficult to define. Some people associate the word "home" with a building; others associate it with a sense of belonging. Regardless, most people know home when they feel it, and know what home isn't when they feel that, too. This is why it's particularly important to teach the concept of home through music. Students should be able to reflect on their home memberships, or lack thereof. They should be able to consider, for themselves through engaging with others, what home might mean and can potentially mean. Doing so is crucial for engaging in "love as action" and therefore enacting social justice in the pursuit of a life well lived.

However, different cultures and communities of people have particular ways of understanding "home." Therefore, it becomes even more imperative that students are afforded opportunities to think through the ways "home" matters and is understood by those closest to them and those who are not. Doing so may yield a better understanding of the values of home membership. Additionally, students may find themselves better understanding themselves through understanding the homes of others.

This unit does not attempt to define "home" for students. Instead, it offers opportunities to engage with the concept of home as felt in communities, families, the cultures of particular peoples, and beyond. Still, the lessons here are just the starting point. They are not "ends" in themselves, and should be considered as the jumping-off point for other lessons in this unit.

Home

Lesson 1

Goal
To assist students to understand the ways in which music is utilized to represent "home."

National Standards
- MU:Re8.1.7a: Describe a personal interpretation of contrasting works and explain how creators' and performers' application of the elements of music and expressive qualities, within genres, cultures, and historical periods, conveys expressive intent.

- MU:Pr4.2.7c: Identify how cultural and historical context inform performance and result in different music interpretations.

Assessment/Evaluation
- **Formative:** The teacher will assess students' abilities to compare and contrast the sounds of some Bollywood music. The teacher will assess students' abilities to draw from Bollywood influences to create an original rhythmic accompaniment to a Sanskrit poem.

YouTube Videos
- Chahunga Main Tujhe—Dosti (1964) (Flute instrumental cover by Maestro V. Hemapala Perera): https://www.youtube.com/watch?v=Ur2wc7ztkF4&feature=youtu.be
- "Gha Aaya Mera Pardesi": https://www.youtube.com/watch?v=Vf334WjKQI0
- "Coming Home," featuring Asha Bhosle: https://www.youtube.com/watch?v=gsid-2VpxPM

Other Materials
- "Jewel of All My Kingdom": Sanskrit poem (Appendix A)
- Instruments typically found in Bollywood soundtracks: drums (e.g., tabla, maracas), bansuri (or other bamboo flute with 6–7 holes), violin, etc.
- Bollywood Informational Guide (Appendix B)

Teaching Process (this may take two or three class periods)

Instruction	Comments/Suggestions
Do Now: Have "Chahunga Main Tujhe," from the film *Dosti* playing as students enter the classroom. Write the following on the board: Listening to the song played, answer the following questions in your Listening Log: • What does this music make you think of? What scene or personal experience comes to mind from the musical selection? • What emotions do you hear in the music? • What is happening in the music that makes you think of these emotions or experiences? For example, how does speed play a part in this? How does, say, volume play a part in this? How does, say, instrumentation play a part in this?	The teacher should keep her/his own Listening Log in order to participate with students if/when possible. Allow students to share their responses. Total time for this activity: 5–6 minutes.

Instruction	Comments/Suggestions
Pair–Share Activity: Where do you live? Can you describe where you live as a series of places, one inside the other, each smaller and more specific? For example: Universe, Galaxy, Earth, United States, New York, Westchester, Tarrytown, etc. With a partner, draw a diagram of concentric circles and try to name all the inner circles. When you are finished, compare your circle with your partner's.	
Pair–Share Activity: Have students read together "Jewel of All My Kingdom." Ask students to "visualize" imagery for each line of the poem. Additionally, ask them to consider "sonic imagery" for each line as related to the visual imagery. So, what sounds/noises might fit with each line of the poem?	The author of the poem is from ancient India, whose identity is unknown. Model the kind of thinking for them. Possible suggestion: *When I read the first two lines of this poem, "Although I conquer all the earth, / Yet for me there is only one city," I am picturing in my mind an Indian city, exotically formed: beautiful stone buildings adorned with turquoise textures and sheet curtains swaying in the breeze. The sounds/noises I imagine would fit with these first two lines are: the sound of thunder in the distance next to wind chimes.*
Help students understand "Bollywood" (see **Appendix B**). Listen to "Gha Aaya Mera Pardesi" and ask students to notice the components (e.g., instrumentation, meter, dancing) of Bollywood.	
Watch the video for "Coming Home." Ask students to take notice of the instruments used, vocal line (What is the gender of the singer? Who is the singer singing to?), and the shape of the melodic line.	As the composer notes on the official video for this song: *"Everyone has a place or person in their life where (or with whom) you feel the most loved, warm and secure with . . . It could be your wife (or husband!), your kids, your country, your pets, etc. and this song is all about that place! After taking all the crap that life hands out to you, this is the song about that place where you go, where you can just let go! BTW, all the 'home footage' used in the video are actual moments of my life, captured over the years. . . ."*[2]

Instruction	Comments/Suggestions
Ask students to relate the sonic imagery/visualizations related to the poem with the sonic imagery/visualizations from the Do Now activity in addition to "Coming Home." What are some similarities? Differences? Ask the students to speculate "why" there are these similarities and differences.	
In small groups (no more than five per group), create a Bollywood "groove" (rhythmic line) that could sit with the poetry. Create musical materials that not only symbolize the words of the poem, but also could potentially symbolize "home" for the speaker of the poem.	Feel free to use GarageBand, Protools, SoundTrap, or some other Digital Audio Workstation (DAW). Find more examples of Bollywood, rhythmically driven, musical examples on our book's website.
Have student volunteers share their creations.	Whenever students are going to share compositions, it is critical that you first lay the groundwork for supportive listening and applause.

Home

Lesson 2

Goal

To consider how spirituals and gospel music can embrace and embody a sense of "home."

National Standards

- MU:Re7.2.6a: Describe how the elements of music and expressive qualities relate to the structure of the pieces.
- MU:Pr4.2.7c: Identify how cultural and historical contexts inform performance and result in different music interpretations.

Assessment/Evaluation

- **Formative:** The teacher will assess students' abilities to compare and contrast the sounds of some spirituals and gospel music. The teacher will assess students' abilities to understand "home" in the content and contexts of some spirituals and gospel music.

YouTube Videos
- Trailer for *The Black Church: This Is Our Song, This Is Our Story*: https://www.youtube.com/watch?v=ULhwJIBnIos
- "Swing Low, Sweet Chariot" by The Plantation Singers: https://www.youtube.com/watch?v=ljup8cIRzIk
- "In the Morning When I Rise" by Sweet Honey in the Rock: https://www.youtube.com/watch?v=ZAJBZXIzKcY&feature=emb_logo
- "I'll Take You There" by The Staple Singers: https://www.youtube.com/watch?v=IhHBr7nMMio&feature=emb_logo
- "Detroit Youth Choir 'Glory' featuring IndigoYaj": https://www.youtube.com/watch?v=EDWsm7lcGXM

Other Materials
- "Spirituals" and "Gospel Music": A Brief Description (Appendix C)

Teaching Process (this lesson could take two or three class periods)

Instruction	Comments/Suggestions
Do Now: Watch the trailer for *The Black Church: This Is Our Song, This Is Our Story*. Ask the following questions: • *From your point of view, what is the relationship between home and spirituality and music?* • *From the point of view of the film trailer, what seems to be the relationship between home and spirituality and music?*	Have a discussion with the class. As students begin to share their thoughts, be sure to help them understand that "spirituality" is different from "religion" or "being religious."
There are important differences between "spirituals" and "gospel music" (see **Appendix C**).	Help students understand the similarities and differences between spirituals and gospel music. Important note: The word "gospel" means "good news."

Instruction	Comments/Suggestions
Here are some songs. As you listen, think about what these songs have in common, as well as what seems different about them. Which seem like a spiritual? Which seem like gospel music? • "Swing Low, Sweet Chariot" by The Plantation Singers • "In the Morning When I Rise" by Sweet Honey in the Rock • "I'll Take You There" by The Staple Singers	Analyze the form of the songs. *Is this a typical verse/chorus form?* Analyze the "instrumentation." *Is this sung with accompaniment or not (a cappella)?* Analyze the lyrics of the song. *Where might this song be sung; outside while working, or in a church? In a rural setting or an urban setting? Is this sacred or not; do the lyrics suggest a biblical theme or not?*
Teach the class to sing one of the previously listened to songs (or another one of your choosing).	Invite a culture/tradition bearer into class (either in person or via technological means – whether through video or audio) to assist in the teaching of either a spiritual or gospel music. Doing so will provide an important contextual understanding for the students.
Have students watch "Detroit Youth Choir 'Glory' featuring IndigoYaj". Ask the students the following question: *Is some of the musical content here similar to "gospel" music? Why?*	"Glory" is also explored in "The American Protest Unit." If you taught this prior, be sure to acknowledge this to students.
Exit ticket: *How might singing this song express "home"?*	Either have students write their answers down on index cards, or have a discussion that addresses this question.

Home

Lesson 3

Goal

To provide opportunities for students to consider what "home" means to them, and how "home in music" can help us understand one another.

National Standards

• MU:Re7.1.6a: Select or choose music to listen to and explain the connections to specific interests or experiences for a specific purpose.

- MU:Re7.7a: Classify and explain how the elements of music and expressive qualities relate to the structure of contrasting pieces.

Assessment/Evaluation

- **Formative:** Teacher will assess students' abilities to discuss the musical/lyrical elements that help them understand a "musical" sense of "home." Teacher will assess students' participation in co-constructing a musical identity through song choices.

Materials

- Playlist Project Information Sheet (Appendix D)

Teaching Process (this may take two class periods)

Instruction	Comments/Suggestions
Do Now: Today we are going to create a "home" playlist of our class. And each student will provide parts of "themselves" to this playlist through understanding "home" and "self." For now, consider the following question: *What are some connections among "home," "love," and "identity"?*	Have a discussion with the class.
List some of the students' ideas on the board. Introduce a new topic: *What places or people mean "home" to you? What does "home" feel like? What feels like "home"?*	Model ideas for students, which will sow the seeds toward their own playlist selections.
How do we think through these questions as related to music? What songs/pieces sound like "home" to you? Think–Pair–Share: Alone, consider your answers to the following questions. Share those answers with a partner: *What song/piece makes you think about your childhood (or your past)? What song/piece makes you think about your adolescence (or your present)? What song/piece makes you think toward your adulthood (or your future)?*	Share **Appendix D** with students.
Create a Google spreadsheet for every student's music/song picks.	

Instruction	Comments/Suggestions
Create and share the class's "playlist"; ask students to listen to three different songs from each category (childhood; present-day; future). In their notebooks and then in discussion in small groups, ask them to comment on the following: *What do you notice about the songs in the childhood, adolescence, and adulthood categories? What do they suggest about your peers' sense of "home" and "love"?*	
Reflection: *What do you appreciate about the class's "playlist"?*	DO NOT SKIP THIS STEP. It is important that youth (who are putting themselves on the line) get positive peer feedback about their sense of self "through music." They need to feel that their efforts were appreciated.

Friendship

Introduction

Adolescents learn a lot about "love" from home. But they learn an equal amount about love—and love-as-action—by having friends and potentially "best friends." But who counts as a friend? Let's look at some of the defining characteristics.

Even though adolescents may learn love at home, they may not feel it fully there (for one reason or another). Because of this, friendships offer adolescents an important window into understanding and feeling connection and love, openness and belonging, trust and comfort. How? When engaged in *real* friendship, among other emotional ways of experiencing ourselves in our worlds, we feel witnessed and we feel at ease. Additionally, friends tend not to lose connection, despite separation; indeed, friends often describe reuniting with one another—whether weeks or years have passed—as if the separation didn't occur; they "pick up" right where they left off. One reason this is the case is that friends see oneself in the other. So, this connection cannot be severed because we ourselves are mirrored in our friendships.

Because of this, the lessons on "friendship" concentrate on building connections, building empathy, and building community. There are numerous ways to build the foundations for friendship-love through music making: song-writing, group singing, and more. The emotional content of music is potentially ripe with this fuel. However, we suggest having students engage with West African drumming, singing, and dancing to learn and explore "friendship" through music making. This kind of musical engagement (quite naturally) provides the foundation for countless positive values. And there are numerous reasons—too numerous to mention—why this is the case. One reason, this music is participatory. Additionally, its aim is to connect each and all. Also, it calls participants to listen intently in order to respond empathetically (note: the lead drummer calls out to the dancers and supporting drummers; the call and response nature of the dialogues forges connection, intentional listening, and empathetic responsiveness).

Some of the many values that West African drumming, singing, and dance yield are: community, care, trust, spirituality, joy, and fellowship. Notably, these values should be noticed and pointed out when they occur. It is not enough to assume that the students are feeling these values. Such values need to be explicitly examined rather than passively received. Additionally, these values are the foundation for practicing any kind of love. Asking students to "love one another" is not a request that is beyond the ability of secondary school students. Still, they need to be given opportunities to practice love. Learning constructive strategies for connecting with others through music may help students cultivate a better world.

Friendship

Lesson 1

Goal
To understand, feel, and engage with "friendship" through West African drumming, singing, and dancing, specifically, "Gahu."

National Standards
- MU.Pr4.2.6c: Identify how cultural and historical contexts inform performances.
- MU:Re8.1.6a: Describe a personal interpretation of how creators' and performers' application of the elements of music and expressive qualities, within genres and cultural and historical contexts, conveys expressive intent.

Assessment/Evaluation
- **Formative:** Teacher will assess students' abilities to engage musically via supporting drum parts, dancing, and singing "Gahu." Through questions and answers, teacher will assess students' awareness of "listening" as a means for (musical and communal) friendship.

YouTube Videos
- "Gahu": https://www.youtube.com/watch?v=lAobzTuWeS4
- "Gahu" (START 15'04" : https://www.youtube.com/watch?v=GU6uiyuf1mY
- "Sounds of Ghana": https://www.youtube.com/watch?v=_MDrb24vfvM&feature=youtu.be

Other Materials

- Information on context of West Africa as it pertains to "Gahu"
- Photographs from Africa and West Africa (see National Geographic for examples: https://www.nationalgeographic.com/photography/article/everyday-africa-instagram-book)
- Audio recordings from "This World Music: Gahu": https://thisworldmusic.com/gahu-african-drumming-and-dance-from-ghana/
- Lyrics to a Gahu song (Appendix E)

Teaching Process (this may take two class periods)

Instruction	Comments/Suggestions
Do Now: Watch "Gahu."	Ask students to pay attention to the various drummers, singers, and dancers. Additionally, together, make inferences about the relationships between the drummers, singers, and dancers.
Show students a map of Africa and particularly West Africa, and photographs of various places in West Africa.	Ask students to explain what they notice about the photographs.
Explain to students the Ewe traditions of communal music making.	The Ewe people are primarily from Ghana (the Volta Region), southern Togo, and southwestern Benin. Dance-drumming is integral to all community life and communal living. So, there is no "audience." Everyone participates; and everyone has a role in their participation, whether as drummers, singers, or dancers.
Show students the instruments used in "Gahu" and explain that the drums used in Gahu, and most of West African drumming and dancing, can be categorized as a "family" of instruments: gankogui (two-toned, iron bell); axatse (gourd rattle); kagan (small drum, or "baby" of the family; high-pitched); kidi (mid-sized drum, or "mom" of the family; medium-pitched); sogo (large-sized drum, or "dad" of the family; low-pitched). The lead drum is typically played on the gboba.	Preferably, have a set of drums in class. If this is not possible, approximate the drum sizes, timbres, and tone qualities. There are "time keeping roles" and "supporting roles." Time keeping roles = gankogui and axatse; Supporting roles = kagan, kidi, and sogo.

Instruction	Comments/Suggestions
Play the bell pattern—the "heartbeat"—for students; have them dance in a circle (which moves clockwise): R, R, L, L. With each step—lined up with the bell—students should feel comfortable leaning into the step accompanied by their same sided shoulder.	As the students dance/move to the bell pattern, explain that Gahu is a social-recreational dance. It's found at gatherings, community functions, and is "performed" in a circle (so it's easier to make friends and meet new people).
Teach, via call and response and without the aid of sheet music or notation, the gankogui and axatse patterns. Add additional drum patterns as is comfortable/accessible for the students.	Lean on the following (as is needed): https://thisworldmusic.com/gahu-african-drumming-and-dance-from-ghana/ Use **Appendix E** as needed (though do not share notation with students; this is more for you as you listen to help "make sense" of the rhythms). Also lean on an additional sharing of "Gahu," particularly to learn the dancing (at 15'04" min.) as needed: https://www.youtube.com/watch?v=GU6uiyuf1mY
Critical Thinking Prompt: *Why is music such a powerful tool in creating community as well as in making connections?*	Examples: Every person can participate; making music together can bring people together.

Friendship

Lesson 2

Goal
To continue the learning and understanding of "friendship," "dialogue," and "community" through drumming, singing, and dancing "Gahu."

National Standards
- MU:Re8.1.6a: Describe a personal interpretation of how creators' and performers' application of the elements of music and expressive qualities, within genres and cultural and historical contexts, conveys expressive intent.
- MU:Pr4.2.6a: Identify how cultural and historical contexts inform the performances.

Assessment/Evaluation
- **Formative**: Teacher will assess students drumming, singing, and dancing "Gahu." Through questions and answers, teacher will assess students' awareness of "friendship" created through drumming, singing, and dancing.

YouTube Videos
- "Highlife Classic Old School," Ghana: https://www.youtube.com/watch?v=s5zycFeyqBE&t=2s
- Another version of "Gahu": https://www.youtube.com/watch?v=PUKknyxfzj4
- Another version of "Gahu": https://www.youtube.com/watch?v=F5SbyBAPlPk
- Another version of "Gahu": https://www.youtube.com/watch?v=_BhrNmIQsho

Other Materials
- Lyrics to a Gahu song (Appendix E)

Teaching Process (this may take two class periods)

Instruction	Comments/Suggestions
Do Now: Have "Highlife Classic Old School" playing as students enter the classroom. Write the following on the board: Listening to the song played, answer the following questions in your Listening Log: • What does this music make you think of? What scene or personal experience comes to mind from the musical selection? • What emotions do you hear in the music? • What is happening in the music that makes you think of these emotions or experiences? For example, how does speed play a part in this? How does, say, volume play a part in this? How does, say, instrumentation play a part in this?	The teacher should keep her/his own Listening Log in order to participate with students if/when possible. Allow students to share their responses. Total time for this activity: 5–6 minutes. Then, explain to students the following: *Highlife music came primarily from the Akan culture in the late nineteenth century (during British colonial rule). It brings together indigenous ways of being musical with Western ways of being musical. In some ways, the popularity of "jazz" music in the United States mirrored the popularity of Highlife music in Ghana. "Clave" patterns are a feature of Highlife music; that which utilizes a clave pattern outside Ghana can find its roots in Ghanian culture. The music features brass bands, a vocal component, as well as a fusion of jazz and indigenous stylizations.*

Instruction	Comments/Suggestions
Have students watch another interpretation of Gahu: https://www.youtube.com/watch?v=PUKknyxfzj4 Ask them to consider some of the similarities between Gahu and Highlife music. Additionally, ask the following question: *What about both Gahu and the Highlife music heard seems like "friendship"?*	Consider helping students realize that both Gahu and Highlife music are sources of inspiration, joy, pleasure, and inclusivity. The music of Ghana is relational; it "makes energy" and "sends energy out"—"Gahu" is no exception. And friendship—authentically conceived and practiced—is relational and it, too, makes energy and sends energy outward.
Friendship is something that is worked on and through over time; much like the learning of music, friendship is experienced from the inside out. *Continue to "work through" the teaching and learning of "Gahu" and aim for connectivity, joy, and friendship-in-action.*	Brief sharing of personal definitions on friendship.
As students hone their drumming and dancing, teach them a song from "Gahu" (see **Appendix E**). Have students watch another interpretation of "Gahu": https://www.youtube.com/watch?v=F5SbyBAPlPk	Encourage students to reflect on their own music making (drumming, singing, and dancing) in relation to the other versions of "Gahu."
What might friendship "feel like" through drumming, singing, and dancing? In pairs, list some of the musical and social features that help students understand "friendship" through West African drumming.	Extension if time permits: Share other West African drumming, singing, and dancing with students (see book's website for additional examples).

Passion

Introduction

Of all the lessons in this unit, "passion" may be the most elusive to teach. Many adolescents have yet to fully experience it, so their frame of reference may be somewhat off. Still, they've likely witnessed "passion" in others. And hopefully, and in addition to witnessing "passion" in home-membership, they see it modeled at school when you, their teacher, are excited to engage with interesting content, the music you love. Hopefully, they witness it in others when they pursue their hopes and dreams. As is likely clear by now, this unit does not explore "passion" in the romantic sense; but rather in dedicating oneself to something fully, to be passionate about someplace or something. This can lend itself nicely to being passionate about "someone," but that is beyond the scope of the lessons here.

More often than not, students hear and have heard: "Love what you do and you will not work a day in your life." In essence, this catch-all phrase suggests that people should figure out what they're passionate about and pursue that by way of a career. But aren't there more useful ways to consider "passion"? And must they lead to careers and making a living? Might passion be about finding ways to build a life? Sometimes being passionate about places and dreams, whether or not they are financially fruitful, are reasons people get out of bed in the morning. So, helping students find their healthful passions, connected to persons, places, things, and dreams, is important in educating "love" through music making.

Because of this, the lessons in this unit are inspired by places and dreams. Why do we love—and are therefore passionate about—the places that are important to us? Why do we love—and are therefore passionate about—the dreams that are important to us? How can we be both passionate about where we are from, yet passionate about "leaving" and moving on? And in what ways are these questions related to social justice matters? For many reasons, our "roots" define us, enliven us, inspire us, and place us. As the Salvadoran poet Roque Dalton writes in "Como Tú" (Like You): "Yo, como tú, amo el amor, la vida, el dulce encanto de las cosas . . ." (Like you, I love love, life, the sweet charm of things . . .). And we learn how to (and how not to) love, how to experience the sweet and the salty, how to struggle and feel joy from the places that matter to us and the dreams we hope to achieve.

Music, poetry, theater, and dance have always given artists a mode of expression to explore passion: to examine and express a love for place and space, as well as an experience of inhabiting the stuff of dreams. The lessons that follow emphasize music as a powerful means for reflecting on passion, love, and love-as-action. The overall point of these lessons is to show students how they can experience passion through the arts; this may then inspire them to create a life where passion is central to everyday living and being with and for others.

Passion

Lesson 1

Goal
To help students understand passion and love through the music of "salsa."

National Standards
- MU:Re8.1.6a: Describe a personal interpretation of how creators' and performers' application of the elements of music and expressive qualities, within genres and cultural and historical contexts, conveys expressive intent.
- MU:Re7.1.6a: Select or choose music to listen to and explain the connections to specific interests or experiences for a specific purpose.

Assessment/Evaluation
- **Formative:** The teacher will assess the students' understanding of the mood of several salsa songs using both narrative and musical terminology. The teacher will assess the students' abilities to learn and engage with the rhythmic pulse, meter, and emotional intent of salsa through students' participation in dancing.

YouTube Videos
- "Salsa y sabor" by Tito Puente: https://www.youtube.com/watch?v=sdJPaDMrxig
- "Salsa": https://www.youtube.com/watch?v=Ws67AP-2dEw
- "Real Grouches Don't Dance" by Sesame Street: https://www.youtube.com/watch?v=xHvtKdlAEUk&t=8s
- "Five(ish) Minute Dance Lesson: Salsa": https://www.youtube.com/watch?v=FdQ87SOfb7Y
- "Un verano en Nueva York" by El Gran Combo: https://www.youtube.com/watch?v=hd0cl2d2ziU
- "Que locura enamorarme de ti" by Eddie Santiago: https://www.youtube.com/watch?v=0sqWOC6bi_Y&feature=emb_logo
- "Vivir mi vida" by Marc Anthony: https://www.youtube.com/watch?v=ziUICCkVL0U

Other Materials
- Background information about Puerto Rico and "salsa" (Appendix F)
- Photo images from Getty of Puerto Rico: https://www.gettyimages.com/photos/puerto-rico

Teaching Process (this may take two or three class periods)

Instruction	Comments/Suggestions
Do Now: Have "Salsa y sabor" playing as students enter the classroom. Write the following on the board: Listening to the song played, answer the following questions in your Listening Log: • What does this music make you think of? What visual scene or personal experience comes to mind from the musical selection? • What emotions do you hear in this musical selection? And how do these emotions play into the scenes or experiences you have imagined? • What is happening in the music that makes you think of these emotions or experiences? For example, how does speed play a part in this? How does, say, volume play a part in this? How does, say, instrumentation play a part in this?	The teacher should keep her/his own Listening Log in order to participate with students if/when possible. Allow students to share their responses. Total time for this activity: 5–6 minutes.
Introduce and explore Puerto Rico (**Appendix F**). For pictures of the island, see the book's website as well as Getty images.	Some students may have been to or are from Puerto Rico. If so, call upon their experiences and expertise.

Instruction	Comments/Suggestions
Watch "Salsa" from Discover Puerto Rico: https://www.youtube.com/watch?v=xHvtKdlAEUk&t=8s *What do you notice about Puerto Rico from the video?* *What do you notice about salsa?* *What are some of the instruments you notice? How do people tend to react to the music? Why?* Teach your students a 3-2 clave and a 2-3 clave beat.	Have an open conversation that is respectful, and also points out some of the characteristics that lead to an understanding of the music. Play the 3-2 clave (Figure 5.1) and the 2-3 clave (Figure 5.2) in unison. **Figure 5.1.** Son Clave, 3-2. **Figure 5.2.** Son Clave, 2-3.
Have students watch "Real Grouches Don't Dance" by Sesame Street: https://www.youtube.com/watch?v=xHvtKdlAEUk&t=8s As they watch/listen to Tito Puente, ask them to consider whether the music uses a 3-2 clave or a 2-3 clave.	Introduce students to Ernesto "Tito" Puente (1923–2010): *Timbale player, songwriter, and band leader, born in New York City and from Puerto Rican descent. Latin musician who was called the "King of Latin Jazz," "El Rey del Mambo," [the King of Mambo] and "El Rey del Timbales," Tito Puente was also a marimbaist, pianist, congo player, bongo player, and saxophonist. Filled with Puerto Rican nostalgia, he loved to dance, and so became a club musician in local clubs. He was drafted into the Army and then attended Juilliard upon returning home. For years, he played the Palladium—a popular club that helped popularize the mambo, the cha cha cha, and other Latin dance crazes. Additionally, the Palladium helped to support the birth of "salsa"—most notably, incorporating Tito Puente's Afro-Cuban rhythms into the mainstream of jazz and popular musics.*
Learn how to salsa with your students. Salsa: https://www.youtube.com/watch?v=FdQ87SOfb7Y Practice and dance to "Un verano en Nueva York" by El Gran Combo: https://www.youtube.com/watch?v=hd0cl2d2ziU	If you do not know this dance, be sure to let students know that you are learning alongside them. For more examples of salsa music, see the book's website.

Instruction	Comments/Suggestions
In pairs or trios, use mobile device to find other examples of "salsa."	Some students may have specific songs in mind. If not, you can facilitate a search by telling students to Google the category of Latin music and dance.
Listen to and dance to "Vivir mi vida" by Marc Anthony: https://www.youtube.com/watch?v=ziUICCkVL0U	If students are unfamiliar with Marc Anthony, explain a bit of his biography: *American musician Marc Anthony (b. 1968; real name, Marco Antonio Muniz) is from New York City and was raised by Puerto Rican parents. He's been a performer since the young age of 12, and started making salsa music in the late 1990s. His 1997 album,* Contra la Corriente *(Against the Current), was incredibly popular; he gained cross-over popularity with his hit "I Need to Know."*
Exit Ticket: *What is the message of "Vivir mi vida"? And how does this relate to "passion" of place and of having dreams?* Give a two- to three-sentence explanation for your answer.	

Passion

Lesson 2

Goal
To help students understand passion and love through the music of "merengue."

National Standards
- MU:Re8.1.6a: Describe a personal interpretation of how creators' and performers' application of the elements of music and expressive qualities, within genres and cultural and historical contexts, conveys expressive intent.
- MU:Re7.1.6a: Select or choose music to listen to and explain the connections to specific interests or experiences for a specific purpose.

Assessment/Evaluation
- **Formative:** The teacher will assess—both through observation and through questions/answers and dialogue—students' ability to describe the mood of several given songs using both narrative and musical terminology. The teacher will

assess students as they feel the rhythmic push and pull of the dance, both as an embodied expression of passionate engagement and also as passionate "wordless" communication.

YouTube Videos
- "Music and Dance of the Merengue": https://www.youtube.com/watch?v=fautemcgU48
- "Five(ish) Minute Dance Lesson: Merengue": https://www.youtube.com/watch?v=daaHi0jtHlw
- Milly y Los Vecinos, "La Guacherna": https://www.youtube.com/watch?v=7VBnE1J6Odk

Other Materials
- Photo images from Getty of the Dominican Republic: https://www.gettyimages.com/photos/ominican-republic?phrase=ominican%20republic&sort=mostpopular
- Background information about Dominican Republic and "merengue" (Appendix G)
- Map of the Caribbean/Dominican Republic (found online)
- Audio file of Joaquin Diaz's "Merengue alegre" (e.g., hosted on Apple music or Spotify)

Teaching Process (this may take two class periods)

Instruction	Comments/Suggestions
Do Now: Have Joaquin Diaz's "Merengue alegre" playing as students walk into the classroom. Write the following on the board: Listening to the song played, answer the following questions in your Listening Log: • What does this music make you think of? What scene or personal experience comes to mind from the musical selection? • What emotions do you hear in the music? • What is happening in the music that makes you think of these emotions or experiences? For example, how does speed play a part in this? How does, say, volume play a part in this? How does, say, instrumentation play a part in this?	The teacher should keep her/his own Listening Log in order to participate with students if/when possible. Allow students to share their responses. Total time for this activity: 5–6 minutes. Then, explain to students the following: The music and dance of *merengue* came from the Dominican Republic. Initially considered "rural," merengue was deemed unsophisticated and unpopular with the upper classes. However, after a political decree in the 1940s, it became the Dominican Republic's national dance.
Introduce and explore the Dominican Republic from the Getty library. Read **Appendix G** on background information on Dominican Republic and the merengue. Ask students: • *What seem to be some characteristics of dancing the merengue?* • *What instruments to do you hear?* Watch "Music and Dance of the Merengue": https://www.youtube.com/watch?v=fautemcgU48	Be sure to ask students if anyone has traveled to or is from the Dominican Republic. If someone has traveled there or is from there, be sure to mine their experiences. Write students' thoughts on the board for a reference point. Some possible answers for characteristics: festive, joyful, freeing, interactive, welcoming, inviting. Answers for instrumentation: accordion, guitar, tambora, güira, bass, voice. Compare answers to the preceding questions with what you and students learn from watching the video on the music and dance of the merengue.

Instruction	Comments/Suggestions
Learn the merengue with your students and practice with them. Merengue: https://www.youtube.com/watch?v=daaHi0jtHlw Practice and dance to Milly y Los Vecinos "La Guacherna": https://www.youtube.com/watch?v=7VBnE1J6Odk	If you do not know this dance, be sure to let students know that you are learning alongside them. For more examples of merengue music, see the book's website.
In pairs or trios, use mobile device to find other examples of "merengue."	Some students may have a specific song in mind. If not, you can facilitate a search by telling students to Google the category of Latin music and dance.
Exit Ticket: *If you were going to choose a song to teach a friend or loved one how to dance the merengue, what criteria would you use when choosing a song?* Give a two-sentence explanation for your answer.	

Passion

Lesson 3

Goal

To explore how Lin-Manuel Miranda's *In the Heights* examines the passion and love of place, while also considering dreaming of a home beyond one's home.

National Standards

- MU:Re8.1.7a: Describe a personal interpretation of contrasting works and explain how creators' and performers' application of the elements of music and expressive qualities, within genres, cultures, and historical periods, conveys expressive intent.
- MU:Pr4.1.8a: Apply personally developed criteria for selecting music of contrasting styles for a program with a specific purpose and/or context and explain expressive qualities, technical challenges, and reasons for choices.

Assessment/Evaluation

- **Formative:** The teacher will assess students' interpretations of *In the Heights*. The teacher will assess students' interpretation of belonging, identity, and expanding identity through musical creation.

YouTube Videos

- *In the Heights* Trailer: https://www.youtube.com/watch?v=U0CL-ZsuCrQ
- Audio recording of the beginning of *In the Heights*: https://www.youtube.com/watch?v=mzWCc9JwZTo
- *In the Heights*, the opening number: https://www.youtube.com/watch?v=RrIAUhmQsXM

Other Materials

- *In the Heights* character list, plot summary, and creators' bios (Appendix H); see also project's website: https://www.linmanuel.com/project/in-the-heights/
- Getty images of Washington Heights: https://www.gettyimages.com/photos/washington-heights?phrase=washington%20heights&sort=mostpopular
- Select quotations about "love" and "dreams" from *In the Heights* (Appendix H)

Teaching Process (this may take two or three class periods)

Instruction	Comments/Suggestions
Do Now: Consider the following in your notebook: In an interview, the composer and creator of *In the Heights* (and *Hamilton*) Lin-Manuel Miranda said the following about this musical: "*In The Heights* is a story about family, of love, of community, of chasing your dreams and, most of all, it is about finding home."[3] *What songs come to mind that make you think of "family, community, dreaming, and finding home"?*	This is a challenging question, so consider having a discussion with the students and model for them your answers to this question. For the full interview with Miranda, see here: https://www.swarthmore.edu/news-events/heights-a-conversation-lin-manuel-miranda
Watch the trailer to the film *In the Heights*. Ask students: *What do you notice? What questions do you have?*	If students are not responding, or if they typically do not watch (or are interested in) musical theater, help them respond by offering your own ideas.

Instruction	Comments/Suggestions
Explore the plot, characters, and select quotes from *In the Heights*. (**Appendix H**). Explore photographs of Washington Heights in New York City. *Ask students: In what ways does the "neighborhood" of Washington Heights seem to "come alive" through its characters? What does the name "Washington Heights" symbolize?*	Possible interpretations: "the heights" means high altitude, but also achieving one's dreams (as in reaching the heights). Consider discussing current events surrounding immigration and the "Dream Act" in relation to a place like Washington Heights (for a review of film and its contexts: https://www.vox.com/ 22440448/in-the-heights-movie-rev iew-miranda-ramos-chu-hudes; for information on the "Dream Act": https:// www.americanimmigrationcouncil.org/ research/dream-act-overview).
Listen to the opening audio file of *In the Heights*: (https://www.youtube. com/watch?v=mzWCc9JwZTo) *From the beginning of this musical, what do we learn about the main character, the context of the musical, as well as the people associated with* In the Heights? *Take notes in your notebook; then turn to the person sitting nearest you and discuss what you learned about this community. Consider, too, does it remind you of any community you know?*	If possible, consider showing students selections from the film version of *In the Heights*.
Watch the following from the first act of the musical: https://www.youtube. com/watch?v=RrIAUhmQsXM *Ask students: Does the setting/context presented on stage seem "authentic" to what you heard via the audio of the opening to the musical? Why or why not?*	After students answer this question, share (selected by you) photographs of Washington Heights in New York City.
Consider the following: *The musical has been described as an "original hip-hop-salsa-merengue musical about two days in the life of Washington Heights, a vibrant immigrant neighborhood at the top of Manhattan."* *Why do you think Lin-Manuel Miranda bridged all these "worlds" of music and culture in this musical theater work?*	Listen intently to the thoughts of the students.

Instruction	Comments/Suggestions
Put students in groups and ask them to create a potential map for a "musical theater song" that celebrates the many musical-cultural identities of your school's community. What worlds of music and culture should be "celebrated" to authentically represent your school and its communities of people?	Visit the groups as they consider their task. Help if needed.
In their groups, and using GarageBand (or other DAW), have students create an "instrumental" track (through loops) that brings together some of the musical worlds and cultures represented across the school's community. If some groups finish early, have them create "spoken word" poetry (or lyrics) that could be read over their looped creations that would celebrate the worlds/cultures of the school's communities.	To assist with this, consider giving students some "restrictions" to focus their creations: Their composition (or "communal looping") should be no more than two minutes in length. They should "marry" at least three different worlds/cultures as exemplified through the sonic qualities of the loops.
When complete, share student creations. Allow for reflective responses about the pieces.	
Exit ticket: In the Heights *is about loving one's home while also trying to dream beyond one's home.* *How can we celebrate "home" and belonging while also trying to expand "where" home is?* Write two to three sentences explaining your thinking.	

Ethics

Introduction

Why include lessons on "ethics" as part of a unit on "love"? Of all the lessons in this unit, "ethics" is the most individualistic, yet possesses the most potential consequences for community living. This is so because one's ethical compass seeks to answer some very tough questions specifically for oneself, namely, "What kind of person is it good to be?" and "How should I live?" And no one can (or should) attempt to answer these questions for another person. These questions are to be internalized, deliberated upon, and asked, answered, and re-answered often throughout one's life. So, there are no "once and for all" answers to these questions. This is the good news, but also the difficult news.

Very often the teaching of "ethical responsibility" is left to parents and religious institutions. However, schools, too, can be sites of students' ethical development. And there is no reason that students cannot consider these questions in relation to music making and musical creation. There are plenty of composers, songwriters, hip-hop artists, performers, and more who have considered such questions in relation to their creative activity. Children and adolescents, too, can harness their creative potentials to explore these first-person ethical questions. Because of this, the lessons in this unit ask students to consider some of the ills of society, while being mindful of ways to "take care of" (or propose solutions to) moral shortcomings in the world. So, the focus is on combating stereotypes, while engaging in musical creation that seeks to answer first-person ethical questions through music making and sharing.

Ethics

Lesson 1

Goal
To help students experience music as a means for noticing ethical matters and the personal choices and decisions to "do good" for oneself and others.

National Standards
- MU:Re8.1.6a: Describe a personal interpretation of how creators' and performers' application of the elements of music and expressive qualities, within genres and cultural and historical contexts, conveys expressive intent.
- MU:Re7.1.6a: Select or choose music to listen to and explain the connections to specific interests or experiences for a specific purpose.

Assessment/Evaluation
- **Formative:** The teacher will assess students' abilities to categorize and describe songs/music using both narrative and musical terminology. The teacher will assess students' abilities to place song within a given category and explain the reasoning for this choice.

YouTube Videos
- "Stereotypes" by Black Violin: https://www.youtube.com/watch?v=WYerKidQGcc
- "Same Love" by Macklemore and Ryan Lewis, featuring Mary Lambert: https://www.youtube.com/watch?v=hlVBg7_08n0

Other Materials

- "Spillane" by John Zorn (audio file)
- Composition Assignment Instructions (Appendix I)
- Diagram of the form of "Spillane" by John Zorn (Appendix J)

Teaching Process (this may take two class periods)

Instruction	Comments/Suggestions
Do Now: Listen and watch the video of "Stereotypes" by Black Violin. As you listen, in your notebook answer the following question: *What musical means are used to support the musical ends of this song?* Take time to discuss the students' "Do Now" activity together as a class. Discuss the various "stereotypes" this performance illustrates and interrogates.	Have the words, "stereotype," "hope," "ethics," "sorrow," "discrimination," and "prejudice" (and so forth) on the board as a reference. Consider noticing with the students the use of counterpoint—another form of "rap battle." Counterpoint = democratic balance: the voicing of various views while still maintaining a sense of the integral whole.
Listen to about three minutes of "Spillane" by John Zorn as a class. Ask the students: *What do you notice? What stands out to you?* In their groups as they listen, ask them to map out (or draw) the "story" behind the music, given what they are hearing.	As the music is playing, create your own "map" of the form of this piece. Essentially, the music is formed in "blocks" of sonic material: sampled sound + musical narrative + sampled sound + musical narrative + sampled sound + musical narrative, etc., etc.
In their groups, ask students to consider and discuss various stereotypes that are problematic for various groups of people: gender stereotypes, ageism, racism, etc. Share with students some music that speaks directly to the problem of stereotyping peoples. Examples beyond "Same Love" may include: "Blackbird" by The Beatles "Changes" by 2Pac "I Can't Breathe" by H.E.R. "Society's Child" by Janis Ian "Q.U.E.E.N" by Janelle Monáe (featuring Erykah Badu)	

Instruction	Comments/Suggestions
Hand out the Composition Activity Instructions. Put students into small groups (of 4 or 5). Have them complete **Part 1** from the instructions together in groups. Ask students to share some of the world's problems and the world's "fixes" to those problems; ask them to share some of the songs/music that seems to illustrate the problems and solutions (as per the handout instructions)	Take time and visit with each group; answer any questions and help facilitate their progress (though without much involvement, if possible).
Have the groups share with the whole class what they discussed in small groups.	Be sure to model active listening while students are sharing.

Ethics

Lesson 2

Goal
To explore how creating music can honor the struggles of others while also providing hope for solutions to those struggles.

National Standards
- MU:Re8.1.7a: Describe a personal interpretation of contrasting works and explain how creators' and performers' application of the elements of music and expressive qualities, within genres, cultures, and historical periods, conveys expressive intent.
- MU:Pr4.1.8a: Apply personally developed criteria for selecting music of contrasting styles for a program with a specific purpose and/or context and explain expressive qualities, technical challenges, and reasons for choices.

Assessment/Evaluation
- **Formative:** The teacher will assess students' understanding of how to take elements from different musical creations to create something new. The teacher will assess students' abilities to engage in ethical considerations as "fuel" for musical creation.

YouTube Videos
- "Obvious Child" by Paul Simon: https://www.youtube.com/watch?v=9HKNAhAxMAk&list=FLTa1yrOAA0BiUWGF57IgoPg&index=681

Other Materials
- Composition Assignment Instructions (Appendix I)
- Music technology software (e.g., GarageBand) and movie-making software (e.g., iMovie)

Teaching Process (this may take two class periods)

Instruction	Comments/Suggestions
Do Now: Write down the following in your notebook: "Love that does not satisfy justice is no love at all. . . . Love at its best is justice concretized."[4] — Dr. Martin Luther King, Jr. List one song you know that relates to this quotation and give reasons why.	Discuss the Do Now activity with students. This should take 3–5 minutes.
Watch the video for and listen to Paul Simon's "Obvious Child." *What is meant by "why deny the obvious child"? And who (or what) is the "obvious child"? Why incorporate Brazilian drumming into this song?*	Have a discussion about this song with students. Consider interpretations like "we can learn from our past mistakes," while aiming to be "better tomorrow." Note: Incorporating Brazilian drumming into this song accentuates "living in the preset" and realizing that as we aim to be better tomorrow, we are better for it right now. The coming together of styles and cultural communities helps this song "celebrate" the here and now.
Put students back into their composition groups from the previous lesson. Review if necessary. Continue onward with the composition assignment until complete.	
When ready, as a class listen to the finished product (see **Appendix I**).	

Instruction	Comments/Suggestions
Allow students to offer their thoughts about the compositional group process as well as experiencing the final product. *How did this process and the creation of your product engage in your ethical growth?*	Ask "feeling-related" questions, such as: *How did you personally feel when you saw your "vignette" showcased on the screen? How did you feel when you saw your name on the screen? How did you feel when you witnessed what your classmates created to challenge the wrongs of the world? How did you feel when you witnessed what your classmates created to offer solutions to fix the wrongs of the world?*

Appendix A

Jewel of All My Kingdom

> Although I conquer all the earth,
> Yet for me there is only one city.
> In that city there is for me only one house;
> And in that house, one room only;
> And in that room, a bed.
> And one woman sleeps there,
> The shining joy and jewel of all my kingdom.
>
> —Sanskrit Poem, author unknown

Appendix B

Bollywood Informational Guide

What Is "Bollywood"?

While some film critics and social commentators find the term "Bollywood" derogatory, others view it as a label to embrace. Essentially, the name itself is a coming together of the "ethos" of two places and a combination of two words: "Bombay" (India) and "Hollywood" (California, USA). The Bollywood film industry, which began in the 1930s, finds its home primarily in Mumbai (formerly Bombay), though the films are representative of the places, spaces, and people across South India. For multiple examples of Bollywood films and music/dance, see the book's website.

Features of Bollywood Films

The multi-million-dollar film industry is as distinctive as it is popular. There are a few characteristics that seem to distinguish Bollywood films. Please note: there are plenty of Bollywood films that defy characterization. Still, what follows might be helpful as you engage with the films:

- Colors galore! Expect to experience a kaleidoscope of colorful clothing, landscapes (flora and fauna), jewelry, set design, and more.
- Music and dancing! Regardless of the content and plot-line of the film, expect catchy songs linked with coordinated and choreographed dance sequences. Music and dance sequences are woven into the plot line of the film.
- Fairy-tale-like plot lines! More often than not, and even when characters engage in troublesome issues, expect those troubles to work out or unravel in a similar way to most fairy tales. While not all Bollywood films feature happy times throughout, the thrust at the end of the film is a vehicle for happiness or a lesson toward moral learning.

Features of Bollywood Music and Dance

Unlike Broadway musicals where actors are expected to be able to sing and dance themselves, Bollywood stars more often than not do not do any of their own singing (though, they do dance when involved in dance-sequences). The singing is prerecoded and actors lip-sync their lines. Still, like the films themselves, the music and dance sequences are colorful. There are a few characteristics that seem to distinguish the music and dancing. Please note: there is a lot of Bollywood music and dancing that defies characterization. Still, what follows might be helpful as you engage with the film scores/soundtracks:

- Both the music and dancing are incredibly important to the plot, character development, and more. Think of the music and dance "on par" with the costumes and set design.
- Singing is a fusion of styles. It combines idioms and stylizations from Indian classical and folk musics with "borrowings" from American jazz, hip-hop, salsa and other Latin-based forms, Arabic forms, and more.
- Dancing choreography is a fusion of styles. It combines idioms and stylizations from Indian classical and folk dancing with "borrowings" from American jazz dance, hip-hop moves, salsa and other Latin-based forms, Arabic dancing forms, and more.
- Because the music takes inspiration from Indian classical music, expect to experience ragas (melody based on specific scale patterns) and talas (meter-cycle based on a specific number of beats).
- Despite the music stemming from Indian classical music, it maintains a "pop"-style (similar to Western popular music).

- The dancing incorporates a lot of hand movement; hands are an integral part of the choreography, and each gesture "means" something specific.
- The dancing incorporates a lot of head movement; whether moving side-to-side or forward and backward, the head and neck create important gestures for choreography.
- The dancing incorporates a lot of foot movement; feet are an integral part of the choreography, and each gesture "means" something specific.

For more information about Bollywood films, film music, and Indian musics, see the work of Natalie Sarrazin and Jayson Beaster-Jones (*Music in Contemporary Indian Film: Memory, Voice and Identity*, Routledge, 2016), as well as Sarrazin's *Indian Music for the Classroom* (Rowman Littlefield, MENC, 2008).

Appendix C

Spirituals and Gospel Music: A Brief Description

There are some similarities between spirituals and gospel music. However, there are some important differences. This very brief guide provides insight into some of the similarities and differences. For a variety of examples of spirituals and gospel music, see the book's website.

Spirituals

The term and concept of "spirituals" came from the New Testament, specifically "The Epistle to the Ephesians" (5:19): "speaking to one another with psalms, hymns, and songs from the Spirit. Sing and make music from your heart to the Lord." There are generally three kinds of spirituals:

- Call and response: A leader/soloist sings (be it a phrase or short melody) something, which is then repeated by the chorus/group (e.g., "Swing Low, Sweet Chariot"; "Got On My Traveling Shoes"; "All Night, All Day")
- Slow, melodic (e.g., "Deep River"; "Sometimes I Feel like a Motherless Child"; "Nobody Knows the Trouble I've Seen")
- Fast, rhythmic (e.g., "Ain't That Good News"; "Who'll Be a Witness for My Lord"; "Fare Ye Well")

The melodies are typically sung a cappella, whether in unison or inclusive of sung harmony. Spirituals maintain, typically, one strain, which gets repeated. Because of this, the lyrics serve a few purposes. Lyrics tend to refer to people from the Old Testament—e.g., Moses, David—who had to overcome adversities, challenges, and some form of persecution; however, some lyrics engage with the New Testament. Additionally, the lyrics provide a language and code to speak/sing about "freedom" from oppression and slavery. The lyrics are group oriented and tell stories that large numbers of people can relate to. Importantly, spirituals were passed on orally and were not written down.

Gospel Music

This music grew from spirituals and maintains some of the same characteristics; however, gospel music is different in a variety of ways:

- Call and response, syncopation, and improvisation (e.g., "Every Praise" by Hezekiah Walker)
- Verse-chorus or strophic forms (e.g., "To God be the Glory" by Fanny Crosby)
- Instrumental accompaniment (e.g., "Nobody Greater" by VaShawn Mitchell featuring Bebe Winans and Tasha Cobbs)
- Rhythmic intensity (e.g., "Old Time Religion" by Mahalia Jackson)
- Melodic lines take inspiration from the blues (e.g., with bent tones, flat thirds and sevenths) (e.g., "Death Come a-Knockin" by The Four Brothers)

For more information, see the following resources:

The Music of Black Americans: A History by Eileen Southern (W. W. Norton)
The Spiritual Database: http://spirituals-database.com/#sthash.PN09NVWx.dpbs
African American Spirituals, from the Library of Congress: https://www.loc.gov/item/ihas.200197495/
The Black Church: This Is Our Song, This Is Our Story from PBS; hosted by Henry Louis Gates, Jr.: https://www.pbs.org/show/black-church/
The Harlem Gospel Choir: http://www.harlemgospelchoir.com
The Mississippi Mass Choir: https://www.malaco.com/artists/gospel/the-mississippi-mass-choir/
"Now What a Time: Blues, Gospel, and the Fort Valley Music Festivals, 1938 to 1943": https://www.loc.gov/collections/blues-gospel-and-the-fort-valley-music-festivals/about-this-collection/

Appendix D

Playlist Project Information Sheet

Think about your life, who you are, and what matters most to you. And, in considering these questions, think about them through music. In other words, what songs or compositions would ultimately answer the question: "who are YOU"?

Choose at least three songs or pieces of music that speak to aspects of YOU. If you need help doing this, you may want to select music by thinking about the following aspects of your life:

- your childhood (your past),
- your current sense of self (your present),
- and your visions about who you'd like to become (the future).

While you should select three songs or pieces of music, you are not limited to three—feel free to include more than three if you wish.

For each song, explain (in your notebook) the following:

- What songs or pieces of music did you choose? Who are the artists/groups? What genres (types) of music might your songs/pieces be classified as?
- Why did you choose these musical selections? What personal meaning do they hold for you?
- What does each song/piece make you think of? What visual scene or personal experience comes to mind from each musical selection?
- What emotions do you hear in your musical selections? And how do these emotions play into the scenes or experiences you have imagined?
- What is happening in the musical selections that make you think of these emotions and experiences?

Appendix E

Gahu

Gahu "welcomes" all participants to join in!

Song
Call: Ga-hu lo . . . ga-hu ah-dog-bay, nawo lo-ay (rough translation: Gahu greets you!) Response: Ga-hu ay . . . ga-hu ah-dog-bay:|| Call: Eh dog-bay Response: Ga-hu ah-dog-bay:||
All: Ga-hu lo . . . ga-hu ah-dog-bay, nawo lo-ay. Ga-hu ay . . . ga-hu ah-dog-bay.
Drum pattern (Figure 5.3)
x = play

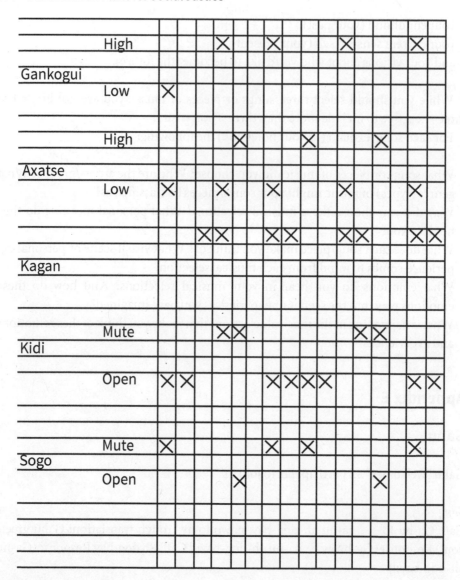

Figure 5.3. Gahu notation.

Appendix F

Puerto Rico and "Salsa"

Puerto Rico is an island in the Caribbean and since 1917, Puerto Ricans have been United States citizens. Originally settled by the Indigenous Tainos (an Arawak people), Puerto Rico was colonized by Spain upon the arrival of Christopher Columbus (in 1493). For centuries it remained under Spanish rule, and during that time, African slaves were brought to the island. The United States acquired it in 1898 after the Spanish-American War. A Puerto Rican identity is layered, a fusion of the Indigenous, Spanish, and African peoples inhabiting the island. So, Puerto Rican culture is an amalgamation of three worlds coming together. Additionally, and all at once, Puerto Rico combines "old world" sensibilities and tempi with modernization and innovation.

Facts: Its capital is San Juan.
Major languages spoken: Spanish and English
Major religion: Christianity (the majority being Catholic)
Major revenue: manufacturing (mainly pharmaceutical) and tourism
Culture: Taino, Spanish, and African elements.

Puerto Rican landscapes vary: from forests to mountains to pristine beaches. Like its land, the cultural heritage of Puerto Rico is exceptionally rich and diverse, too: its food, traditions, dance, and music!

"Salsa"

Tito Puente (recall: one of the biggest names and legends of salsa music) is claimed to have said: "Salsa is something you put on spaghetti; it's not music." Despite this, the term "salsa" is acknowledged and utilized to categorize dance and music of Latin American heritage. But where did the term "salsa" come from? The term *salsa* was coined as a marketing idea in the 1970s in New York City by a company called Fania—a small, independent record label that focused on various music of Latin American musicians. Hence the term "salsa dancing" emerged to sell records. The label caught on, as did salsa dancing and its music, and the rest is (sort of) history.

At its core, salsa is an amalgamation of various dance styles/music: cha-cha, pachanga, guaracha, bolero, and more. Its vibe is upbeat, "loud" (in content and essence), and seductive; noticeably, the feeling of listeners is a need to get up and dance! Because of the hybridization of diverse musical styles, salsa combines the spirit of diverse peoples and places across Latin America: Cuba, Puerto Rico, and the Dominican Republic. What links these peoples and places? A shared ancestry from Africa.

As the Fania label expanded in popularity, so did its roster of artists. Because of this, early prolific salsa musicians include: Celia Cruz, Tito Puente, Willie Colón, as well as an amazing group, the Fania All-Stars. For examples of salsa music and dancing, see our book's website, including scenes from a Fania All-Stars concert, which was organized as part of the George Foreman/Muhammed Ali African-based fight, "Rumble in the Jungle," in 1974 in Kinshasa, Zaire.

Appendix G

Dominican Republic and the Merengue

The Dominican Republic—or DR—is in the Caribbean. Originally settled by the Indigenous Tainos (an Arawak people), the DR shares its geography with Haiti on the island of Hispaniola (coined "Little Spain" by Christopher Columbus in 1492). Due to diseases brought by Europeans, the Taino population declined. After more than 300 years of Spanish rule, in 1821, the DR gained its independence.

Facts: Its capital is Santo Domingo.

Major language spoken: Spanish

Major religion: Christianity

Major revenue: tourism, sugar, coffee, and other exports

Culture: African and Taino elements

The DR landscapes vary: from forests to deserts to mountains to beautiful beaches. Like its land, the cultural heritage of the DR is exceptionally rich and diverse, too: its food, traditions, dance, and music!

Merengue

The merengue is considered by most native Dominicans the national music and dance of the DR. The lyrics tend to embrace the values of the people, while focusing on "everyday stories." The instruments typically used in merengue music showcase the diversity of the DR people: the *güira* (from the Taino people), the *tambora* (or drum from Africa), and the accordion (from Spain). To see photographs and videos of these specific instruments in action, see our book's website.

There are numerous well-known merengue artists from the DR: Milly Quezada, Juan Luis Guerra, Johnny Ventura (AKA El Caballo Negro), Wilfrido Vargas, Fernando Villalona, Eddy Herrera, among many, many others. However, this popular style emigrated beyond the country's parameters, and finds new homes in other Latin American countries, as well as in the United States. To experience more merengue music and dancing, see our book's website.

Appendix H

In the Heights: Plot Summary, Character List, and Select Quotations

In the Heights, book written by Quiara Alegria Hudes and music and lyrics by Lin-Manuel Miranda (creator of *Hamilton*), is a two-act musical (and now a feature-length film) that explores three days in the Dominican and Puerto Rican community of Washington Heights in New York City. During the Fourth of July weekend, a particularly hot time of year in New York City, we learn about the neighborhood and its people. The themes of the musical span the human experience: love, family, faith, belonging, home, sacrifice, and the "American Dream."

USNAVI DE LA VEGA (24 years old, Latino)
The "narrator" and eyes and ears of the Heights. Dominican owner of De La Vega's Bodega. His parents immigrated from the Dominican Republic. He is in love with Vanessa.

SONNY (15 years old, Latino)
Usnavi's young, smart-alecky, wise cousin, who is able to avoid trouble. Tough and smart Dominican, has big dreams for himself and his neighborhood and the city.

NINA ROSARIO (19 years old, Latina)
Young, smart college student who just finished her first year at Stanford University, but is quitting school. Daughter of Kevin and Camila, she is a brave and strong Puerto Rican girl. Emotional and conflicted, she is the "star" of the neighborhood and represents "getting out" of the community.

VANESSA (19 years old, Latina)
Sexy, strong, and smart shampoo girl at Daniela's Salon. She grew up with Benny and Usnavi. Has a troubled home life, and wishes get out of Washington Heights and find something better. Tired of being chased by men; looking to be loved.

BENNY (24 years old, any ethnicity)
Strong, smart driver at the Rosario Car and Limousine Service. Very ambitious, full of dreams. Handsome, bright, and harbors a crush on the "boss's daughter."

ABUELA CLAUDIA (late 60s, Latina)
Has raised Usnavi since his parents died. Cuban American matriarch of the neighborhood. Takes care of everybody, has lived "in the Heights" the longest; she possesses a wise character with strength, passion, and a fine memory.

KEVIN ROSARIO (40–50 years old, Latino)
Born and raised in Puerto Rico, he is Nina's father. Owns and runs Rosario Car and Limousine Service with his wife, Camila. Traditional, hard-working Latin father, overprotective, loving, with a temper.

CAMILA ROSARIO (40–50 years old, Latina)
The smart co-owner with her husband Kevin of the Rosario Car and Limousine Service. She takes care of the bills and business, but usually holds her tongue in the presence of her husband. Dynamic Puerto Rican woman, with a powerful sense of self that comes undone when she's been pushed too much. (This character appears in the musical theater work, but not in the filmed version.)

DANIELA (30–40 years old Latina)
Puerto Rican owner of "Daniela's," the neighborhood hair and nail salon. Sassy, witty, she loves to gossip, has a tough exterior, but enjoys being a no-nonsense kind of woman. Her salon rent keeps going up, so she must move out of the neighborhood.

CARLA (20–30 years old, Latina)
Up-beat, funny, sweet best friend of Daniela. Born and raised in Queens, New York. Very kind; religious. Supportive friend to the salon trio; easily taken advantage of because of her naïve nature.

GRAFFITI PETE (18 years old, any ethnicity)
Wiley graffiti artist of the neighborhood and nemesis of Usnavi. Always hangs out on the streets, though has a good heart. He wants to make a difference while making a living.

PIRAGUA GUY (30–50 years old, Latino)
The town crier. Sells shaved ice from a cart, talks about how people "keep scraping by."

MEN AND WOMEN OF WASHINGTON HEIGHTS
(20–50 years old, Latino, Latina, Black, Asian, White)
Diverse people of the community. All of these people have their own stories and troubles.

Quotations[5]—See our book's website.

Appendix I

Composition Assignment Instructions

Part 1

What songs/pieces point out what is wrong with the world? What songs/pieces show how we should fix the world?

In groups of 4–5 people, come up with at least 5 songs for the negative interpretations (i.e., what is wrong with the world) and 5 songs for the positive interpretations (i.e., how we should fix the world). Write down your choices. (Use your phone or laptop for inspiration if need be.)

Across all these songs/pieces, what issue seems to be the most concerning to you and your group members? Why?

In relation to the preceding, what sounds or noises are indicative of the issue that concerns you the most?

Across all these songs/pieces, what solution seems to be the most inspiring to you and your group members? Why?

In relation to the preceding, what sounds or noises are indicative of the solution that inspires you the most?

Part 2
Pre-composition Assignment

1. Given your answers to the preceding questions, select an aspect (either harmony, melody, bass line, etc.) from one of the songs that illustrates the issue that concerns your group the most. Decide in your groups which of these musical aspects you'll highlight in your composition (see Part 3).
2. Given your answers to the preceding questions, select an aspect (either harmony, melody, bass line, etc.) from one of the songs that illustrates the solution that seems to be the most inspiring to your group. Decide in your groups which of these musical aspects you'll highlight in your composition (see Part 3).

Part 3

Composition Assignment

Given your answers to the previous questions, you will compose two (very short) musical "blocks" (or musical vignettes).

1. Compose 15–20 seconds of music that bring together (a) a sound/noise indicative of the issue that concerns your group the most WITH (b) an aspect (e.g., a melodic fragment, bass line, chords, a rhythmic component) from one of the songs that illustrates the issue that concerns your group the most. Save as an independent file (as .mp3, .wav, .aiff, etc.).
2. Compose 15–20 seconds of music that bring together (a) a sound/noise indicative of the solution that seems to be the most inspiring to your group WITH (b) an aspect (e.g., a melodic fragment, bass line, chords, a rhythmic component) from one of the songs that illustrates the solution that seems to be the most inspiring to your group. Save as an independent file (as .mp3, .wav, .aiff, etc.).

Use GarageBand, Protools, or any other music composition software to do this.

Then, take your 2 sonic vignettes and upload to iMovie (create two iMovies; one for each sonic vignette). Create visualizations to go along with your creations. Save the "issue" vignette and the "solution" vignette separately.

Think back to John Zorn's *Spillane*.

At the end of class, e-mail both of your creations. Along with your e-mail, be sure to e-mail me the name of the songs you've been inspired by to create your "issue" vignette and the "solution" vignette.

Note to the Teacher: Once complete and once you have all students' video vignettes, you will then, using iMovie, create a unified project. Place all the videos in an order of your choosing. Consider having a small group of students help you "edit" this project (note: consider including additional sounds/musical moments to "round out" and sonically organize all videos under one creation; include, too, video transitions, title page, credit list, etc.).

Appendix J

"Spillane" by John Zorn

Form Map, Biography, and Program

Sampled sound +
musical narrative +
sampled sound +

musical narrative +

sampled sound +

musical narrative, etc., etc.

John Zorn (b. 1953)

If one were to "categorize" John Zorn's music, as well as his influences and life experiences, it would become clear that it's almost impossible to box him into any category. Largely considered a composer and saxophonist, Zorn's musical stylings cross genres from jazz to pop to punk to classical to klezmer to . . . well, you name it! Inspired by the music of Frank Zappa, Philip Glass, Steve Reich, Duke Ellington, the Beatles, Edgar Varese, Anthony Braxton, the Doors, Ennio Morricone, and Lou Reed, Zorn makes a term like "eclecticism" seem trite.

He was born in New York City and studied at the United Nations International School, where he studied piano, guitar, and flute. After hearing Anthony Braxton, he began seriously studying the saxophone. He dropped out of college, moved to the West Coast, then back to New York City where be played in small clubs, bars, and theaters. Before turning 20, he already had defied each and every genre he engaged with as a musician, composing, performing, and producing music that blended, bent, and redefined genres as tools for creative musical possibilities.

See the following article for more information: https://www.rollingstone.com/music/music-features/john-zorn-jazz-metal-interview-naked-city-1015329/.

Zorn on "Spillane"

Because I write in moments, in disparate sound blocks, I sometimes find it convenient to store these "events" on filing cards so they can be sorted and ordered with minimum effort. After choosing a subject, in this case the work of Mickey Spillane, I research it in detail: I read books and articles, look at films, TV shows, and photo files, listen to related recordings, etc. Then, drawing upon all of these sources, I write down individual ideas and images on filing cards. For this piece, each card relates to some aspect of Spillane's work, his world, his characters, his ideology. Sometimes I wrote out only sounds: "Opening scream. Route 66 intro starting with a high hat, then piano, strings, harp." Other times I thought of a scene from a movie like Year of the Dragon, and I wrote: "Scene of the crime #1 - high harp harmonics, basses and trombone drone, guitar sonorities, sounds of water dripping and narration on top." . . . Sorting the filing cards, putting them in the perfect order, is one of the toughest jobs and it usually takes months. . . . I set up the overall arc, but there's a real give and take with the musicians in the studio. Sometimes I bring in written music and I run it down to the players, layering and molding it as it is being played. Other times I'll simply say something like "Anthony, play some cheesy cocktail piano." Or, "Bill, go and improvise My Gun Is Quick" [an early Mickey Spillane novel], and we'll do take after take until we're all happy that every note is perfect. . . . My works often move from one block to another such that the average person can hear no development whatsoever. But

I always have a unifying concept that ties all the sections together. . . . —John Zorn (http://www.thrillingdetective.com/more_eyes/triv353.html)

Notes

1. https://kinginstitute.stanford.edu/king-papers/documents/where-do-we-go-here-address-delivered-eleventh-annual-sclc-convention.
2. https://www.youtube.com/watch?v=gsid-2VpxPM.
3. https://www.swarthmore.edu/news-events/heights-a-conversation-lin-manuel-miranda.
4. King, Martin Luther, *Where Do We Go from Here: Chaos or Community?* Boston: Beacon Press, 1968, 95.
5. All quotations are taken from the musical *In the Heights*; music and lyrics by Lin-Manuel Miranda; book by Quiara Alegria Hudes. Premiere July 23, 2005, Eugene O'Neill Theater Center (Waterford, CT); original Broadway cast recording, GHOSTLIGHT, 2008.

6

Climate Change Unit

Introduction

Humans are only one part of this huge ecosystem that we call Earth. Plants, animals, oceans, deserts, rivers, and mountains also share space with us in what is now approaching a crisis of environmental safety. It is "The House That Jack Built" scenario in which the function of each piece determines the health and welfare of the whole. When harmful gases overload the earth's ability to absorb them, temperatures rise, glaciers melt, islands disappear as sea levels rise, animal habitats are disrupted . . . human habitats are disrupted. Until we take seriously the damage that just one malfunctioning piece can create, we will continue to experience a domino effect that, in some cases, may not be reversed.

And there's more. The people who are affected most by changing environmental conditions are the poor, those who live in Cancer Alley (Louisiana) near the line of industrial plants that spew toxins into the air from recycling plastics, or those in towns where the only source of water is tainted with lead. Wealth buys choices—different places to live, nourishing food to eat, bottled water to drink. Herein lies the crux of social justice: For now, those with economic means can find a space with clean air, travel by plane, own several cars, and shop for organic, fresh food, while rising oceans displace islanders who have nowhere else to go and environmental toxins shrink animal habitats toward extinction. In essence, climate change is not just about the inconvenience of warmer temperatures; it is a global phenomenon that has an unequal impact on groups of people and animals.

This unit is a series of lessons organized into four categories that highlight the different dimensions of climate change. The first cluster is an introduction to Earth as an ecosystem. Like an orchestra, each piece of the ecosystem is interdependent upon the others. Each piece plays a role in helping or harming the planet. Lessons in this first cluster are intended to portray the big picture before moving on to others that focus on specific issues of climate change. The second and third clusters of lessons examine the impact of toxins and pollutants on humans and animals. The last cluster, "Advocacy," introduces the youth movement, given a rich life through Greta Thunberg's powerful presence, and ways that youth can advocate for a healthier ecosystem.

Music plays a central role in each cluster, from singing and analyzing "Petroleum Distillation" by Fifteen to creating a video about the right to a healthy environment via music and spoken word. Teachers will find a range of music, inclusive of classical, popular, punk, jazz, and deep house genres. Other art disciplines are represented as

Music Lesson Plans for Social Justice. Lisa C. Delorenzo and Marissa Silverman, Oxford University Press. © Oxford University Press 2022.
DOI: 10.1093/oso/9780197581476.003.0006

well. Each lesson involves some type of music making, much of it compositional in nature.

The role of the arts in climate change cannot be underestimated. It is through the arts that we see/hear expressions of loss, hope, anxiety, and fear that speak directly to environmental concerns as they exist today and in the future. Salvador Dali's famous painting, *The Persistence of Memory*, known to many as the "melting clocks," was probably not created as a response to climate change, yet the images are ruthless in portraying a world where only memories and time remain. Jazz and the blues become a perfect medium for composing songs about loss and frustration as a healthy environment seems to slip away. Artists are realists, idealists, soothsayers, and seekers of knowledge. While the science dimension of climate change is integral to understanding the changing world, it is the arts that provide a medium for human expression and advocacy. Consequently, this unit blends science and music in a course of study that moves students from understanding the social repercussions of climate change to active response as musicians.

Graphic Organizer: Climate Change

Climate Change: Our Warming Planet

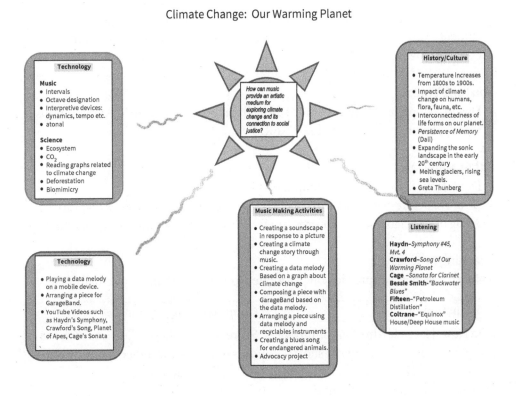

Climate Is Everything

Lesson 1

Goal
To examine the interconnectedness of our ecosystem as a basis for creating music that heightens awareness of the effects of climate change.

National Standards
- MU:CR2.1.6a: Select, organize, construct, and document personal musical ideas for arrangements and compositions within AB or ABA form that demonstrate an effective beginning, middle, and ending, and convey expressive intent.
- MU:Cr3.1.7a: Evaluate their own work, applying selected criteria such as appropriate application of elements of music, including style, form, and use of sound sources.

Assessment:
- **Formative:** The teacher will assess students' choice and range of musical ideas when using recyclable objects as sound sources. In addition, the teacher will assess students' verbal and musical contributions in creating a class composition with recyclable objects.

YouTube Video
- Haydn, Symphony #45 in F# Minor, Farewell Symphony—Fourth Movement: https://www.youtube.com/watch?v=kjFeDk6Kr3U

Other Materials
- Digital projector with sound amplification
- (Prepare before class) How to Collect Images and Sound Sources (Appendix A)
- A bag of recyclable sound sources (preferably a variety of timbres) for each group

Teaching Process
* Note to teacher: Scripted lesson plans often look longer than they actually take.

Instruction	Comments/Suggestions ...
Do Now: Have **Haydn's Symphony** #45 playing (Movement 4). Play a short excerpt and ask students to write two adjectives that describe the music.	Share some of these adjectives with the class to find out whether someone else had a similar adjective.

Instruction	Comments/Suggestions . . .
There is a joke at the end of this symphony. To understand the joke, you need some background: There was a prince who hired Haydn to compose music for the court. Every summer, the prince and his court moved to the palace. One particular summer, the prince decreed that only the male musicians could move, and the women and children had to stay behind. Toward the end of the summer, the musicians were homesick, especially when the prince made no move to return home. The musicians pleaded with Haydn to do something, so Haydn wrote a symphony that ended with a solution for the musicians. Play the adagio movement, which starts about 2'40" into the piece.	
The title of the symphony is The Farewell Symphony. Critical thinking prompt: *How is the end of this symphony like climate change?*	Discuss how the ending of the symphony relates to the projected outcomes of climate change.
What causes climate change? *When the sun warms the earth, some of this heat is absorbed and some of it is reflected back to space. When this is in balance, we have a healthy planet. However, now we are in a situation where harmful gases cannot escape back into space and are trapped within the atmosphere around the planet. Carbon dioxide and water vaper do most of the trapping and the warming rays cannot reflect back to space.* Bottom Line: *The earth is emitting more harmful gases than it can absorb, which creates, among other things, a big rise in temperatures.*	Students share what they know, but be careful to distinguish the cause of climate change from the effects of climate change.

Instruction	Comments/Suggestions . . .
What happens when temperatures rise around the globe?	Students identify consequences of hot temperatures, such as rising sea levels, extinction of animals, drought, more intense storms, flooding, wildfires, etc.
How would climate change affect our sonic environment? Pause for 30 seconds to listen to the classroom sonic environment. *What did you hear? If you were living on an island, how might the soundscape change?*	
I am going to give you a picture that shows a scene you might find in the world. Your job is to imagine the sounds that characterize the picture and create a soundscape for the picture. Create an episode of sound that has no clear beginning or ending—as if you just walked into the picture. Break into groups of four or five. Give each group a climate scenario (see **Appendix A**).	It is difficult for students to *not* add an ending; however, they will need only a segment of sound for the next activity.
Give each group a **bag of recyclable sound sources**. Students will use these sound sources to create musical episode that depicts their scenario.	
When finished, each group explains the decisions they made in composing the episode. Then they perform for the class.	Either project the picture or, if it is large enough, have a volunteer display the picture while the group is performing.
On teacher's cue, ask every group to play at one time. Ask students to play exactly as they did before without adjusting tempo, dynamics, etc. *Were you able to listen to everyone at once?* If not, do it again, focusing on the whole sonic soundscape.	It will sound like a hot mess.
Ask for student responses and discuss what they heard. *What is the matter with this?*	e.g., "One group was too loud," "I couldn't hear the sounds in my own group. . . ."

Instruction	Comments/Suggestions . . .
This is what the earth sounds like today. Each of you is a piece of the earth. In a healthy ecosystem, there is a sense of balance where all the pieces work together. How could we create a sense of musical balance with all of your sound excerpts?	Explore balancing two of the groups in terms of their music. *What needs to be softer? . . . louder? How else can we blend these two groups? Should one instrument start before the others?* These are prompts to help students listen carefully for balance and make decisions about how to adjust their sounds.
Let's create a climate story. In the beginning of the world, everything was in balance.	At this point the class piece will start to unfold as students get ideas like, "We should start with that sound because it's like the beginning of the world." Or, "I think these three people should play at the same time." Try to keep the groups intact, but do not worry if the music evolves differently. The students are the main decision-makers.
As the piece comes together, the teacher or a student can begin to cue or cut off different sound sources.	
I *wonder if we could end this piece like Haydn ended his symphony. Different sound sources could stop playing until we are left with just one sound. What would that be?* *When the world as we know it comes to an end, what is left?* (e.g., the ocean)	
Perform entire piece up to the very last sound.	Then, just pause for a time in silence.
Reflect on an artist's way of interpreting the world—music is one way of expressing one's ideas and feelings.	

Making a Data Melody

Lesson 2

Goal
To use music as a way of interpreting graphs about climate events over time.

National Standards
- MU:Cr3.1.6a: Evaluate their own work, applying teacher-provided criteria such as application of selected elements of music, and use of sound sources.
- MU:Cn11.0.6a: Demonstrate understanding of relationships between music and the other arts, other disciplines, varied contexts, and daily life.

Assessment
- **Formative:** The teacher will assess students' understanding of basic terminology (interval, melodic range) by verbal responses and choices of pitch on the keyboard app. In addition, the teacher will assess students' ability to translate a climate change graph to musical sound through the student's composed data melody.

Video
- "Song of Our Warming Planet" by David Crawford: https://vimeo.com/69122809

Part 1 [stop at 1′32″]; Part 2 [start at 1′32″ and play to the end of the piece]

Other Materials
- Earth's Rising Temperature (Appendix B)
- US Heat Waves (about four handouts) (Appendix C)
- US Wildfires (about four handouts) (Appendix D)
- Arctic Sea Ice Extent (about four handouts) (Appendix E)
- US Sea Level (about four handouts) (Appendix F)
- Students will need their mobile phone
- "Piano" App on Apple Store (iPhone) or find an alternative keyboard app for a different mobile phone. Keyboard must have letters on the keys and, if possible, octave designation such as "C-5"
- Data projector for video

Additional Resources (for teachers)
- https://www.smithsonianmag.com/science-nature/this-song-composed-from-133-years-climate-change-data-180956225/.
- *Fourth National Climate Assessment Report*, USGCRP, 2018: *Impacts, Risks, and Adaptation in the United States: Fourth National Climate Assessment*, Volume II [Reidmiller, D. R., C. W. Avery, D. R. Easterling, K. E. Kunkel, K. L. M. Lewis, T. K. Maycock, and B. C. Stewart (eds.)]. US Global Change Research Program, Washington, DC. https://nca2018.globalchange.gov/chapter/front-matter-about/.

Teaching Process

Instruction	Comments/Suggestions
Do Now: Have **Appendix B** projected or as a handout. *Take some time to look at this graph and write one or two ideas that the graph depicts.*	Review graph reading skills. *How do you make sense of a graph? What do you look for?*
How could you use this graph as a basis for a musical composition? *When David Crawford was a college student, he took a graph of temperature changes over time and assigned pitches to the peaks and valleys of the graph.* **Video:** "Song of Our Warming Planet" View just the first part of (**narrative portion**). Ask students to explain in their own words how he created the music. Play actual piece of music (part 2). *What did you notice about this music? Do you need to see the graph in order for the music to make sense?*	e.g., Translate the message of the graph for a musical piece (temperatures keep rising): replicate the graphic picture with a percussion instrument (rubbing finger nails across the head of a drum with increasing tempo and/or dynamics). Some students are baffled by atonal music when they have only listened to tonal music. You may need to prepare them for the unfamiliar pitches of this piece.
Music Making Activity *Let's make our own data melody. If we look at* **Appendix C**, *what is the graph telling us? If we assign a pitch (e.g., A♭) to the first bar, would the second bar be higher or lower? A lot higher or a little higher?*	
Have each student or pairs of students get out their mobile device and open the app called **"Piano."** Give students some time to freely explore the keyboard. Preparation: 1. *How are the black keys arranged* (in 2's and 3's). 2. *Which direction do you go to make the pitches higher?* 3. *The distance between two pitches is called an interval. Starting on A♭, find the smallest interval you can play going higher (A). Going lower (G). Starting on A♭, play a large interval. It can be a black or white key.*	Have students load this free app before starting the lesson. If the app is not available, find an alternate app that has a piano keyboard with the pitches identified. The purpose of this is to establish some common vocabulary and orientation to a piano keyboard.

Instruction	Comments/Suggestions
Return to **Appendix C**. Find the lowest and highest point on the graph. Ask one student to play a corresponding interval with a black and white key. *This is called the "melodic range."* Task: In pairs, compose a data melody using white and black keys (no need to alternate white and black as long as there are some of each). Identify the range pitches first (highest and lowest note).	Arrange students in pairs. Have them choose one of the graphs for their data melody (**Appendices C–F**).
Perform data melodies for the class in order of the Appendices. Display the appendix for each shared data melody. *IMPORTANT: Collect completed data melodies for next class.	No discussion needed. This serves as a check point for the culminating project.
Final Question: *Look at your own climate change graph. What might be some of the consequences if temperatures continue to increase? How might these changes affect the environment, animals, or people?*	

Refining the Data Melody

Lesson 3

Goal
To create an expressive data melody through dynamics, rhythm, tone color, articulation, etc.

National Standards
- MU:Cr3.1.6a: Evaluate their own work, applying teacher-provided criteria such as application of selected elements of music, and use of sound sources.
- MU: Cr3.1.6b: Describe the rationale for making revisions to music based on evaluation criteria and other feedback from the teacher.

Assessment
- **Formative:** The teacher will assess students' music analysis skills by having them verbally compare and contrast two pieces that use twentieth-century compositional techniques.

- **Summative:** The teacher will assess the students' revised data melody by having them explain their musical choices in comparison to the original melody.

YouTube Videos

- *Sonata for Clarinet, First Movement* by John Cage: https://www.youtube.com/watch?v=CHshVZ_tppU
- "Song of Our Warming Planet" by David Crawford: https://vimeo.com/69122809

Other Materials

- Mobile phones with keyboard app
- Students' data melody handouts from last class

Teaching Process

Instruction	Suggestions/Comments
Do Now: Listen to the first movement of *Sonata for Clarinet* by John Cage. Respond to the following question: *How is this piece similar as well as different from the data melodies that you started in our last class?*	Although this piece is not related to climate change, it provides an aural context for listening to early twentieth-century music. Students should be aware that other composers used various techniques for expanding the music soundscape.
Compare the Cage piece with David Crawford's piece. Play about 30 seconds of "Song of Our Warming Planet." After a brief discussion, play part of the Cage piece again. Repeat in small listening chunks as needed. Think about the performance of Crawford's piece in comparison to Cage's piece. *Cage went beyond playing one note on every beat.* What are some ideas for making your data melody more interesting? List some elements that they could vary: rhythm, tempo, articulation, dynamics, or timbre (if the app has that capability). ** Important: Do not change the intervals unless you want to play it in a different octave.	Introduce the term "atonal." Talk about how dynamics, rhythm, tempo, and pitch change a performance. Which of these two pieces is more interesting? Why? Help students find the different octaves on their keyboard. Play C5 then C4 or C3.

Instruction	Suggestions/Comments
Music Making Activity In same pairs, students review their data melodies. Explore some of the compositional techniques discussed (e.g., rhythmic, tempo changes).	If a student is absent, either have the student work alone, or join another group with the same graph.
Ask a few students to perform their "original" and then "revised" data melody.	Here's a point where the teacher might comment on the interesting techniques that the performers used to revise their melody as a way of reinforcing terminology.
When students are finished, they should record their revised melody on the phone. There is a recording button on the piano app. Save the recording as an MP3 file and, if time, transfer to GarageBand. Add 1 or 2 atonal or ambient loops to enhance the data melody.	

Living in a Toxic World

Lesson 1

Goal
To analyze the lyrics and musical characteristics of the song "Petroleum Distillation," as it relates to pollutants that create a toxic world.

National Standards
- MU:Cn11.0.7a: Demonstrate understanding of relationships between music and the other arts, other disciplines, varied contexts, and daily life.
- MU:Cr1.1.6a: Generate simple rhythmic, melodic, and harmonic phrases within AB and ABA forms that convey expressive intent.

Assessment
- **Formative:** The teacher will assess students' understanding of lyrics of the song "Petroleum Distillation" through a verbal discussion and song analysis. In addition, the teacher will assess students' ability to connect the notated bass line with its aural equivalent by having students hum, sing, and reproduce the bass line on a pitched instrument.

YouTube Video

- "Petroleum Distillation" by Fifteen*: https://www.streetdirectory.com/lyricadvisor/song/cjouao/petroleum_distillation/

Other Materials

- Lyric sheets for "Petroleum Distillation" by Fifteen*: https://www.streetdirectory.com/lyricadvisor/song/cjouao/petroleum_distillation/
- Music descriptors on board (see "Do Now" activity)
- Three examples of a bass line in standard notation on the board (see "Music Making" in the teaching process)
- A few pitched instruments capable of playing the pitches, B-flat, E-flat, F
- Some snare drum sticks (optional)

Additional Resources

- Song analysis of "Petroleum Distillation" (see Appendix H)
- Fracking: https://www.theguardian.com/news/2018/feb/26/fracking-the-reality-the-risks-and-what-the-future-holds
- Distillation Process: https//www.e-education.psu.edu/eme801/node/470

* This is the "clean" version, but always check for questionable language before presenting in class.

Teaching Process

Instruction	Suggestions/Comments
Do Now: Read the **lyrics** of the song "Petroleum Distillation" and circle all the words that refer to pollutants. *After reading the lyrics, what would you expect the song to sound like:* • *Driving tempo or relaxed tempo* • *Moderate/soft dynamics or moderate/loud dynamics* • *Traditional orchestra instruments or electronic instruments*	This activity should be completed before students hear the music. "Petroleum Distillation" is a complex song. See **Appendix H** for a helpful overview.

Instruction	Suggestions/Comments
Listen to the song and discuss musical characteristics from the "Do Now" activity: *Can you guess in which decade the song was written? (e.g., 1990s, 2000, 2010, present day)* Historical context: This song falls in the category of punk. The punk music style is an angry response to authority. It is often described as "in-your-face" music. *What about the music or lyrics create this mood?*	The song was written in 1994 and performed by the band Fifteen.
With a partner, make a list of all the machines or products that use gas or oil. *Where does gas/oil come from? What does petroleum distillation mean?*	Oil is formed in rocks deep in the earth where they are under intense pressure (like fossils). To get the oil, you have to drill down to the rocks and infuse with high pressure water which fractures the rocks (fracking). The crude oil is then transferred to an industrial plant where it is broken down into chemicals (distillation) which result in products like gas, plastics, etc.
Listen to the "Petroleum Distillation" again and discuss the pollutants that are toxic to the planet. Discuss some of the more abstract lyric phrases such as "Paying for four walls leaves slavery intact," or "The ground is my body."	Refer to students' circled lyrics from the "Do Now." Paying rent keeps me a slave to capitalism. The earth is my body.
Music Making Listen to the bass line for the introduction. Hum the bass guitar line. Show **three notated examples** on the board using bass clef (two of them should be grossly incorrect such as F – E♭ – F – E♭). *Which of these examples is correct? Does the bass line change in the first verse?*	B♭ – E♭ – F – E♭ The purpose of this reading activity is to connect the ear with the eye in terms of melodic contour without needing to know a lot about standard notation.

Instruction	Suggestions/Comments
Recreate bass line on a pitched instrument. Write a treble clef version as well (optional) Using a non-traditional sound source, create a driving beat of sixteenth notes. Play along with the recorded music until the lyrics "I know, I know, I know . . ."	Guitar, ukulele, piano, vocal, computer keyboard, Boomwhackers, piano keyboard app on cell phone. Some students may want to improvise their own rhythms instead.
Some songs are about love, loss, greed, etc. What do you think the message is from this song? Petroleum is the main source of energy today. *What are the benefits of petroleum distillation? What are the consequences?* Social Justice Question: *Do the benefits outweigh the consequences in terms of a healthy planet?*	Benefits: Fuel for transportation, economic growth for oil companies, heating homes, etc. Consequences: Air pollution, toxic chemicals, desecration of land, etc.

Living in a Toxic World

Lesson 2

Goal
To reconsider recyclables as musical instruments.

National Standards
- MU:Cr2.1.6a: Select, organize, construct, and document personal musical ideas for arrangements and compositions within AB or ABA form that demonstrate an effective beginning, middle, and ending, and convey expressive intent.
- MU:Re7.1.6a: Select or choose music to listen to and explain the connections to specific interests or experiences for a specific purpose.

Assessment
- **Formative:** The teacher will assess students' musical decision-making in terms of organizing sound material for a large group improvisation. In addition, the teacher will assess students' problem-solving skills when presented with the ethical dilemma of what to do with plastic bags that were used as sound sources.

YouTube Videos

- "How Plastic Bags Are Made": https://www.youtube.com/watch?v=24wb7Kz4j2Y
- "The Landfill Harmonic Orchestra": https://www.youtube.com/watch?v=UJrSUHK9Luw&t=150s

(There are several different YouTube videos about this orchestra. You may want to choose a longer video.)

Other Materials

- A plastic grocery bag for each student (other recyclable containers can be used if plastic bags are no longer available)

Other Resources

- "Three Unexpected Effects of Plastic Pollution": https://www.youtube.com/watch?v=X4uefUtvLpc

Teaching Process

Instruction	Suggestions/Comments
Do Now: Have an ordinary grocery **plastic shopping bag** in front of the room where all can see. *Imagine all the sounds you can make with this plastic bag. With a partner, think of five different ideas for making sound from this plastic bag.*	Students engage in a quick Pair–Share Activity.
Pass the bag around the room, or ask a small group of volunteers come to the front of the room. Each person produces a different sound with the bag. *Any sound is ok, except something that puts a hole in the bag.*	This exercise must be done in complete silence including passing the bag to the next person.
Choose two students who have similar (but different) sounds. Listen to each sound event several times as students find words to describe what they hear. Introduce some musical vocabulary such as pitch, loudness, decay, rhythmic, arhythmic, etc.	The purpose is to build a vocabulary for describing sound. Choosing similar sounds rather than sounds that are very different: this makes listening discrimination more acute.

Instruction	Suggestions/Comments
Music Making Activity • Give each student a plastic bag. Students should find a quiet place in the room where they can experiment making different kinds of sounds.	Give students an opportunity to share their favorite sound.
• Explore the following techniques: (1) Teacher conducts students in a short episode using gestures that will create different sounds (e.g., shaking the bag in the air). Have a few other students act as the conductor.	These conducting gestures are physical movements that demonstrate how to produce the sound rather than a traditional beat pattern. Do all of this without talking.
• Ask one student to create a simple rhythm. Cue in other students to play rhythms that complement the basic beat. Create a jam session so that students are playing rhythms that synchronize. Teacher might add cues for solos, volume, stopping.	Here, the teacher may need to conduct a steady beat.
• Conduct a large group improvisation with a beginning, middle, and end.	Let the following question prompts guide the design of the composition: *Who has a good starting sound? How could we add to that? How can we build excitement in the piece?*
Discussion: *Was this a piece of music? Does the mere presence of sound mean that it is music? What makes sound become music?*	Contemplate the meaning of music and whether the plastic bag improvisation constitutes music.

Instruction	Suggestions/Comments
An ethical dilemma: *Does the harm caused by making and throwing away plastic bags override their usage as musical instruments?*	This question can also be asked after students learn about the life of a plastic bag.
Tracing the life of a plastic bag: *Where does a plastic bag come from?* **Video**: "How Plastic Bags are Made"	Plastic is made from breaking down crude oil and fossil fuels. This process creates considerable *air pollution* and results in a product that is *not biodegradable*.
Where does a plastic bag go when you throw it away? *What about recycling?*	It goes from a trash container to a landfill. It takes *500–1,000 years* to break down. Or, it gets *dumped in the ocean* where marine animals can swallow it, feel full, and starve to death. The most dangerous form of plastic is when it breaks down into small crumbly pieces called *microplastics*. These are easier for fish to eat, and eventually end up on our dinner plate when we eat fish, crabs, clams, lobsters, etc. Recycling is *expensive* and it is getting harder to keep up with the demand. Also, the *fumes* from recycling plastic are harmful to humans.
Video: "The Landfill Harmonic Orchestra"	*Here is a way that some people in Paraguay turned garbage into music.*
Discussion: *The people of Paraguay used things that people threw away to make instruments similar to traditional instruments that we would see in an orchestra today. We used the bags as they were. Does that make our music more or less valid than the Landfill Harmonic Orchestra Project?* *What should we do with the plastic bags that we used today?*	Ethical dilemma

Living in a Toxic World

Lessons 3–4

Goal

To recognize how people are affected by human-created toxins and to compose a piece in the style of Deep House music, that sends a warning message about increasing pollution of our earth.

National Standards

- MU:Cr2.1.8a: Select, organize, and document personal musical ideas for arrangements, songs, and compositions within expanded forms that demonstrate tension and release, unity and variety, balance, and convey expressive intent.
- MU:Cr3.1.7a: Evaluate their own work, applying selected criteria such as appropriate application of elements of music including style, form, and use of sound sources.

Assessment

- **Formative**: The teacher will facilitate a discussion related to the video "Plastics and Poverty," as a means of gauging student comprehension regarding the impact of disposable plastics on people living in poverty.
- **Summative**: Student compositions will be assessed according to the guidelines on the handout and the effective use of digital media.

You Tube Videos

- TED Talk, "Plastics and Poverty": https://www.ted.com/talks/van_jones_the_economic_injustice_of_plastic?language=en
- "Petroleum Distillation" by Fifteen*: https://www.streetdirectory.com/lyricadvisor/song/cjouao/petroleum_distillation/
- "Old School Chicago House Mix": https://www.youtube.com/watch?v=uQze4dTsVjM
- *Toxic Earth* by Mike Byrd: https://www.youtube.com/watch?v=q53YmYhqjf4

Other Materials

- Lyric sheets for "Petroleum Distillation" (see Lesson #1)
- "What Should Your Friends Know?" (Appendix I)
- Culminating Project Guidelines for "Living in a Toxic World" (Appendix J)

Related Resources

- "World's Top Ten Toxic Pollution Problems": https://www.conserve-energy-future.com/top-10-worst-toxic-pollution-problems.php

This is a short article that describes the impact of toxic pollutants in our world.

Teaching Process

Instruction	Suggestions/Comments
Do Now: Watch part (about 6 minutes) of the Ted Talk: "Plastics and Poverty." Choose one prompt for the Pair–Share Activity: • *Why is plastic both a good thing and a bad thing?* • *In what ways can recycling be helpful or harmful?* • *Why are low-income families affected most by the production and disposal of plastics?*	The second part of the video could be viewed at the beginning of the next lesson. Students work in pairs before discussing the video in a large group.
How do we contribute to the toxicity of the earth? • Re-listen to the beginning of "Petroleum Distillation." List some of the outcomes of our dependence on unsustainable products (e.g., gas/oil engines and air pollution; plastic distillation and toxic chemicals, etc.) • *How do some of these toxins affect human health?*	*What is the message that this music is trying to convey? A warning? Helpful solutions?* Increase in asthma. Increased lead poisoning from water. Illness from ingested plastic particles.
Small Group Research (**Appendix I**) Choose or assign a short research project that involves reading for groups of three or four. *What should people know right now?* Topic 1: Coal as Fuel Topic 2: Plastic Pollution of Oceans Topic 3: Hazardous Waste from Industries Topic 4: Contaminated Water from Lead Topic 5: Pesticides from Agriculture	Using a computer or phone, type in your topic to find information. Emphasize that students write only key words or short phrases, not complete sentences. For efficiency, have each person tackle one question on the handout (**Appendix I**). This information is preparation for the culminating project. Collect papers if needed for the next class.

Instruction	Suggestions/Comments
Music Making Project (Appendix J) *House music is a kind of dance music that originated in Chicago during the 1970s. If House Music were a recipe, it would include a fusion of gospel, disco, blues, jazz, funk, and new wave.* • Play about 2 minutes of Old School Chicago House Mix. *See if you can identify most of the elements that give this music its special sound.* Keep listening in short segments until all the key elements are identified. • Play to 1′30″ of *Toxic Earth* by Mike Byrd. *This is an example of deep house music. How would you compare in terms of style and elements that you just that we have listed on the board?*	e.g., electronic instruments, bass line, drop-kick beat, lively percussion, fuzzy electronic background, synthesizer chords. Mike Byrd is an artist musician and producer from the windy northern city of Manchester in the United Kingdom.
In groups of three or four, explore loops for house or deep house music. Explore some loops for the following instruments: electric bass, drums, synthesizer, electric guitar. Write the name of the loop(s) that you like on the back of the research handout (**Appendix I**).	Students should select the prompt, "GENRE," for house or deep house. Put the names of these instruments on the board for reference.
Save the rest of this strategy for the next class because students will need a lot of exploration time with the loops.	
Hand out the project guidelines (**Appendix J**) and review with the class. To prepare for composing with GarageBand, select some of the basic beats provided, demonstrating how to move the loop into the working grid. Show how to extend the loop for a long period of time and how to add loops at different points in the piece.	This step can be eliminated if students are familiar with GarageBand or equivalent composition software. Once students are in their small working groups, you will have time to answer questions that arise.
Students work on compositions in their original small groups.	There are three different tasks which can be divided among the students: spoken verse, music, slides.

Instruction	Suggestions/Comments
Once all groups are finished, create a sharing session where students can listen to each piece and answer the following discussion prompts: *What did you like about this piece? What made it particularly effective?* To the composers: *Tell us about the decisions you made when creating this piece. Is there anything you would change if you had more time?*	This is an important piece of the project because it gives the composers a chance to self-reflect and it gives the listeners a chance to provide positive feedback.

The Shrinking Animal Habitat

Introduction

"The Gwich'in elders long ago predicted that a day would come when the world was warm, and things would not be the same for animals. That time is now."[1] In his chapter, "Farewell, Sweet Ice," Matthew Gilbert writes about the plight of the caribou and how their struggle to survive is essential to the survival of his tribe, located along the northernmost regions of Alaska and Northwest Canada. The tribe relies on caribou for food, but because of global warming, the "Porcupine River Caribou Herd" has decreased in numbers from 178,000 to under 129,000.

As with most shrinking animal habitats, the caribou are no longer supported by their environment. The warming temperatures have melted the glaciers and ice where caribou subsist on lichen and plants of the tundra. In addition, the caribou need the coldest regions to birth their calves. The need to travel north is so strong during birthing season, that hundreds of caribou risk their lives trying to cross a treacherous river that was once solid ice. Because they are migratory animals that travel up to 600 miles to find suitable habitat, any changes in their route, such as warming rivers or man-made fences, create life-sustaining problems.

Climate change has had a devastating effect on animal life which, if we consider ourselves part of this giant biosphere, also has a devastating effect on humans. Like the domino effect, when the earth's climate changes, it not only has an impact on food and water needed to sustain animal life, but also forces many animals to find new environments where they can survive. People who deeply depend on animals for food or their livelihood are particularly vulnerable. Climate change, however, is not the only threat to species: poaching, oil spills, wild fires, and human-directed deforestation also wreak havoc on the animal kingdom.

This cluster of lessons examines animals' shrinking habitats as inspiration for songwriting in the blues style. The first lesson focuses on birdsong and bird calls in the tropical rainforest. Many Western composers, such as Olivier Messiaen (1908–1992) and Ottorino Respighi (1879–1936), have incorporated bird song into their compositions. It is fitting, then, to explore musical ways of imitating birdsong for building not only listening discrimination but also a level of appreciation for the tunefulness of the Amazon rainforest in its natural state.

The second and third lessons focus on characteristics of the blues as a form for writing songs from the perspective of endangered animals. These lessons might easily pair with lessons in the sciences, with documentary films, such as *Chasing Ice*[2] and *Our Planet*,[3] or with politics, such as the US Endangered Species Act (ESA). The underlying assumption—that many forms of knowledge add to the richness of music composition—also embraces the humanness of music as a personal expression about the world around us.

Amazon Rainforest

Lesson 1

Goal
To examine the shrinking animal habitat in the Amazon rainforest and its effect on birds as well as the changing soundscape.

National Standards
- MU:CR2.1.7b: Use standard and/or iconic notation and/or video recording to document personal simple rhythmic phrases, melodic phrases, and harmonic sequences.
- MU:Re7.2.6a: Describe how the elements of music and expressive qualities relate to the structure of the piece.

Assessment
- **Formative**: The teacher will assess students' ability to discriminate bird songs by playing the game "Birdsong Hero." In addition, to assess the soundscape performance, students will give feedback on how to adjust and revise the improvisation before performing it again.

YouTube Videos
- "Relaxing Rainforest Sounds": https://www.youtube.com/watch?v=sXFceFu-3k0
- "Rainforests 101" (National Geographic): https://www.youtube.com/watch?v=3vijLre760w
- "Bird Song Hero": https://www.youtube.com/watch?v=8xH2GjHKYj0

Other Materials
- Answer boards, cloth eraser, marker. You can make an answer board by stuffing a stiff piece of cardboard or half of an oaktag folder into a plastic sheet liner.

Erasers can be small pieces of cloth. Students can pick up each item on their way in the door.

- Instruments: Melodic (mallet instruments, slide whistle, kazoos, recorders, piano app on mobile device, vocal sounds or whistles) and percussion instruments in two bags for the waterfall group and the rainstorm group. Always add a few extra instruments so that students have more choices.

Other Resources

- Composers have been fascinated with bird calls and have used them in their music. Here are some examples: Respighi, Messiaen, Elgar, Prokofiev (*Peter and the Wolf*).

Teaching Process

Instruction	Suggestions/Comments
Do Now: *John James Audubon was one of the first persons to identify and paint birds in North America. He is attributed to have said:* "If only the bird with the loveliest song sang, the forest would be a lonely place."[4] *What did he mean?*	Students could write their response in a journal or discuss their ideas with a partner. Example response: There are many sounds in the forest besides the loveliest bird song.
Listening: "Relaxing Rainforest Sounds" (audio only) Stop the video after 15 seconds and ask: *Where are we?* Start the video where you stopped it. Listen silently for the last two questions below: *How many different sounds do you hear?* *Where do these sounds come from?* *How is this soundscape different from where we live?*	When students are completely silent, turn off lights and play only the sound portion of the video. Do not talk during the listening.
What do you already know about the rainforest? Video: "Rainforests 101 (National Geographic)" Sample prompts: *What did you see that you've never seen before? How would you describe a rainforest to someone over the phone? Why is the rainforest the biggest eco-system?*	Assess prior knowledge but no need to have a conversation.

Instruction	Suggestions/Comments
Listen to "Relaxing Rainforest Sounds" again for 30 seconds: *How many bird calls/songs can you identify? How can you tell the difference between one bird and another? You may need to play an excerpt several times.* Graph one of the more distinctive bird calls on the board. Like this: Whoo – oop	Play a short excerpt of the video again and have students put a thumbs up when they hear that bird call.
Here is a game called "Bird Song Hero." You will hear different bird calls but you have to identify the call to get it right. Use your **Answer Board** *to write down your answer. Hold it up when you are finished.* **Video:** "Bird Song Hero"	Remind students that it goes fast so write your answer immediately.
Video: Listen to 20 seconds of "Relaxing Rainforest Sounds." *Here's the ultimate challenge for $6,000. I will play 20 seconds of the rainforest video that you heard before. Listen for one bird call that you can identify easily.* Play another 20 seconds and ask students to follow their bird call by putting a tally mark on their answer board. *Now make a graphic picture of the call. Think about the graphics from Bird Song Hero.*	
There are indigenous tribes that live in the rainforest. They can identify every sound because their ears are so sensitive to the forest sounds. Ask a student to replicate a bird sound from the rainforest on an instrument. It could be the one he/she/they graphed or an earlier graphed example.	Student should choose an instrument from those displayed (see: Other Materials for examples).

Instruction	Suggestions/Comments

Music Making Activity
10 students create their bird call on a melodic instrument.
  5 students create a waterfall with percussion instruments.
  6 students create a 15-second rainstorm.
(adjust the numbers as needed)
	Have two bags of selected percussion instruments for the waterfall group and the rainstorm group. They will work together in different corners of the room.

Experiment with creating a tropical rainforest. Start with the waterfall, softly in the background. Cue bird calls at different times. If needed, you can cut out different birds calls and bring them back in. Ask students their opinion about when to play the thunderstorm. Make any adjustments according to student feedback and play again. You can choose to play "Relaxing Rainforest Sounds" in the background. Evaluate the performance and describe how a soundscape can also be a musical composition.	The bird call musicians should repeat their call every three seconds. Consider asking a student to conduct while you take his/her/their place.
Rainforests are shrinking. Trees are cut down for wood and forests are destroyed to increase land for agriculture. *What are the consequences of deforestation for birds? In what ways do humans benefit? In what ways do humans hurt themselves?*	Social Justice Question

Endangered Animal Blues

Lesson 2

Goal
To examine the shrinking animal habitat and its effect on wildlife as a basis for composing music to that of John Coltrane.

National Standards

- MU:Re7.2.6a: Describe how the elements of music and expressive qualities relate to the structure of the piece.

Assessment

- **Formative**: The teacher will assess students' music listening acuity through discussion that focuses on describing the introduction and phrase structure of the tune for "Equinox." In addition, the teacher will assess students' connection between endangered animals and equinox; students will create lyrics about the consequences of deforestation to the tune "Equinox."

YouTube Videos

- "Deforestation in the Tropical Rainforest: Impact on Animals": https://www.youtube.com/watch?v=pH31fEOTI9U
- "Equinox" by John Coltrane: https://www.youtube.com/watch?v=5m2HN2y0yV8
- *Chasing Trane: The John Coltrane Documentary*: https://www.youtube.com/watch?v=xApMCjrc-VQ

Other Materials

- "The Impact on Animals" (Appendix K)
- Melodic instruments that have C#, E, D#, F#, or voice
- Piano app on students' phone

Teaching Process

Instruction	Suggestions/Comments
Do Now: Follow directions on **Appendix K. Video** - "Deforestation in the Tropical Rainforest." Discuss responses as a class. *Let's play an imagination game. Imagine that you would earn thousands of dollars from deforestation of your land. What would your music sound like? If you were the animal that suffered from the loss of your habitat, would your music sound different?*	Students should read the questions first, then watch the video before responding. e.g., upbeat, fast tempo, forte

Instruction	Suggestions/Comments
When people/animals are oppressed, music takes on a completely different mood. The blues is a form of jazz that can express agitation or sadness, as well as courage and overcoming adversity. Ask a few questions to create the context for the lesson: *Where do the blues come from? Why might the blues serve as a possible style for a song about endangered animals?*	
Video: Listen to a short episode of "Equinox" (30–60 seconds). *The name of this tune is "Equinox." The equinox is the time when the sun's position is exactly over the equator and the day and night are of equal length. This happens twice a year around the start of spring and the start of autumn.* Second Listening (15 seconds): *Pay close attention to the introduction and how this might set up a scene about endangered animals.*	On first short listening, talk about the images that students "see in their head." Starts out with a lot of rhythmic movement in the bass, followed by a repeating low pitch that leads into the sax entrance. One interpretation might be that a healthy biosystem anticipates impending danger (low repeating piano pitch).
Third Listening (the original tune): How many musical sentences (phrases) do you hear? Which phrases have the same melodic material? Sing or play on **Piano app** the first two phrases along with the recording (everything by ear—no notation). Some students may be able to find the third phrase by ear.	Draw the three phrases (in the air) with the students to show the longer phrases that include the repetition of the first motive. Add a graphic to the board to show repeating material. Phrases 1: (C#), E, C#, C#, E, C# Phrase 2: (C#) F#, C#, C#, E, C# Phrase 3: D# (repeat 4x), E, C# (optional) – After they are secure with the listening, you might show the notation just to show what it would look like on a score.

Instruction	Suggestions/Comments
Music Making (creating lyrics) Think about the scenes you saw in the video at the beginning of class. Review the dangers for animals when their home is destroyed. Make a list of words or short phrases from the perspective of the endangered animal. Using these words or phrases as ideas, create lyrics for the first phrase. Continue to create lyrics for the rest of the phrases. Sing finished version with the original tune on the recording.	e.g., I need another home; I can't find any food; I miss my clan; I am fearful. e.g., I'm hungry, I'm tired.
A piece of music is like a jigsaw puzzle. You have to find all the pieces in order to know the form. Once you know the form, it is easier to listen because you have an idea of what's coming next. *You already know the first two parts of this music (introduction and main tune). What happens after the original tune is presented?* Listen a bit further. *What is going on? I'll play some more and tell me what happens when I stop the music (stop a little way into the piano improvisation).* *Play to the end. Give me a thumbs up when the original tune comes back. How does the piece end?* (Optional) You may want to identify the form of the piece, but it is not necessary.	The tune appears twice before going into an improvisatory section.
Time permitting: Watch the short documentary excerpt: *Chasing Trane*.	

Endangered Animal Blues

Lessons 3–4

Goal

To advance knowledge of the blues style by identifying the 12-bar blues chord structure and relating this, through music, to the plight of endangered animals.

National Standards

- MU:RE7.2.6B: Identify the context of the music from a variety of genres, cultures, and historical periods.
- MU:Cr3.2.7a: Present the final version of their documented composition, song, or arrangement, using craftmanship and originality to demonstrate unity and variety, and convey expressive intent.

Assessment

- **Formative**: To assess understanding of blues style, students will compare "Backwater Blues" with "Equinox" and discuss the similar/different characteristics.
- **Summative**: To assess understanding of blues song form, students will perform a new song in the blues style from the perspective of an endangered animal.

YouTube Videos

- "Backwater Blues," Bessie Smith: https://www.youtube.com/watch?v=4gXShOJVwaM
- "Equinox," John Coltrane: https://www.youtube.com/watch?v=5m2HN2y0yV8
- "Backwater Blues," Joe Izen: https://www.youtube.com/watch?v=XVKCQ-01HFU

Other Materials

- Lyrics to "Backwater Blues": https://www.google.com/search?client=firefox-b-1-d&q=lyrics+for+backwater+blues
- Class lyrics and video for "Equinox" from last session
- Mobile phones with Piano app or equivalent piano keyboard app
- Endangered Animals World Wildlife Fund (Appendix L): https://www.worldwildlife.org/species/directory?direction=desc&sort=extinction_status
- Prepare to project a picture of the endangered animals that students choose for their project. You can find the pictures on the preceding website
- Have an A Major scale notated on the board, using chromatics rather than a key signature. Add a whole note in each bar using the chart for "Backwater Blues" (see Teaching Process)

Teaching Process

Instruction	Suggestions/Comments
Sometimes it's fun for the teacher to start the class (without any explanation) by singing a blues song related to you or the class. Use the tune from "Backwater Blues," as the melody. *So . . . what is the name of this jazz style that we talked about in the last class? Here's another blues song performed by a famous jazz artist named Bessie Smith.* **Video:** "Backwater Blues" with the **lyric sheet.**	e.g., "When I woke up this morning, I was feeling so blue (repeat) But then I remembered that I'd soon see you."
What is this song about? Why do you suppose Bessie Smith chose the blues as the style for her song?	Discussion: Students might retell the story or they might talk about themes of loss, desperation, class distinction.
We've also been talking about how rising temperatures and deforestation affect animal habitats. Can you think of any animals that are in danger of becoming extinct? Polar bears are on a vulnerable animal list. They live on glaciers in the northern oceans so they can eat dolphins and other marine animals that surface in the water. However, what is happening to glaciers in the northern oceans due to climate change? If we wrote a song about the vulnerability of polar bears or other endangered species, the blues might be a perfect style for the song. Why is that? In our last class we created a blues song for endangered animals. Play the beginning of "Equinox" and sing or hum along. *What do you remember about the phrases of the original tune?* Play the first verse of **"Backwater Blues"** so students can refresh their memory. Draw the phrases in the air. *How would you compare this to the beginning verse of* **"Equinox?"** *What musical ideas seem similar . . . different?*	e.g., three phrases; last phrase completely different from the first two.

Instruction	Suggestions/Comments
The sequence of chords is one telling indicator of a blues song. *Listen to this performer (**Video -** "Backwater Blues," Joe Inez) and watch his hands for the chord changes when he starts to sing. (He will play a lot of single notes in between but you can tell the chord has changed when he puts all 3–4 fingers down at once.)* *Sing the bass line and tap 3 beats in between. Reinforce with piano and chords.* Invite a student pianist to play the bass line while you play the chords. Refer to the chart on the board. *The musical term for this is chord structure is the 12-bar blues. Why do you think it is called that? How many chord changes? Put chord function on every chord change, and then look at the* *A scale written on the board. See if you can figure out why I used those roman numerals?* *Often a musician will sneak in another IV chord like this in the last phrase –* *E- - - D - - - A - - - A - - - This is how musicians add their own touch to the blues.*	The students will see a lot of chord changes but this chart shows the main chords: Chart A - - - A - - - A - - - A - - - D - - - D - - - A - - - A - - - E - - - E - - - A - - - A - - - Joe sneaked in a second IV chord in the second bar. (D) A - - - A - - - D- - - A - - -
Listen to a few verses one more time (Joe Izen) just to enjoy it.	
Small Group Music Making Project Divide the class into small groups of three or four. Give each group a link to a list of critically endangered animals. See **Appendix L**. Create lyrics from the perspective of the animal, using either "Equinox" or "Backwater Blues" as the tune. Practice the song as a group (optional: use a melodic instrument to play the chords or a baseline).	

Instruction	Suggestions/Comments
Ask students to record their song when finished.	Tip for Teacher: The room will never be completely quiet but you should be able to put the microphone or mobile device in the center of the group and still hear that group. For the best recording, sing with a full voice and enunciate the words. Check each group to remind them about this.
Share the recordings or live performances and project pictures of the endangered animal while students are performing.	It may be necessary to do this in the next class if students are not finished.
Reflective discussion about the songs. *How could we use these recordings to make other people aware of all the animals that may become extinct without some intervention?*	Social Justice Question

Introduction to Advocacy for Climate Change

There is an important distinction between talking about climate change and doing something about it. It is also noteworthy that many advocacy movements in all areas were started by youth. Take, for example, the National School Walkout, which was initiated by the students of Marjory Stoneman Douglas High School in April 2018 as a dramatic response to the tragic shooting at their high school.

Students should know that they are not too young for their voices to be heard. This cluster of lessons, consequently, focuses on how young artists can have a voice in working toward an equitable and just climate future. Because this unit has such a strong visual component, the final project reflects a student-created video that presents images, music, and spoken word to convey different messages about climate change. In addition, there is special emphasis on the work of Greta Thunberg, a 16-year-old Scandinavian student at the time, who single-handedly launched a series of climate strikes and marches for environmental justice throughout the world. Her advocacy for climate change has rocked the world, so much so that she was chosen as Person of the Year for *Time Magazine* in 2019. In addition, Greta's work has inspired other youth to speak out against fossil fuels, industries, and other human overload of the carbon cycle that add to the increasing temperatures around the planet.

The lessons presented here have four main intentions: (a) to tie together all the lessons in the Climate Change unit, (b) to recognize that problems with the climate are human-centered, (c) to understand that people are affected differently depending on where they live and what they do for a living, and (d) to give students an artistic challenge in advocating for climate change. Through creating a video with music and spoken word, students have an opportunity to speak out against the many and varied dimensions of climate change. Although music is selected rather than composed, it still requires critical musical judgment to find a piece that not only sets the mood of the video but also works in balance with poetry and visual imagery.

This culminating project is one that can serve in many capacities, such as the beginning for a concert program based on environmental themes, or a showcase for another class in the school. It is a way for students to experience some level of activism and to engage in several art forms. Hopefully, the learnings from this unit will transform the way students think and behave regarding their own place on the planet.

Advocating for a Just and Equitable Climate Future

Lesson 1

Goal
To recognize climate change as having unequal effects on different communities.

National Standards
- MU:RE7.1.6a: Describe how the elements of music and expressive qualities relate to [the video experience].
- MU:Cn11.6a: Demonstrate an understanding of relationships between music and the other arts, the disciplines, varied contexts, and daily life.

Assessment
- **Formative:** The teacher will assess students' understanding about the arts as a tool for advocacy through their participation in discussions.

YouTube Videos
- Ted Talk: "The Economic Injustice of Plastic": https://www.youtube.com/watch?v=wrjhnpFepCw
- "Man vs. Earth" with Prince EA (spoken word artist): https://www.youtube.com/watch?v=B-nEYsyRlYo

Other Materials
- "Topics for a Final Project" (see Appendix M)
- Computers, mobile devices, iPads

Additional Resource
- *A Vision for an Equitable and Just Climate Future*: https://ajustclimate.org

This document is the work of environmental justice and environmental advocates who participated in *The Climate Forum* during October 2018, launched by the Center for Earth, Energy and Democracy, the Center for American Progress, and the Natural Resources Defense Council, with support from the Midwest Environmental Justice Network and the New Jersey Environmental Justice Alliance. It is a very accessible read for teachers and provides important background knowledge on the advocacy movement for climate change.

Teaching Process

Instruction	Suggestions/Comments
Do Now: Write this quote on the board and play some quiet instrumental background music while students are writing their response to the question. "It is the poor and vulnerable communities that are most deeply affected by climate change." Do you agree or disagree with this claim? Write down at least two reasons why this statement is true or false, in your opinion. Briefly discuss student reasoning for the validity or ineffectiveness of the claim.	Students will write their responses in a journal or on paper.
Video: "The Economic Injustice of Plastic" Ted Talk. Questions for discussion: • *How does this video better inform your ideas about climate change and economic justice?* • *What is the problem with the creation of plastics or other disposable items?* • *What is biomimicry and what can a clam teach us about sustainability?*	
What are ways that we can advocate for climate change? *How can we use the arts to advocate for change?*	List ideas such as petitions, marches, strikes, adjusting personal habits like recycling, etc. Brainstorm ideas (e.g., song, dance, writing, making a video, painting).
Here is one way that an artist advocated for a healthy earth: **Video**: "Man vs. Earth." *What different art forms are used in this video? What makes this video powerful?*	Discuss the poetic form of delivery, the background music, and the visual images.

Instruction	Suggestions/Comments
Preparation for Project (see **Appendix M**). Divide into class into groups of four or five. For this assignment it is best to have friends working with friends. Choose a topic area and complete worksheet. Topic Areas <ul><li>The Right to Clean Water</li><li>The Right to Clean Air</li><li>The Right to a Good life</li><li>The Right to Safety from Violent Storms</li><li>The Right for Preservation of Animals</li><li>The Right for Preservation of Trees</li><li>The Right for Preservation of the Ocean</li></ul>	Use internet-capable devices to gather research for the selected topic area. Designate a person in each group to record information. Be sure to collect a paper from each group at the end of class. Note to teacher: We suggest that you do not use these papers as a grading opportunity.
Closing One person from each group gives a brief overview of what the group accomplished. Collect all work.	

Advocating for a Just and Equitable Climate Future

Lesson 2

Goal
To explore the meaning of "A Just and Equitable Climate Future" as the grounding for a climate change project.

National Standards
- MU:Cn11.06a: Demonstrate an understanding of the relationships between music and the other arts, other disciplines, varying contexts, and daily life.

Assessment
- **Formative:** The teacher will assess student work on the project handout from their completed worksheets.

YouTube Video
- "Climate Change: A Spoken Word Poem": https://www.youtube.com/watch?v= UlRybPymylc

Other Materials
- Student-completed worksheets from last class
- Project Guidelines Handout (teacher constructed) (Appendix N)

Teaching Process

Instruction	Comments/Suggestions
Do Now: *The Marshall Islands are located in the Pacific Ocean, roughly between China and Australia. These islands and the people who live there are in great danger of rising sea levels. Most of them live in the capital city which is barely 6 feet above sea level.* **Video:** "Climate Change—A Spoken Word Poem." Listen to this spoken word poem of a woman speaking to her baby about climate change. In the video, the poet is addressing the United Nations on climate change. *Is this a poem of comfort or of warning? What did you see or hear that helped you make that choice?*	The author and speaker is Ms. Kathy Jetnil-Kijiner, a Civil Society Representative from the Marshall Islands to the United Nations.
How is a spoken word poem different from a typical speech? What makes the spoken word poem as powerful as a good speech?	
Brainstorm ways of creating a spoken word poem to advocate for climate change. Use this information and prompts in the right column to determine a good starting place: There are approximately 584,000 people who are homeless in the United States. For these homeless people, their bed is a concrete sidewalk or subway bench. Many have to find a YMCA or other places to use the toilet and take a shower.	Some ways to begin: • Write as a letter, "Dear . . ." • Start with startling statistics or start with a short, strong phrase, "All humans have a right to . . ."
Hand out the **project guidelines**. Discuss the meaning of the title: "Advocating for a Just and Equitable Climate Future."	
In their small groups from the last class, students will need a lot of time to make their decision about the advocacy activity. Determine what equipment is needed.	Distribute project worksheets from the last class. The students must consult with the teacher before working on their advocacy activity.
Closing Each group takes a minute to share what they did in their small groups. IMPORTANT: Collect all work.	

Advocating for a Just and Equitable Climate Future

Lessons 3–4*

*This lesson will need two class sessions.

Goal
To complete the project, "Advocating for A Just and Equitable Climate Future." Share with the class and discuss other possible venues for publicizing students' work.

National Standards
- MU:Cr3.2.6a: Present the final version of their documented personal composition, song, or arrangement, using craftsmanship and originality to demonstrate an effective beginning, middle, and ending, and convey expressive intent.
- MU:Cn11.0.7a: Demonstrate understanding of relationships between music and the other arts, other disciplines, varied context, and daily life.

Assessment
- **Formative**: Students will receive verbal feedback based on the demonstration of critical thinking and questions raised during the discussions throughout the lesson(s).
- **Summative**: Students will receive feedback on their final project in the form of a rubric that includes the following criteria: How well does the project communicate the group's topic? Does the project include all parts of the project guidelines? How well do the different parts (speaking, background music, pictures) complement each other? Is there a balance of individual contributions to the project as a whole?

YouTube Videos
- "Greta Blasts World Leaders in an Emotional Speech at the U.N. Climate Summit": https://www.youtube.com/watch?v=DYqtXR8iPlE
- "Greta Thunberg Inspiring Others to Take a Stand against Climate Change"; The Daily Show with Trevor Noah: https://www.youtube.com/watch?v=rhQVustYV24

Other Materials
- Worksheets and other related materials for the projects

Additional Resource
- "Person of the Year Greta Thunberg [Cover Story]," *Time Magazine*, December 13, 2019: 46–47.

Teaching Process

Instruction	Suggestions/Comments
Do Now: Watch the **video**: "Greta Blasts World Leaders . . ." *How old do you think Greta is in this video? (16 years old). What makes Greta's speech so powerful?*	No need to play the entire video.
Greta Thunberg is a young citizen of Sweden. When she was in elementary school, her teacher played a video that depicted starving polar bears and the ravage of wild storms to help students understand the impact of climate change around the planet. Greta was so disturbed that she fell into a depression and stopped talking for months. She ate so little that her growth was stunted. Gradually she got better as her parents started to make changes in their eco-lifestyle, like installing solar panels, growing their own vegetables, avoiding travel by plane. When school started again, Greta told her parents that she would strike in front of the Swedish Parliament every Friday to pressure the government to make changes for the health of the planet. She sat, at first, alone, with her homemade strike sign and flyers that said: "My name is Greta, I am in ninth-grade, and I am striking for the climate. Since you adults don't give a damn about my future, I won't either." The Friday strikes grew from one girl to thousands of people. Children in other countries began following Greta's example. She came to the United States (by sailboat) to address the United Nations. In December 2019, Greta was featured on the cover of *TIME* magazine as Person of the Year. Here is a clip from an interview with Trevor Noah. **Video:** "Greta Thunberg Inspiring Others . . ." *Do you think Greta was (is) successful in her advocacy for climate change? Why? What does it mean to you that Greta was so close to your age when she began her climate strikes? Can you think of other movements where young people initiated action for change (e.g., school shootings)?*	It may be more appealing if the teacher presents this information as a story, rather than reading it from the lesson plan. It is written in story form as a helpful guide. Depending on the discussion, the teacher may want to explain that Greta has Asperger's syndrome, which may account for her strong emotional response to the video she watched in school. Should the opportunity arise, this is a good story for demonstrating that many people with special needs do powerful things for the world.

Instruction	Suggestions/Comments
Work on the final project. Students will probably need the next class to complete their project.	This may require the next class and homework.
When complete, share group projects with the class. Have group members talk about their thinking process and decisions in making or performing this project. Then, use the following prompts to facilitate a critical evaluation discussion: • *What did you especially like about this performance?* • *Was this a convincing presentation for climate change? In what ways?*	It is important that the presentations be handled with care. Teachers should establish a safe, respectful setting where students can speak knowledgeably about their experiences as creators and thoughtfully about other group projects.
Final Discussion: How has this project had an impact on your thinking about climate change? What are some things that you learned from these lessons on climate change? In what way could we reach others about taking action toward a healthy planet?	The intent of this discussion is to help students pull together all that they've learned throughout the unit, as well as making a connection to the arts as a viable form of action.

Appendix A

How to Collect Images and Sound Sources

Images

Go on Google Images for photographs, using keywords like "nature" or "natural scenes." Try to show scenes that are fairly simple, like just ocean waves or a parrot in a tropical jungle. However, also look for different geographical settings, like camels crossing a desert, Niagara Falls, a wheat field in the wind, bustling city traffic, children playing a game in Ghana, a lone island, a pagoda in the rain.

The best outcome is an 8 × 10 color picture of the image. You may want to staple it to oaktag and laminate (if needed) so the pictures can be used year after year. Have two additional pictures than you need for the class. One person from each group should come up to the displayed pictures and choose one for the group. There are two extras so that everyone has some kind of choice.

Recyclable Sound Sources

Look around the house for recyclable objects (different types of plastic containers, newspaper, empty cans, old garment items, glass bottles, etc.). Try to have a variety of timbres because too much plastic limits the sound possibilities.

With five students to a group, approximate how many groups will need bags of sound sources. Putting the sound sources in bags is an efficient way of distributing and cleaning up. Plus, the bag itself may also be a recyclable sound source.

Appendix B

Earth's Temperature Record

This link, https://climate.nasa.gov/climate_resources/9/graphic-earths-temperature-record/, will take you to an interesting graph that shows the rising temperatures on earth over the past six and a half decades. This graph can be enlarged to fit a full screen. The purpose of this activity is threefold: (a) to find out how much students know about reading a graph, (b) to demonstrate a scientific image of dramatically rising temperatures, and (c) to prepare students for the video: "Songs of Our Warming Planet."

Credit: "NASA Global Climate Change," https://climate.nasa.gov.

Appendix C

US Heat Waves

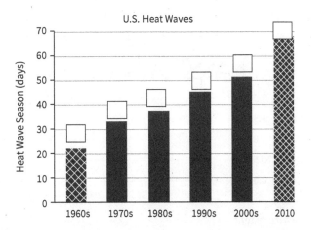

Figure 6.1. US heat waves.

Source: Fourth National Climate Assessment, Vol. II. https://nca2018.globalchange.gov.[5]

Appendix D

US Wildfires

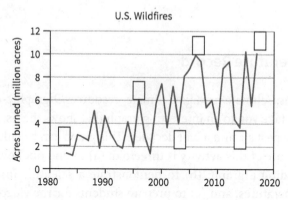

Figure 6.2. US wildfires.

Source: Fourth National Climate Assessment, Vol. II. https://nca2018.globalchange.gov.[6]

Appendix E

Arctic Sea Ice Extent

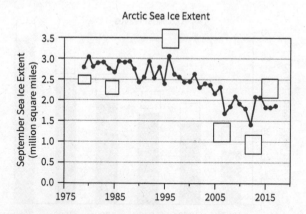

Figure 6.3. Arctic sea ice extent.

Source: Fourth National Climate Assessment, Vol. II. https://nca2018.globalchange.gov.[7]

Appendix F

US Sea Level

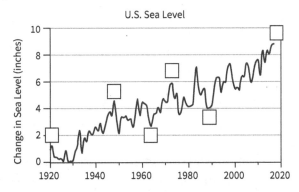

Figure 6.4. US sea level.

Source: Fourth National Climate Assessment, Vol. II. https://nca2018.globalchange.gov.[8]

Appendix G

Culminating Data Melody Project

Your goal is to create a piece of atonal music using your data melody and GarageBand loops (if this technology is available, or using percussion instruments).

GarageBand Project

1. Load your mp3 file (data melody) into GarageBand.
2. Explore some atonal loops such as ambient sounds, sound effects, etc. Select two loops that enhance the data melody.
3. Create a piece that has a beginning, middle, and end, using loops and your data melody. You can use the melody more than once if it makes musical sense to you.
4. Save in a folder.

or: Percussion Project

1. Select some percussion instruments to use with your data melody.
2. Create a piece that has a beginning, middle, and end using your recorded data melody and percussion instruments. One person will need to start and stop the recording (on phone or computer) when performing the piece.
3. You can use the melody more than once if it makes musical sense to you.
4. Record if possible and save.

Appendix H

Lyric Analysis for "Petroleum Distillation"

Background Information

Fifteen was a punk band formed in 1988 which produced numerous albums including *The Choice of a New Generation*, featuring "Petroleum Distillation."[9] Musically, punk is "loud, fast, and angry." Punk musicians sought to expose oppression, social injustice, and the authorities who created these conditions. Characterized as "in your face" music, punk music expresses the following attitude: "I don't care what you say. I will do it anyway and do it the way I want." Although "Petroleum Distillation" was released in 1992, the message is still relevant to the current day. A mouthpiece for social justice, Fifteen performed in many benefits that called for social action.

The Lyrics

Both the lyrics and the music play a commanding role in "Petroleum Distillation." According to Furness, "We can't really learn anything significant about the significance of songs by pulling the lyrics apart from the music. In the same way, we can't really learn anything significant about a piece of music by extracting it from the larger social, cultural, and political context in which it was written."[10]

In terms of the lyrics, Furness identifies three interlacing themes in the song: (a) capitalism as the oppression of society, (b) pollution as humanity's oppression of the earth, and (c) autonomy as freedom from oppression. Because this unit focuses on ecological justice, we will turn our attention to that particular theme.

"Petroleum Distillation" brings awareness to the range of pollutants that toxify our earth. By emphasizing the word "we," Fifteen clarifies that clean air, water, and other affected areas are the responsibility of everyone. Having said that, pollution is as much a personal issue as it is a political one. The second verse, for example, draws a connection between abusing one's self (e.g., drugs, alcohol) and abusing the Earth: "The water's my heart, it's been broken with booze and drugs and shooting up paste. The sun is my spirit, it belongs to all of us, I guess we're all one sick race." Essentially, the song points to the strong connection between humans and the earth.

Metaphors and Phrases Explained

1. "Paying money for four walls which leaves slavery intact." The four walls represent housing in our society. Slavery means that one must work to pay for the privilege of having a home—a reference to capitalism.
2. Pollutants, specifically fumes from cars, lead, and toxic waste point out the many ways that humans harm the earth. The reference to "booze, drugs, and paste [heroin]" represents how humans harm themselves, suggesting that abuse to one's self and abuse to the earth are one in the same.

3. The final verse offers hope that, with autonomy, humility, and integrity, people will recognize their responsibility for preserving the world community and natural environment.

Appendix I

What Should Your Friends Know?

TOPIC: _____

What can you find about the following questions? You do not need to write complete sentences.

1. Describe your topic and use interesting statistics to reinforce the urgency of the problem.

2. Who or what is affected by this problem? In what way?

3. What else should we know in order to understand the importance of this topic?

Appendix J

Culminating Project

Living in a Toxic World
Let's create a "Top-Of-The-Billboard" piece that invites listeners to think and act more responsibly about our toxic environment.

Everyone should have a say in each part of the project.

Writer/Poet (**two students**): Review the handouts that you completed in the last class. Circle some information that would catch someone's attention.

Write a three-line spoken word poem that you can read over the music. A spoken word poem doesn't have to rhyme and is meant to be a powerful statement to the listener.

Composer (**two students**): You are going to create a piece in the style of house or deep house music. You need to use GarageBand (or compatible software) for this project. Make sure you choose house or deep house music for the genre.

Listen to three loops for the following instruments: backbeat or drum set, electric bass guitar, and synthesizer. Write these on a piece of paper, then choose two that you like the best. Create a different track for each instrument. The music should be 30 seconds long.

All finished? Listen to the music and decide where to put the poem. You do not have to read the whole poem at once. Or, you could decide to put the poem in two different places. The choice is yours.

Choice 1: Record your voice over the music.
Choice 2: Read the poem live during the music.

Appendix K

The Impact on Animals

DO NOW: Watch the video, "Deforestation in the Tropical Rainforest: Impact on Animals." and consider the following questions. After the video, write down your responses to the following questions:

1. How do humans benefit from deforestation?

2. Are animal species worth saving? Why?

Appendix L

Critically Endangered Animals

There are 12 critically endangered animals listed on the *World Wildlife Fund*. When students go to the website https://www.worldwildlife.org/species/directory?direct ion=desc&sort=extinction_status, they will be able to choose an animal for their project. Students can find a picture and information by clicking on the name of the animal.

Appendix M

These Are Our Rights, Right?

NAMES: _____

Circle your topic below:

- The Right to Clean Water
- The Right to Clean Air
- The Right to a Good life
- The Right to Safety from Violent Storms
- The Right for Preservation of Animals
- The Right for Preservation of Trees
- The Right for Preservation of the Ocean

You can use the same topic as another group, but it should be something you care about. Using a computer or mobile device, do some research on this topic. The following questions should help you. Ask one person in the group to be the writer. Just write key ideas—no need for complete sentences. Use the back of this paper to take notes. You must hand this in to me before you leave class.

Prepare your argument:

1. Why is this an important topic?
2. What is the main problem? (statistics can be convincing).
3. How does this harm people?
4. What can you or others do to eliminate the problem? How would you solve the consequences of your solution? (e.g., if we eliminate cars to lessen air pollution, how would people travel?)

Appendix N

Advocating for a Just and Equitable Climate Future

Note to Teacher: In many of the units we have described a flexible final project for the students. In this unit, advocacy might have more meaning if students created their own project.

What Would This Entail?

- A level of comfort that, with some guidance and stated boundaries, the students are capable of creating a project that demonstrates their best work.
- Allowing students to work on projects that are different from other students.
- Revisiting the discussion on how to use the arts to advocate for change.
- Using the ideas from that discussion, to craft a handout that lists the students' ideas and some of your own. Here are some examples—choreographing a dance with music related to climate change; a spoken word poem with images projected or recorded on composing software (e.g., GarageBand, Soundtrap); a video project that involves music; compose a song or instrumental piece with a spoken/written introduction that explains the composition; write a letter to a congressional leader who represents your state and attach a recording of the musical project.
- It's ok to have more than one group doing the same activity because they have different topics.
- Create a project handout with guidelines for all the groups. Each group must involve music in some way.
- Provide any relevant materials that students cannot provide themselves.

What If I Am Not Comfortable with Multiple Projects?

- Create a project for small groups or the class where you set flexible working guidelines that involve music making and advocacy for climate change.

What Else?

Projects become social justice actions when they are made public. There are big ways to go public and there are, just as valuable, small ways to go public. The "public" can be a class of younger students, teachers, a school assembly, a presentation for parent's night, or a community organization. You could write an article for the local newspaper with pictures of the students' work, or you could invite a community journalist to visit the class. Anything that goes beyond the classroom is an opportunity to bring social awareness to other people.

Notes

1. Mathew Gilbert, "Farewell, Sweet Ice." In *A People's Curriculum for the Whole Earth: Teaching Climate Change and the Environmental Crisis*, edited by Bill Bigelow and Tim Swinehart, 74–76. Milwaukee, WI: Rethinking Schools, 2014, 74. Matthew Gilbert resides in the Arctic Village, where he was raised by his grandparents.
2. https://www.youtube.com/watch?v=uEb1FmsS9ec.
3. *Our Planet* is a powerful series of Netflix episodes that capture the devastation of animal habitats over time. Here is the URL for the episode "Jungles": https://www.youtube.com/watch?v=um2Q 9aUecy0.
4. https://artofquotation.wordpress.com/2018/01/13/if-only-the-bird-with-the-loveliest-song-sang-the-forest-would-be-a-lonely-place/.
5. The chart/graph in this appendix comes from the following source: Jay, A., D. R. Reidmiller, C. W. Avery, D. Barrie, B. J. DeAngelo, A. Dave, M. Dzaugis, M. Kolian, K. L. M. Lewis, K. Reeves, and D. Winner. Overview. In *Impacts, Risks, and Adaptation in the United States: Fourth National Climate Assessment*, Volume II, edited by D. R. Reidmiller, C. W. Avery, D. R. Easterling, K. E. Kunkel, K. L. M. Lewis, T. K. Maycock, and B. C. Stewart. Washington, DC: US Global Change Research Program, 2018. doi: 10.7930/NCA4.2018.CH1.
6. The chart/graph in this appendix comes from the following source: Jay, A., D. R. Reidmiller, C. W. Avery, D. Barrie, B. J. DeAngelo, A. Dave, M. Dzaugis, M. Kolian, K. L. M. Lewis, K. Reeves, and D. Winner. Overview. In *Impacts, Risks, and Adaptation in the United States: Fourth National Climate Assessment*, Volume II, edited by D. R. Reidmiller, C. W. Avery, D. R. Easterling, K. E. Kunkel, K. L. M. Lewis, T. K. Maycock, and B. C. Stewart. Washington, DC: US Global Change Research Program, 2018. doi: 10.7930/NCA4.2018.CH1.
7. The chart/graph in this appendix comes from the following source: Jay, A., D. R. Reidmiller, C. W. Avery, D. Barrie, B. J. DeAngelo, A. Dave, M. Dzaugis, M. Kolian, K. L. M. Lewis, K. Reeves, and D. Winner. Overview. In *Impacts, Risks, and Adaptation in the United States: Fourth National Climate Assessment*, Volume II, edited by D. R. Reidmiller, C. W. Avery, D. R. Easterling, K. E. Kunkel, K. L. M. Lewis, T. K. Maycock, and B. C. Stewart. Washington, DC: US Global Change Research Program, 2018. doi: 10.7930/NCA4.2018.CH1.
8. The chart/graph in this appendix comes from the following source: Jay, A., D. R. Reidmiller, C. W. Avery, D. Barrie, B. J. DeAngelo, A. Dave, M. Dzaugis, M. Kolian, K. L. M. Lewis, K. Reeves, and D. Winner. Overview. In *Impacts, Risks, and Adaptation in the United States: Fourth National Climate Assessment*, Volume II, edited by D. R. Reidmiller, C. W. Avery, D. R. Easterling, K. E. Kunkel, K. L. M. Lewis, T. K. Maycock, and B. C. Stewart. Washington, DC: US Global Change Research Program, 2018. doi: 10.7930/NCA4.2018.CH1.
9. The information in this appendix comes from the following source: Furness, Zach. "Petroleum Distillation by Fifteen." In *Rebel Music: Resistance through Hip Hop and Punk*, edited by Priya Parmar, Anthony J. Nocella II, Scott Robertson, and Martha Diaz. Charlotte, NC: Information Age, 2015. This is an excellent resource for music teachers who want short accessible information on various hip hop and punk songs.
10. Furness, Petroleum, 15.

7

Peace Unit

Introduction to the *Peace* Unit

Should schools be responsible for helping students understand and embody the aims and ideals of peace? This is an important question, and it is up to each school—actually, each classroom—to decide whether or not "peace" is teachable. We believe it is. Moreover, any teacher committed to social justice should consider connections between "peace education" and teaching toward social justice. Why? If we are committed to confronting antagonistic forces that prohibit social justice, we are, in essence, enacting a commitment to confronting the antagonistic forces that prohibit peace.

Indeed, worldwide organizations such as the United Nations provide viable tools that exhibit provocative illustrations of being with one another. For example, look no further than the Preamble to the United Nations Charter:

We the peoples of the United Nations, determined

to save succeeding generations from the scourge of war, which twice in our lifetime has brought untold sorrow to mankind, and

to reaffirm faith in fundamental human rights, in the dignity and worth of the human person, in the equal rights of men and women and of nations large and small, and

to establish conditions under which justice and respect for the obligations arising from treaties and other sources of international law can be maintained, and

to promote social progress and better standards of life in larger freedom,

And for these ends

to practice tolerance and live together in peace with one another as good neighbors, and

to unite our strength to maintain international peace and security, and

to ensure, by the acceptance of principles and the institution of methods, that armed force shall not be used, save in the common interest, and

to employ international machinery for the promotion of the economic and social advancement of all peoples,

Have resolved to combine our efforts to accomplish these aims.[1]

Education, in schools and beyond, is integral in attempting to achieve such ideals. However, an impulse-reaction to the preceding may be: This kind of education should be reserved for "social studies" classes. Instead, we believe that music educators should not be devoid of such responsibilities, and all teachers—regardless of content area specialty—must contribute in their own unique ways to aiming for peace and reconciliation. But how?

Music Lesson Plans for Social Justice. Lisa C. Delorenzo and Marissa Silverman, Oxford University Press. © Oxford University Press 2022.
DOI: 10.1093/oso/9780197581476.003.0007

While there is no consensus on "what" peace education is, or what it should look like, this should not deter us from attempting to create our own versions of peace education in our school classrooms and communities. Yet despite this lack of consensus, we know that teaching for "peace" necessitates encouraging and enacting a culture of peace. In attempting to enact a culture of peace, we, teachers, should model the following:

- Teaching about war and its avoidance as evidenced in, about, and through music and music making;
- Teaching and encouraging cooperative and harmonious relationships and relationship building (between individuals and groups of people) as evidenced in, about, and through music and music making.

So, what do we mean when we use the term "peace" in this book? For us, peace means "doing no harm," whether directly or indirectly. Peace is evidenced when there is an absence of direct or indirect violence. However, we would like to point out that simply an absence of "violence" is not necessarily the goal of peace. Rather, active cooperation and harmonious living as well as advocating on behalf of cooperation and harmonious living—all components for achieving social justice—are goals of peace.

Notes to Teacher

As we've been explaining throughout this book, social justice is "action-oriented." So, it's not enough to discuss social justice; we must attempt to make positive changes in ourselves, our communities, and the world around us. "Peace," a goal of social justice-action, is no exception here. Like social justice, peace, too, is action oriented. We might consider the oxymoron "fighting for peace." What this implies is that the lessons in this unit not only help students understand components of peaceful being; they also ask students to engage actively towards creating peaceful habits and habitats with and for others.

Although the lessons are labeled in sequence, there may be places where the teacher should insert a lesson (or two or more) according to the needs of the class. For instance, some of the lessons include creating music based on a scale or mode. If your students have not engaged in considering such musical components, it may be important to insert a lesson on "modes and scales," "intervals," "how to listen for modes/scales," and so forth. Please note: the reason for doing so is not to focus on the elements of music; rather, in order for students to create music based on a particular mode (specifically as explored in this unit) given a mode's propensity for it to seem/feel "meditative"—a tool for peaceful being—students might benefit from understanding how modes and scales work.

Here are some specific points for each section to keep in mind when teaching some or all of the Peace unit:

Mediation and Meditation

1. Social justice "action" takes on different forms in understanding music as a means for mediation and meditation.
2. There are too many songs/pieces of music to choose from for these lessons. Teachers may substitute other relevant songs that seem more appropriate for the class.

Forgiveness and Freedom

1. In order to achieve freedom, we must learn how—often under challenging circumstances—to forgive. Because of this, we can start by acknowledging our own flaws, missteps, and misjudgments, and forgive ourselves.
2. Sometimes, we must practice forgiving others. The lessons in this unit explore what that might feel like through selected music listening and music making activities. The hope here is that students will, through empathy and experiencing others' forgiveness, understand how important forgiveness of another is as a foundation for freedom.

Globalization and Community

1. We highlight some of the tensions and possibilities that present themselves in globalization through music listening and music making, namely cultural appropriation and cultural appreciation.
2. Because you—the teacher—know what might be good to assist your students in these lessons, we leave it to you to "fill in" the gaps and/or supplement the musical understanding your students will need to participate most fully in the musical activities. You might find doing so important to teach, not only toward musical matters, but also sociocultural matters.

Pedagogy for Peaceful Being

There are a few ways to build a more peaceful classroom. Primarily, teachers provide a model for more peaceful living inside the classroom in order for students to consider peaceful living outside the classroom. The first is by deciding that "peace" and peaceful being is important; the second is through the types of assignments and music making/listening experiences we create *with* students and their worlds in mind. Because conflict is inevitable—especially when children and adolescents are concerned—we must explicitly teach toward forgiveness, for without forgiveness there is no peace.

Helping Students Build a Peaceful Classroom in the Upper Grade Levels

Here are a few strategies that may help students engage with the themes of this unit:

- Have students discuss the following themes as they relate to their lived experiences, and also as they relate to the music they enjoy: forgiveness, receiving forgiveness, and reconciliation.
- Model humility and help students recognize and become humble when warranted. For example, put the needs of others in your classroom above your own.
- Teach students healthy ways to engage in conflict resolution (e.g., through discussing issues openly; de-escalating the "temperature" of a conflict by deep breathing and/or physically moving).
- Aligned with humility, the teacher should model dispositions of integrity. For example, admit any wrongdoing by showing your imperfection; ask for forgiveness when necessary; and show that you are willing to wait to be forgiven if necessary.
- Show that you are willing to change if/when necessary; teach students that sometimes we need to change the ways we engage with one another.
- Practice random acts of kindness.
- When warranted, allow time in class to focus on breathing, listening, movement, and reflection: in other words, focus on mindfulness.

None of these strategies in and of itself is indicative of peace making. Rather, the intent is to help students pay attention to more mindful ways of engaging with and for each other through mindful music making that aims to engage with and for oneself and each other.

Graphic Organizer: PEACE

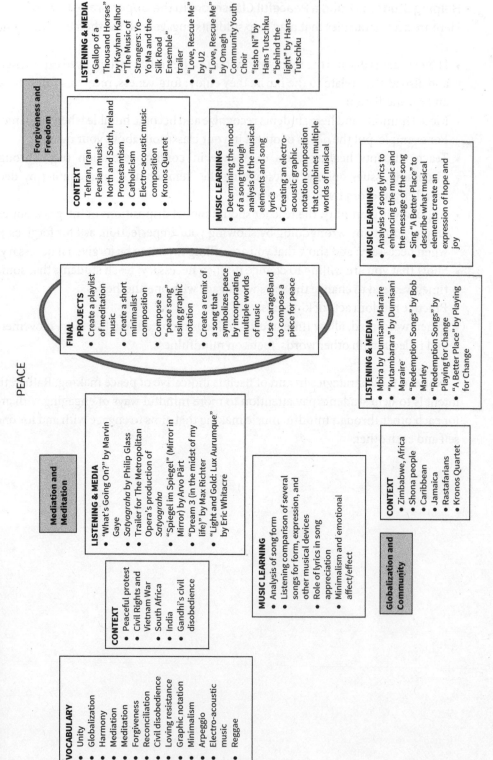

PEACE

Forgiveness and Freedom

Mediation and Meditation

Globalization and Community

VOCABULARY
- Unity
- Globalization
- Harmony
- Mediation
- Meditation
- Forgiveness
- Reconciliation
- Civil disobedience
- Loving resistance
- Graphic notation
- Minimalism
- Arpeggio
- Electro-acoustic music
- Reggae

CONTEXT (Mediation and Meditation)
- Peaceful protest
- Civil Rights and Vietnam War
- South Africa
- India
- Gandhi's civil disobedience

LISTENING & MEDIA (Mediation and Meditation)
- "What's Going On?" by Marvin Gaye
- Satyagraha by Philip Glass
- Trailer for The Metropolitan Opera's production of Satyagraha
- "Spiegel im Spiegel" (Mirror in Mirror) by Arvo Pärt
- "Dream 3 (in the midst of my life)" by Max Richter
- "Light and Gold: Lux Aurumque" by Eric Whitacre

MUSIC LEARNING (Mediation and Meditation)
- Analysis of song form
- Listening comparison of several songs for form, expression, and other musical devices
- Role of lyrics in song appreciation
- Minimalism and emotional affect/effect

FINAL PROJECTS
- Create a playlist of meditation music
- Create a short minimalist composition
- Compose a "peace song" using graphic notation
- Create a remix of a song that symbolizes peace by incorporating multiple worlds of music
- Use GarageBand to compose a piece for peace

CONTEXT (Forgiveness and Freedom)
- Tehran, Iran
- Persian music
- North and South, Ireland
- Protestantism
- Catholicism
- Electro-acoustic music composition
- Kronos Quartet

LISTENING & MEDIA (Forgiveness and Freedom)
- "Gallop of a Thousand Horses" by Kayhan Kalhor
- "The Music of Strangers: Yo-Yo Ma and the Silk Road Ensemble" trailer
- "Love, Rescue Me" by U2
- "Love, Rescue Me" by Omagh Community Youth Choir
- "Issho Ni" by Hans Tutschku
- "behind the light" by Hans Tutschku

MUSIC LEARNING (Forgiveness and Freedom)
- Determining the mood of a song through analysis of the musical elements and song lyrics
- Creating an electro-acoustic graphic notation composition that combines multiple worlds of musical

MUSIC LEARNING (Globalization and Community)
- Analysis of song lyrics to enhancing the message of the music and the message of the song
- Sing "A Better Place" to describe what musical elements create an expression of hope and joy

LISTENING & MEDIA (Globalization and Community)
- Mbira by Dumisani Maraire
- "Kutambarara" by Dumisani Maraire
- "Redemption Songs" by Bob Marley
- "Redemption Songs" by Playing for Change
- "A Better Place" by Playing for Change

CONTEXT (Globalization and Community)
- Zimbabwe, Africa
- Shona people
- Caribbean
- Jamaica
- Rastafarians
- Kronos Quartet

Introductory Lesson to Peace

Goal
To introduce "peace" as an activity (verb) as well as a "state" (noun). Importantly, "peace" itself is not an *issue* of social justice but rather a *movement* toward advancing a socially just nation.

National Standards
- MU:Re7.6a: Select or choose music to listen to and explain the connections to specific interests or experiences for a specific purpose.
- MU:Cn10.0.6a: Demonstrate how interests, knowledge, and skills relate to personal choices and intent when creating, performing, and responding to music.

Assessment/Evaluation
- **Formative:** Teacher will assess students' thinking about connections between musical "moods" and peace as a form of action for social justice by responding to specific discussion questions. Teacher will assess students' insights—musical, political, and social considerations—of potential issues as they relate to achieving peace.

YouTube Videos
- "Where Is the Love?" by The Black Eyed Peas (from 2003): https://www.youtube.com/watch?v=WpYeekQkAdc
- "Where Is the Love?" by The Black Eyed Peas featuring The World (from 2016): https://www.youtube.com/watch?v=YsRMoWYGLNA&t=6s

Teaching Process

Instruction	Comments/Suggestions
Do Now: Have "Where Is the Love?" (from 2003) playing as students enter the classroom. Write the following on the board: Listening to the song played, answer the following questions in your Listening Log: • What does this music make you think of? What scene or personal experience comes to mind from the musical selection? • What emotions do you hear in the music? • What is happening in the music that makes you think of these emotions or experiences? For example, how does speed play a part in this? How does, say, volume play a part in this? How does, say, instrumentation play a part in this?	The teacher should keep her own Listening Log in order to participate with students if/when possible. Allow students to share their responses. Total time for this activity: 5–6 minutes.

Instruction	Comments/Suggestions
Discussion Questions: • *What did you notice in this video? Who participated?* • *What were some of the questions posed in this video?* • *Consider how the issues raised in this video/song relate to "peace": What are the relationships between love and peace?* • *How did the music seem to provide an understanding of "peace"? What was happening musically that could suggest "peace-seeking"?* • *How do your thoughts related to these questions connect to "social justice"?*	These are open-ended questions to facilitate a range of responses. Love (note: this is explored in the "Love Unit") is both a verb and a noun; peace, too, can be both a verb and a noun. Consider providing your own examples to help students consider this more fully. Help the students think through the music—coming together of genres/styles. "Where Is the Love?" was first released by The Black Eyed Peas as a response to the 9/11 terror attacks. In addition to terrorism, the lyrics address numerous social ills that run counter to "loving your neighbor": racism, sexism, war, violence, pollution, discrimination of many kinds, etc. They re-released the song in 2016: #WHERESTHELOVE.
Watch the 2016 remake of "Where Is the Love?" Pair–Share Activity: Consider the following questions with a partner: *What is different about this remake? What issues does this version highlight more strongly? Why do you think this might be the case?* AND: *In what ways do we need to consider the issues raised in this remake in order to move toward peace and therefore social justice?*	Have a full-class sharing of student responses.
With a partner, choose songs that seem to point out issues that should be addressed if we are to move toward a more peaceful union. Listening Activity • Have some students share their songs with the class. • Identify the issues that run counter to world "peace." • Compare the songs and discuss how the music sets the mood for the lyrics.	This is an opportunity to talk about how the music conveys a certain mood.

Instruction	Comments/Suggestions
Exit Ticket: On an index card, write down one or two issues that are important in your life which could be addressed via a peaceful intervention (think back to the unit on "protest").	Collect cards as students leave the room and use this information as a springboard for subsequent lessons.

Mediation and Meditation

Introduction

Adolescents often experience predicaments with relationships—whether with friends or family—or other conflict in growing toward adulthood. Additionally, the news is riddled with various kinds of conflict. Because of this, it is imperative that adolescents experience other ways of navigating the world; one where negotiation, communication, and mediation are paramount to rectifying issues. Notably, when mediation is not an option, allowing adolescents to "step back" and clear their minds can be of help.

Conflict is as old and pervasive as civilization itself. When two or more parties—or people—disagree or are in conflict with each other, they may need a third party to intervene and assist in mediating—or negotiating—a more peaceful union. A mediator can steer tension into a more peaceful engagement; sometimes, the mediator can help the parties involved come to an agreement, even when no agreement seemed to be possible. Ground rules of engagement are typically established by the mediator; all parties can state their issues, though it is the mediator who helps the parties come to an agreement that benefits both parties, through compromise on both sides. Mediation can progress in a number of ways: through more open, honest communication, or through more direct means in establishing potential outcomes in which parties can agree. Sometimes, it takes an outsider to read a situation and to point out the irrational nature of the conflict. Other times, things are not so cut-and-dried or simple. So, what to do? Thus, the lessons in this section suggest the mediative and meditative approaches toward conflict resolution.

Mediation and Meditation

Lesson 1

Goal
To understand how "mediation" can work in music making through the creation of a remix/arrangement of a song.

National Standards
- MU:Pr4.2.7c: Identify how cultural and historical contexts inform performance and result in different music interpretations.
- MU:Cr2.1.8a: Select, organize, and document personal musical ideas for arrangements, songs, and compositions within expanded forms that demonstrate tension and release, unity and variety, balance, and convey expressive intent.

- MU:Re8.1.7a: Support personal interpretation of contrasting programs of music and explain how creators or performers apply the elements of music and expressive qualities, within genres, cultures, and historical periods, to convey expressive intent.

Assessment/Evaluation

- **Formative:** The teacher will assess students' abilities to work musically with one another. The teacher will assess students' understanding of the Playing for Change video as it relates to mediation and resolving potential conflicts.

YouTube Videos

- "What's Going On?" by Marvin Gaye, featuring Sara Bareilles and Playing for Change: https://www.youtube.com/watch?v=JEp7QrOBxyQ
- "What's Going On" by Marvin Gaye: https://www.youtube.com/watch?v=H-kA3UtBj4M\

Other Materials

- Percussion instruments from around the world: congas, bongos, tambourines, guiro, rainstick, maracas, clave, shakere, afuche, axatse, djembe, talking drum, table, etc.

Teaching Process

Instruction	Comments/Suggestions
Do Now: Have students do an online search on Marvin Gaye. Ask them to find three interesting facts about Gaye's life. Prior to explaining the story behind "What's Going On?" have students share what they uncover about the singer/songwriter.	Review of pertinent aspects about the Vietnam War (see the "War" unit if need be), as told in "story" form. This will be helpful to put the lesson's activities into proper context. Note: It is more effective when the teacher tells this as a story, rather than reading from a script or having the students read it silently. *Upon returning home from his tour of duty in Vietnam, Frankie Gaye and his brother Marvin Gaye stayed up all night talking, with Frankie describing the horrors of the Vietnam War: death, destruction, combat, and unfair and unjust relationships between countries at odds. This experience inspired Marvin Gaye's "What's Going On?" An outstanding political assessment that captures a most volatile period of US history, Gaye in "What's Going On?" showcases a time frame riddled with poverty, environmental concerns, war, gendered politics, racism, and more. Additionally, a lot was "going on" in Gaye's personal life: drug addiction, the death of his singing partner (Tammi Terrell), the end of his marriage, and his brother serving in the Vietnam War.*

Instruction	Comments/Suggestions
Revisit Marvin Gaye's "What's Going On?" (listened to during the "War" unit), this time as performed as a remix via Playing for Change. What do you notice about this version of "What's Going On?" How is it created? Who seems to be part of the performance? From where? And why do you think this performance of this song was created this way?	The Playing for Change (2014) video opens with an acoustic guitarist (Louis Mhlanga from Harare, Zimbabwe), who is soon joined by an electric guitarist (Vasti Jackson, from Hattiesburg, Mississippi, USA), bassist (Matt Thompson, from Chicago, USA), drum set player (James Cadson, from Los Angeles, USA), and conga player (Leo Batera, from Los Angeles, USA). The singer begins (Clarence Bekker, from Amsterdam, Netherlands) and is joined by another conga player (Paulo Heman, from Rio de Janeiro, Brazil) and a female singer (Titi Tsira, from Gugulethu, South Africa); together they form a powerful union. Additional musicians join in: • electric keyboardist Sean "POW" Diedrick: St. Ann, Jamaica; • guitarist Bobby Broom: Chicago, USA; • percussionist Jim Palmer: London, England; • percussionist Jorge Luiz Germano: Rio de Janeiro, Brazil; • the Novi Sad String Trio: Novi Sad, Serbia; • cellist Cécile Girard: Paris, France; • singer Sara Bareilles: New York, USA; • tabla player D. Chandrajit: Kanchipuram, Tamil Nadu, India The song ends with various percussion and stringed instruments supporting a vocal trio, namely Clarence Bekker, Titi Tsira, and Sara Bareilles. The last sound is that of conga player Paulo Heman. The smile Heman yields at the end of the performance is as warm as it is infectious. The cross-pollination of musical styles and the sites of video production and filming (e.g., Buenos Aires, Argentina; New York, NY; Paris, France; Los Angeles, California; Kingston, Jamaica; and Kanchipuram, Tamil Nadu, India) give the viewer a heightened awareness of issues/social concerns from around the globe.

Instruction	Comments/Suggestions
What does "mediation" mean? In what ways can music help bridge gaps between people and create spaces for "getting along"?	Take answers/suggestions from the class. If students have a difficult time answering these questions, allow them to reflect more on the Playing for Change video of "What's Going On?"
Listen to the original "What's Going On?" After listening, have students choose a percussion instrument—each one should represent different parts of the world—and start experimenting with different grooves that could "sit with" the original recording of "What's Going On?"	
Put students in three groups where each student needs to each create a distinctive rhythmic pattern that can join in rhythmic "harmony" with those in their groups, while also joining in harmony with "What's Going On?" Assign the groups to a particular "verse" of "What's Going On?" The students should analyze the lyrics and create their rhythmic parts based on the lyrics and also on "getting along" with each and every group participant. Teach the students the chorus, too, in unison. Put the parts together; student groups should play along with the recording when their verse is sung. All students should join in and sing the chorus along with the original track.	Have the original of "What's Going On?" playing in the background for the students' musical decision-making processes. If the teacher can play the guitar or keyboard, consider doing so instead of having students play along and sing along with the recording.

Instruction	Comments/Suggestions
Exit Ticket: *In what ways might what we did seem like nonviolent action or mediation?* Write two to three sentences on an index card and turn in before leaving class.	

Mediation and Meditation

Lesson 2

Goal
To consider that meditation can alleviate conflict by offering ways to "clear the mind" through musical means.

National Standards
- MU:Re7.2.6a: Describe how the elements of music and expressive qualities relate to the structure of the pieces.
- MU:Re7.2.8a: Compare how the elements of music and expressive qualities relate to the structure within programs of music.

Assessment/Evaluation
- **Formative:** The teacher will assess the students' understanding of minimalism and musical meditation as evidenced through their music making. The teacher will formatively assess the students' examination of musical meditation as connected to "peaceful being" as evidenced through their music making and music listening.

Videos
- The Metropolitan Opera trailer for *Satyagraha*: https://www.metopera.org/discover/video/?videoName=satyagraha-trailer&videoId=1223824668001
- *Satyagraha* from the *New York Times*: https://www.youtube.com/watch?v=PCGmbzRz9Ws
- "Evening Song" from *Satyagraha*: https://www.youtube.com/watch?v=qBIw017cq4k
- "Spiegel im Spiegel" (Mirror in Mirror) by Arvo Pärt: https://www.youtube.com/watch?v=z8ZScAdV8qE&t=14s
- "Dream 3 (in the midst of my life)" by Max Richter: https://www.youtube.com/watch?v=AwpWZVG5SsQ&t=16s
- "Light and Gold: Lux Aurumque" by Eric Whitacre: https://www.youtube.com/watch?v=0j2JRcC6wBs&t=8s

Other Materials

- Text and selected quotes from *Bhagavad Gita* and beyond (Appendix A)
- Synopsis of *Satyagraha* by Philip Glass: https://www.metopera.org/user-information/synopses-archive/Satyagraha
- "Two Ways of Looking at Philip Glass's 'Satyagraha'" by Joshua Barone in the *New York Times*: https://www.nytimes.com/2018/11/05/arts/music/philip-glass-satyagraha-bam-la-opera.html

Teaching Process (this lesson may take two or more class periods)

Instruction	Comments/Suggestions
Do Now: "In the still mind, in the depths of meditation, the Self reveals itself.[2]" —*Bhagavad Gita* *If you were to write music to match the above quotation, what would the music sound like? Why?*	Share responses with the class.
Consider the following vocabulary words: simplicity; purity; transcendental; balance; loving resistance. *Can you think of any person, past or present, who illustrates these words?* In small groups, students should research (via the Internet) three to five interesting facts about Mohandas K. Gandhi.	Explain to students a little bit about the *Bhagavad Gita*: Hindu scripture, written around second century BCE. Essentially, the text is an epic in which the end goal is "enlightenment." This text is central to the beliefs of Gandhi. Share responses with the class. Put select facts on the board for students to recall if need be.
Watch both the trailer and making of Philip Glass's *Satyagraha* (from the Sanskrit; an approximate translation is "truth force"). *What do you notice about the music you hear in the background of both the trailer and the making of the opera's production? How might what you hear relate to "meditation" and to peaceful being?*	*Satyagraha* is sung in Sanskrit, and is based on text from the *Bhagavad Gita*. Consider sharing the opera's synopsis (found online, among other locations, on the Metropolitan Opera's website). Most importantly, each act of this opera showcases one of Gandhi's "guardian spirits": all people from history involved in peaceful protest and nonviolent resistance and love-as-action: Russian writer and thinker Leo Tolstoy (1828–1910); Indian poet and activist Rabindranath Tagore (1861–1941); and civil rights leader Dr. Martin Luther King, Jr. (1929–1968).

Instruction	Comments/Suggestions
	Additionally, share Philip Glass's biographical details: *He was born (b. 1937) in Baltimore, Maryland. Studied composition at the University of Chicago and Juilliard, but became frustrated with "modern music" as explored and taught in the United States. He moved to Europe, studied composition with Nadia Boulanger in Paris, and worked and composed alongside virtuoso sitar player Ravi Shankar. He traveled extensively (throughout India and North Africa), and returned to New York City, where his creativity blossomed. A prolific composer, most known from his work for films such as* Kundun, The Hours, *and* Notes on a Scandal.
Listen to some of the opening of *Satyagraha*, Act 1, Scene I: "The Kuru Field of Justice"; also the closing aria, "The Evening Song" (from Act III, scene III). Ask students: *What do you notice?*	Help students by pointing out the repetitions of "cells"; Philip Glass called this kind of composing "wheel-work": short patterns of musical materials repeat, change slightly, repeat again, change slightly again, and build and build in cycles. Help students pay attention to the musical "cell patterns" (for examples, see our book's website) as well as a melodic line (another pattern; Phrygian scale) in the tenor voice (which is repeated 30 times): E – F – G – A – B – C – D – E

Instruction	Comments/Suggestions
Composition activity, the aim of which is to create something "musically meditative": Students will read through quotations from the *Bhagavad Gita* (**Appendix A**). In groups of three to four students, they will "compose" a cell/arpeggio/ short three- to four-note phrase. Using some of the techniques found in Philip Glass's *Satyagraha*, students will then manipulate the cell/arpeggio/short three- to four-note phrase in NoteFlight (or Finale or Sibelius) as follows: • Have a minimum of four voices in octaves stating the same cell/ar-peggio/short three- to four-note phrase; • Repeat it four times; • Repeat the rhythm but raise each repetition by a half-step or whole step; • Repeat this new step-wise addition four times; • Go back to **Appendix A** and choose a quotation that speaks directly to the musical content of the phrase; • Include the quotation (either spoken above or somehow mixed in) into their composition.	Provide students with an understanding of the following musical concepts: ar-peggio, octave, half and whole steps. Also, be sure to teach this activity in two parts after reading the quotations from *Bhagavad Gita* and forming a general "interpretation" of its ethos. First create the music, then add the *Bhagavad Gita* quotation. So, teach this composition ac-tivity in stages: (1) create the cell phrase; (2) transpose half/whole step; (3) include the *Bhagavad Gita* quotation. If need be, students can use the transposition key on the Digital Audio Workstation (DAW) or GarageBand, etc.
Have students share their creations with each other.	Student-listeners should provide comments on student-composers work. Model the kind of reflective listening that results in relational being.

Instruction	Comments/Suggestions
Listen to additional meditative music. As you listen, think about what these performances have in common. What makes them different/unique from one another? "Spiegel im Spiegel" (Mirror in Mirror) by Arvo Pärt "Dream 3 (in the midst of my life)" by Max Richter "Light and Gold: Lux Aurumque" by Eric Whitacre Ask students to search online for more musical meditation. Share with the class some of the music.	Facilitate discussion about the music. Analyze the form/structure of the music. Explain to students the nature/concept of "minimalism." *How does this music make you feel?* *What makes this music sound meditative?* Depending on the class, consider engaging in breathing exercises while listening to meditative music.
Exit Ticket: *How can musical meditation be mediative?* Students should write down two to three sentences on index cards.	

Forgiveness and Freedom

Introduction

This cluster of lessons examines, among other things, a few concepts that relate directly to "peace" and therefore social justice. Namely: forgiveness and freedom. Forgiveness and freedom are intimately related to one another. Without forgiveness, people cannot find freedom. And without the freedom—or choice—to forgive, we cannot lead health-filled lives in pursuit of social justice and equitable change.

Social ills exploit inequality and inequities. Too often issues do not get addressed in schools, and students do not know how else to react, other than to take out their anger and grief on classmates and friends. Finding ways and means for students to voice their feelings, hurt, and the pressures they are navigating through allows for more healthful being.

It may seem simplistic to mention this, but many adolescents hold on to resentment. Often, that resentment lives alongside love, and such dualism can cause emotional stress and distress. For example, a teenager can resent his/her/their mother (or sister or brother or friend) while also claiming to love that person. Such emotional weight is complicated and therefore confusing. Indeed, teenagers can be intensely angry at a loved one, yet be fiercely loyal, too. How to rectify such odds? One way is to teach toward forgiveness: to teach adolescents to forgive those they believe have wronged them—flaws and all. As no one is perfect, teach adolescents to forgive themselves for their anger toward those they love. And even when adolescents are "too close" to painful situations, and the anger is too fresh for forgiveness, they can learn that forgiveness is possible someday. That is a powerful lesson to learn.

The possibility of granting (and receiving) forgiveness yields a sense of "freedom." When we share our lived experiences, we are more likely to build communal ties, to create spaces for vulnerability, to allow collectivity to blossom and spread its outgrowth—namely, trust. And where there is trust, freedom is possible.

Will our students in our classrooms be able to experience freedom? Perhaps. Freedom is, more often than not, an ideal; therefore, it is fleeting and illusive. However, this doesn't mean we shouldn't teach for it. Educating our students in, about, and through music is a means toward a potentially freer end. Seeking freedom—whether personal, social, cultural, or political—is not beyond the reach of middle and high school students. So, there are several instances in this unit that introduce ways that teens can experience freedom. Even if only while the music lasts.

Forgiveness and Freedom

Lesson 1

Goal
To consider what "forgiveness" can feel like through music listening and music making.

National Standards
- MU.Pr4.2.6c: Identify how cultural and historical contest inform performances.
- MU.Re7.7a: Classify and explain how the elements of music and expressive qualities relate to the structure of contrasting pieces.

Assessment/Evaluation
- **Formative:** Teacher will assess students' sensibilities on "forgiveness" through their answers to questions, engagement in dialogue/conversations, and their creation of song lyrics. Teacher will assess students' abilities to connect their own life experiences to the meaning behind "Love Rescue Me" primarily through their own contributions—verbal and lyrical—to classroom content.

YouTube Videos
- "Love Rescue Me" by U2: https://www.youtube.com/watch?v=ZDZEqr5LR_g
- "Love Rescue Me" by Omagh Community Youth Choir: https://www.youtube.com/watch?v=P1Q8C9pMopY

Other Materials
- Forgiveness quotes: Appendix B

Teaching Process

Instruction	Comments/Suggestions
Do Now: Write the names of two people throughout history (or whom you know personally) who deserve to be forgiven. *What did these people do wrong?* *What do you think we would need to do to forgive these people?*	Consider completing this exercise, too, to model the ways to approach these questions.
Students share responses with others in the class.	Ask students to explain how they came to their conclusion.
Hand out poetry and/or quotations on "forgiveness" (see **Appendix B**). *In what ways can we relate these words of forgiveness to the people who deserve to be forgiven (from the Do Now)?*	Consider adding your own ideas about forgiveness, as well as adding song lyrics and additional quotes/poems that speak to forgiveness that you know will speak directly to the minds/hearts of your students.
Listen to U2's recording of "Love Rescue Me."	Song was cowritten, primarily by Bono and Bob Dylan; it was released on U2's album *Rattle and Hum* (1988).
Think–Pair–Share: Discuss the content of the song, its message, its means for delivering this message.	You might lead the students into considering how sometimes, people attempt to help others, but do little to help themselves; and sometimes the opposite is true. This song tries to help us see we all—no matter our station in life—need help and forgiveness; need to love and accept love.
Consider with students: *Why might some people need help?* *Why might some people need help with forgiveness?*	
Teach students to sing this song.	

Instruction	Comments/Suggestions
Watch "Love Rescue Me" by Omagh Community Youth Choir. Have a short discussion about this version of the song.	Revisit (or visit: depending on whether or not you taught the "War" unit) the Bogside Massacre, as well as the history of the "Troubles" in Ireland. Explore the context of this community group's singing of this song: https://www.irishtimes.com/news/ireland/irish-news/omagh-bombing-key-events-before-and-after-the-attack-1.3593660.
Have students write their own set of lyrics (an original verse) to "Love Rescue Me" to a person (or people) who deserves forgiveness.	
Share verses with the class.	Student-listeners should provide comments on student-composers' work. Model the kind of reflective listening that results in relational being.
Critical Thinking Prompt: *Why is music such a powerful tool in creating community as well as showing forgiveness?*	Examples: Every person can sing a song; singing the same song brings people together; when a community of people sing a song to support others, they show peaceful signs of coming together.

Forgiveness and Freedom

Lesson 2

Goal
To compose forgiveness and freedom using graphic notation while including electroacoustic components.

National Standards
- MU:Re8.1.6a: Describe a personal interpretation of how creators' and performers' application of the elements of music and expressive qualities, within genres and cultural and historical contexts, conveys expressive intent.
- MU:Pr4.2.6a: Identify how cultural and historical contexts inform the performances.

Assessment/Evaluation

- **Formative:** Teacher will assess students' understanding of "freedom" and "forgiveness" through music listening and music making (primarily through observation and dialogue).

YouTube Videos

- Ten thousand horses gallop in snow-covered grassland: https://www.youtube.com/watch?v=MvUnAsJdJ9E
- "Gallop of a Thousand Horses" performed by the Kronos Quartet: https://www.youtube.com/watch?v=eg9slDGtp-0
- "Gallop of a Thousand Horses" performed by A Far Cry and Silkroad Ensemble: https://www.youtube.com/watch?v=V8JXRXEvMKg
- "The Music of Strangers: Yo-Yo Ma and the Silk Road Ensemble" trailer: https://www.youtube.com/watch?v=qvFjOw9K8eo
- "Kayhan Kalhor: NPR Music Tiny Desk Concert": https://www.youtube.com/watch?v=jMEjPKBvhzE&t=8s
- "Issho Ni" by Hans Tutschku: https://www.youtube.com/watch?v=ofkz7yEzjvw

Other Materials

- "After U.S. Immigration Battle, Musician Kayhan Kalhor Returns to Iran" by Anastasia Tsioulcas: https://www.npr.org/2021/02/10/955787443/after-u-s-immigration-battle-musician-kayhan-kalhor-returns-to-iran
- Appendix C: "Peace Piece"
- Appendix D: Compositions Guidelines

Teaching Process (this may take three or more class periods)

Instruction	Comments/Suggestions
Do Now: Play the video of ten thousand horses galloping over the snow-covered grassland. Keep the sound of this video muted while having the audio of Kayhan Kalhor's "Gallop of a Thousand Horses" playing to accompany the video of the horses running. Ask students to comment on the emotional characteristics of the video of the horses as well as Kalhor's music.	Consider helping students if need be. Of "Gallop of a Thousand Horses," Kalhor writes, "This piece is influenced by Turkoman folk melodies which are intrinsically linked to nature, especially horses. I have tried to evoke a feeling of horses roaming freely."[3]

Instruction	Comments/Suggestions
Have students read and think through with the class the story from NPR on Kalhor's journey: "After U.S. Immigration Battle, Musician Kayhan Kalhor Returns to Iran" by Anastasia Tsioulcas. *In what ways might Kalhor seem free, despite immigration troubles and status (as explained in this article on NPR)? Despite these immigration troubles, in what ways might Kalhor seem like he has forgiveness in his heart?*	This is a sensitive area and teachers should not require students to share their thoughts. Students should not mention names or give details that might reference particular people they know who might be negotiating similar issues regarding immigration. Still, if possible, stick to the inspirational aspects of Kalhor's journey, and relate it back to the thousand horses when possible.
Watch "The Music of Strangers: Yo-Yo Ma and the Silk Road Ensemble" trailer, as well as some of "Kayhan Kalhor: NPR Music Tiny Desk Concert."	The *kamancheh*, the word literally meaning a "little arc," is an instrument found across the musical traditions/cultures of the area and land bordering Iran, Kalhor's homeland. This spike fiddle is also found, usually under other names, in Armenia, Azerbaijan, Egypt, Georgia, and Turkey. Despite political turmoil, musics of Iran and the Iranian diaspora blossom. From the centuries-old courtly tradition of Persian classical music to diverse folk music to a rich pop scene (created by pre-Revolutionary and young artists performing in the exile communities of Los Angeles and elsewhere), Iranian musics are flourishing. While Persian classical music seems to be on the rise (in part thanks to the touring and recording efforts of such groups as the Masters of Persian Music and The Silk Road Project), other genres are not quite as well-known abroad to non-Iranian listeners. While Persian classical music sits primarily among city-dwelling audiences, folk music continues to flourish in rural areas and across many ethnic minority populations.

Instruction	Comments/Suggestions
Questions for discussion: • *What does freedom sound like?* • *What places around the world need freedom songs? Why?* • *What are some examples that you know of where freedom is expressed through sound?* Listen to (selections from) "Issho ni" by Hans Tutschku. Questions for discussion: • *In what ways might this piece seem "meditative" and "peaceful" (and peace-filled)?* • *In what ways do you hear "unity" and "rejoicing"?* • *What are the "acoustic" and "electronic" components?* • *What seems "forgiving" and "freeing" in this piece?* • *How might this relate to issues of social justice?*	Introduce the students to the music and creativity of Hans Tutschku. A professor of music composition at Harvard University since 2004, Tutschku has overhauled electro-acoustic composition there. Aside from composing instrumental and electronic music, he has realized several multi-media productions, conceiving video and choreography. The human voice finds its way in most of Tutschku's compositions from the past 25 years. Tutschku has composed works that incorporate "folksongs, lullabies, prayers and children [*sic*] songs from many cultures."[4] The voice recordings are recreated and adjusted (i.e., he adjusts the pitches and tunings to "create harmony"). He juxtaposes vocal phrases, pitched and non-pitched percussion instruments, and instrumental sounds into "utopian musical works," so various ethnicities come together in unified moments of musical experiences. A 31-minute electro-acoustic composition, "Issho ni (translation from Japanese: 'together') . . . proposes an intense sound ritual. . . . It surrounds and submerges the listener, who becomes a witness and passive participant in a slow[ly] evolving illusory celebration. Elements from secular and religious sources are joining to memorialize unity and to rejoice."[5] If students are interested, consider sharing another piece, "Behind the Light": https://tutschku.com/behind-the-light/

Instruction	Comments/Suggestions
Music making (**Appendix C**: "Peace Piece") Re-perform "Peace Piece" by adding an electronic component.	Model how to conduct/interpret this graphic notation score. Consider inviting student "conductors" to interpret the score differently, too. After performing "Peace Piece," ask students: What sounded "peace-like" to you? If they are not sure, or are not convinced, that is not a problem. Ask students to include an "electronic" component to an interpretation of "Peace Piece" (they can find a "peace sound" online; record something "peace sounding" on their phone to include, etc.) and re-perform the piece.
In small groups, create an electro-acoustic graphic notation score (**Appendix D**).	
Perform electro-acoustic graphic notation scores for the class. Students will explain their composition process.	Whenever students are going to share compositions, it is critical that you first lay the groundwork for supportive listening and applause.
Reflection: *What did you like about each students' piece? Where would each song fit in understanding peace and social justice? Why?*	DO NOT SKIP THIS STEP. It is important that performers (who are putting themselves on the line) get constructive peer feedback. They need to feel that their efforts were appreciated.

Globalization and Community

Introduction

We cannot possibly know and embody "peace" or enact its possibilities unless we recognize and engage with one another as a worldwide globalized community; a global space where we engage in equity-work, justice, and ethical action, while recognizing the tensions that exist between "individuality" and "community." Because of this, the lessons in this unit explore and examine connections between music and the globalization of music as community. The hope is that by thinking through these concepts, students will make connections between peace and social justice. Teaching for social justice implies a quest for humanity and dignity. On the surface, this seems obvious; yet humanity and dignity for each and all are difficult to achieve. Why?

Notions of "globalization" and "community" are not fully innocent or positive. For instance, colonization and appropriation can and do occur, even with the most altruistic intent. Because of this, it is important to present the issues that arise when we attempt to engage with cultures, traditions, instruments, and spaces that are not "our own." On one hand, the world has gotten smaller and smaller. The internet, mass migrations, global trade, and global travel make so many aspects of the world "obtainable" and exist as potential fuel for "use" and "capital." Notably, the sharing of ideas, traditions, and cultural capital helps provide one another with a wealth of resources. On the other hand, national identities, cultural authenticities, and geographic sensitivities must be understood and honored. And when identities, cultures, and traditions are not properly understood and honored, unequal power relationships develop between and among groups. Cultural exchange must not be a one-way process where dominant groups "take" without understanding, honoring, and being sure no offense or harm have occurred.

Globalization and Community

Lesson 1

Goal
To help students understand globalization and, therefore, community through the ways in which musical traditions take root and evolve.

National Standards
- MU:Re7.2.8b: Identify and compare the context of programs of music from a variety of genres, cultures, and historical periods.
- MU:Re8.1.6a: Describe a personal interpretation of how creators' and performers' application of the elements of music and expressive qualities, within genres and cultural and historical contexts, conveys expressive intent.
- MU:Cr2.1.8a: Select, organize, and document personal musical ideas for arrangements, songs, and compositions within expanded forms that demonstrate tension and release, unity and variety, and balance, and convey expressive intent.

Assessment/Evaluation
- **Formative**: The teacher will assess students' understanding of how music can embody unification, globalization, community, and freedom through questions, answers, and dialogue. The teacher will assess students' musical reimagining of how instruments can provide a sense of unification, globalization, community, and freedom.

YouTube Videos
- Mbira music: https://www.youtube.com/watch?v=7tg8FXW79Tk

- Dumisani Maraire—Mbira: https://www.youtube.com/watch?v=6CrFfw4RTpg
- "Kutambarara" by Dumisani Maraire with the Kronos Quartet: https://www.youtube.com/watch?v=VF9OgOp6ZIo
- "Kutambarara" by Dumisani Maraire: https://www.youtube.com/watch?v=8P3RGXwLXl0

Other Materials

- Images of Zimbabwe, Africa (from Getty images): https://www.gettyimages.com/photos/zimbabwe?phrase=zimbabwe&sort=mostpopular
- African instruments (especially from Zimbabwe), such as mbira and hosho

Teaching Process

Instruction	Comments/Suggestions
Do Now: Watch and listen to the first minute (or so) of "Mbira music." *What words describe the mood and characteristics of the mbira instrument?*	Have the words "meditation," "hope," "spirituality," etc., on the board as a reference.
Students should Google search "mbira" and uncover three interesting details about the instrument.	Be sure students understand the following about this instrument: With the mbira, the class will explore the culture of the Shona people of Zimbabwe, Africa. It is considered an instrument that beckons the ancestral spirits. The instrument is said to connect generations—those deceased with those alive—of people. According to Shona traditions, this instrument "communicates" communion and unification. If unsure of this instrument, visit websites to illustrate its purposes (such as: https://mbira.org/what-is-mbira/mbira-music/the-mbira-instrument/).

Instruction	Comments/Suggestions
Listen to Dumisani Maraire—Mbira. Notice how this song embodies its lyrics: Haa ndozotambarara *I will thrive* Hiya iya iya ndichitambarara *As I grow* Hayaya ndozotamba *I will dance*	Listening to more mbira and vocal music will be helpful prior to listening to the Kronos Quartet's recording of "Kutambarara" by Dumisani Maraire. According to a translator of the Shona, Moyo Rainos Mutamba: "**Kutambarara** has multiple meanings. The direct meaning is: sitting with legs stretched forward and horizontal-rhizomatic growth of a plant. . . . Metaphorically, this translates to freedom and relaxation when one has the space to do so. Additionally, it implies thriving, growth, and the joy and freedom that comes with it. The song speaks to the liberation of Zimbabwe. It invokes freedom as the foundation for growth, thriving and joyful abandon. It also implies the spreading of Zimbabwean culture around the world. This is all worth celebrating (*I dance, dance, and dance*)."[6] For the lyrics and the translation from Shona, see our book's website.
Listen to "Kutambarara" by Dumisani Maraire. Dumisani Maraire, lead vocals and mbira Dan Pauli, hosho Oakland Interfaith Gospel Choir, Terence Kelly director Kronos Quartet Discussion questions: • *How does this piece, "Kutambarara" by Maraire, symbolize the piece's title?* • *What is the difference between "appropriation" and "appreciation"?* • *What is the relationship between "globalization" and "appropriation"?*	"Kutambarara" (Shona: Spreading), written in 1990 Be sure students read or have read the following from the composer: "*What is spreading is African concepts, perspectives, philosophies, traditions and cultures through African music. This is now being done by Africans themselves. It is true that African traditions, cultural norms and aspects have been spread for years all over the world. However, this spreading was by non-Africans which in some ways was an interpretation of Africa by non-African scholars, writers, film makers and so on. Africa and Africans have been suppressed for a long time. It was only around the 1950s that Africans resisted and fought for their rights in their own land and started gaining the political power to rule themselves and try to determine their own future.*"[7]

Instruction	Comments/Suggestions
	"The other message of the song is that not all non-Africans oppressed Africans. Actually, there were and still are non-Africans who fought and fight to free Africa from oppression financially, education-ally and politically. Music can dismantle cultural, political and racial barriers."[8] Given the preceding, help students under-stand "appropriation" and "appreciation." Appropriation means, primarily, "the unac-knowledged or inappropriate adoption of the customs, practices, ideas, etc. of one people or society by members of another and typically more dominant people or society" (Oxford Dictionary). Spreading Zimbabwean music was part of Maraire's mission while alive; he moved to the United States and taught ethnomusicology at the University of Washington. However, "cultural appropriation" concerned Maraire.
Listen to another version of "Kutambarara" as performed solo by the composer, Maraire (vocals and mbira). Compare/contrast it to the preceding version by Kronos. Think–Pair–Share Activity: Do you think the Kronos Quartet's recording of "Kumabarara" is appropriation or appreciation? Why? In what ways can we "ap-preciate" mbira music (e.g., Maraire's solo version of "Kumbarara") while also rec-ognizing our "globalized" world and our interconnected "spreading"?	The Think–Pair–Share Activity utilizes open-ended questions to facilitate a range of responses. Consider helping students think through the following issues when encountering questions about "appropriation": • *Is the Kronos Quartet's interpretation of Maraire's "Kumabarara" respectful, learned, and sincere?* • *In what ways is Maraire important to the Kronos Quartet's version?*

Instruction	Comments/Suggestions
Small Group Music Activity: Create a mixed-media work that utilizes and combines photographs and musical materials of Zimbabwe, its people, its landscapes (see Getty Images), sounds from its traditional instruments, and land with the people, landscapes, and traditional instruments of where YOU'RE from.	Students will need to engage in online research for ideas. Potentially students can create: • a slide show with a "soundtrack"; • a soundscape composition based on particular images • rap track inspired by Zimbabwe images that samples Zimbabwean instruments (for inspiration, see Maraire's son, rap artist Tendai "Baba" Maraire, particularly the single "Zimbabwe" featuring Nadine Stoddart)
Share creations with class.	Student-listeners should provide comments on student-composers' work. Model the kind of reflective listening that results in relational being.

Globalization and Community

Lesson 2

Goal

To explore how musicians from around the world can be a united, globalized community through music making for freedom and peace.

National Standards

- MU:Re8.1.7a: Describe a personal interpretation of contrasting works and explain how creators' and performers' application of the elements of music and expressive qualities, within genres, cultures, and historical periods, conveys expressive intent.
- MU:Pr4.1.8a: Apply personally developed criteria for selecting music of contrasting styles for a program with a specific purpose and/or context and explain expressive qualities, technical challenges, and reasons for choices.

Assessment/Evaluation

- **Formative:** The teacher will assess students' understanding of how music can embody unification, globalization, community, and freedom through questions, answers, and dialogue. The teacher will assess students' musical reimagining of how instruments can provide a sense of unification, globalization, community, and freedom.

YouTube Videos

- "A Better Place" by Playing for Change: https://www.youtube.com/watch?v=ZVHOqrw3Jks
- "A Better Place" tutorial by Jason Tamba and Mermans Mosengo: https://www.youtube.com/watch?v=utYPMwShykA&t=45s
- "Redemption Song" by Bob Marley and The Wailers: https://www.youtube.com/watch?v=yv5xonFSC4c
- "Redemption Song" by Playing for Change: https://www.youtube.com/watch?v=55s3T7VRQSc

Other Materials

- Chord list for "A Better Place" (Appendix E)
- Hand-held percussion instruments from around the world
- Keyboards, ukulele, guitar, any additional instruments that you have previously taught students or would consider teaching your students

Teaching Process (this may take three or more class periods)

Instruction	Comments/Suggestions
Do Now: Listen to and watch "A Better Place" by Playing for Change.	According to the creators of this song/video, Playing for Change (PFC): "Released on International Human Rights Day in 2012, this video was created through a partnership between PFC and the United Nations Millennium Development Goals Achievement Fund. We realize that true change for the good of everyone always comes from the hearts of the people, and with music we can unite together to make the world a Better Place."[9]

Instruction	Comments/Suggestions
Discussion Questions: • *What did you notice in this video?* • *Who participated?* • *Why? And what message does this send?* • *What musical styles/genres are included?* • *Why? And what message does this send?* • *How does this song—its people united and its music—seek and celebrate "freedom" through globalization and community?*	These are open-ended questions to facilitate a range of responses.
Music making of "A Better Place." Watch "A Better Place" tutorial. Play along and sing along with Playing for Change (and/or with you accompanying them on piano).	Depending on the students in your class, teach them the chords (see **Appendix E**) to the chorus of "A Better Place" and teach them to sing the song. Have students add/arrange hand-held percussion parts using instruments from around the world. Additionally, consider having students work in groups to write their own verses to include when singing the song as a whole.
Listen to "Redemption Song" by Bob Marley and The Wailers. After listening, separate the class into small groups. Think–Pair–Share Discussion: • *In what ways does this song celebrate emancipation?* • *What musical "means" does Bob Marley employ and why do you think this might be the case?*	If in their groups students are not picking up on the fact that Bob Marley sings this song without the aid of percussion—as is typical of reggae music; recall from the unit on Love—feel free to help them hear this and discuss this aspect. Marley was inspired by the folk music of the 1960s (especially Bob Dylan); this, in some way, marries folk music to the reggae community. When Marley wrote this song, he knew he was dying (of cancer). So this "anthem" was written, in no small way, to point a way forward. In this song, he wanted to be sure to teach people about the importance of overcoming not only physical slavery, but also mental oppression and domination. Only when we free ourselves of all forms of slavery can we find ourselves free.

Instruction	Comments/Suggestions
As a class watch "Redemption Song" by Playing for Change. After watching/listening, separate the class into small groups. Think–Pair–Share Discussion: • *In what ways does this video celebrate emancipation?* • *What musical "means" does this version employ and why do you think this might be the case?* • *In what ways does this version engage in globalization and community?*	Point out to students the following statement made by Playing for Change: "This video is a version of 'Redemption Song' performed around the world in honor of Bob Marley's birthday [2/6/1945]. We have reunited Bob with his son Stephen and the support of the entire planet. In this song, there is a feeling of rising above the past and moving forward with love in our hearts and hope in our eyes."[10] Help students consider the use of various musical communities from around the world (and inclusive of, e.g., instruments, clothing, dance).
Sing "Redemption Song."	Teach the students to sing the song. Consider recreating your own version of a "worldwide" inclusive re-creation of this song; mine the various identities in your school community/classroom community. Include instrumental accompanying parts that celebrate distinct musical cultures in order for students to further engage with "globalization" through music.

Appendix A

From the *Bhagavad Gita* and Beyond

Written in the second century BCE, *The Bhagavad Gita*[11] is an epic tale of war, sacrifice, and spiritual enlightenment. Set on a battlefield, a warrior, the Prince Arjuna, seeks guidance when faced with significant questions such as: What is the purpose of war? Can there be justice if death is the result? What are our responsibilities toward others? What is the relationship between justice and obligation? Is transcendence possible during times of crisis?

The following are selected quotations that represent a cross section of this spiritual dialogue between "master"—Lord Krishna—and "student":

How can we know happiness
if we kill our own kinsmen? (p. 25)

When family is ruined,
the timeless laws of family duty
perish; and when duty is lost,
chaos overwhelms. . . . (p. 26)

Be intent on action,
not on the fruits on action;
avoid attraction to the fruits
and attachment to inaction! (p. 36)

From anger comes confusion;
from confusion memory lapses;
from broken memory understanding is lost;
from loss of understanding, he [she/they] is ruined. (p. 38)

Whatever a leader does,
the ordinary people also do.
he [she/they] sets the standard
for the world to follow. (p. 44)

. . . the senses are superior
to their objects, the mind superior to the senses,
understanding superior to the mind;
higher than understanding is the self. (p. 47)

When ignorance is destroyed
by knowledge of the self,
then, like the sun, knowledge
illuminates ultimate reality. (p. 59)

Without doubt, the mind
is unsteady and hard to hold,
but practice and dispassion
can restrain it. . . . (p. 67)

Persistence in knowing the self,
seeing what knowledge of reality means—
all this is called knowledge,
the opposite is ignorance. (p. 116)

They reach the highest state
who with the eye of knowledge know
the boundary between the knower and its field,
and the freedom creatures have from nature. (p. 119)

What Is Life (Attributed to Mother Teresa)

Life is an opportunity, benefit from it. Life is a beauty, admire it. Life is bliss, taste it. Life is a dream, realize it. Life is a challenge, meet it. Life is a duty, complete it. Life is a game, play it. Life is costly, care for it. Life is wealth, keep it. Life is love, enjoy it. Life is mystery, know it. Life is a promise, fulfill it. Life is a sorrow, overcome it. Life is a song, sing it. Life is a struggle, accept it. Life is a tragedy, confront it. Life is an adventure, dare it. Life is luck, make it. Life is too precious, do not destroy it. Life is Life, fight for it![12]

Salvation of the Dawn (Attributed to Kalidasa)

Look to this day,
For it is life,
The very life of life.
In its brief course lie all the truths
And realities of your existence;
The bliss of growth
The glory of action, and
The splendor of beauty;

For yesterday is but a dream
And tomorrow is only a vision,
But today well lived makes
Every yesterday a dream of happiness
And every tomorrow a vision of hope.
Look well, therefore, to this day.
Such is the salvation of the dawn.[13]

Appendix B

Forgiveness

The weak can never forgive. Forgiveness is the attribute of the strong.[14] — Mahatma Gandhi

We must develop and maintain the capacity to forgive. He who is devoid of the power to forgive is devoid of the power to love.[15] —Martin Luther King Jr.

If we really want to love we must learn how to forgive.[16] —Mother Teresa

To err is human; to forgive, divine.[17] —Alexander Pope

For me, forgiveness and compassion are always linked: how do we hold people accountable for their wrongdoing and yet at the same time remain in touch with their humanity enough to believe in their capacity to be transformed?[18] —bell hooks

In the act of forgiveness we are declaring our faith in the future . . . we are saying here is a chance to make a new beginning.[19] —Desmond Tutu

Poems about "Forgiveness" and "Empathy"

"Forgiveness" by Christopher Soto
"This Is Just to Say" by William Carlos Williams
"I Think Just How My Shape Will Rise" by Emily Dickinson
"Forgiveness" by Emily Dickinson
"Do Not Be Ashamed" by Wendell Berry
"The Peace of Wild Things" by Wendell Berry
"What Changes" by Naomi Shihab Nye
"Kindness" by Naomi Shihab Nye
"Allowables" by Nikki Giovanni

Appendix C

Peace Piece

Paying homage to jazz legend Bill Evans (see our book's website, and also: https://www.billevans.nl/peacepiece/) while simultaneously being somewhat "genre-less," this score utilizes graphic notation to help inspire music making that is as inclusive as it is possibility-less.

Peace Piece

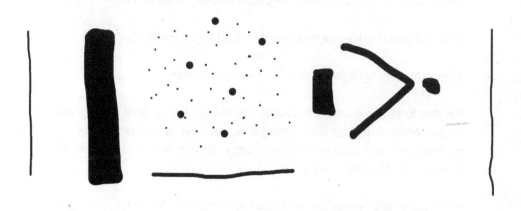

> 1 min < 2min

Figure 7.1. "Peace Piece."

Appendix D

Composition Guidelines: Forgiveness and Freedom

First consider: What does forgiveness sound like? What does freedom sound like?

Second: Find three distinct sound samples—you can use your voice, your iPhone, or anything else in the room as the basis for your electro-acoustic (graphically notated) composition.

Third: Be sure that your composition will employ all participants in this room. It should be less than one minute in length. Remember: "electro-acoustic" means the combination of electronic and acoustic sonic materials.

Fourth: The form/structure and compositional details of your piece are as follows:

- Your graphic notation piece must begin the same way it ends.
- Your graphic notation piece must include silence in some way.
- Your graphic notation piece must include one climax.
- Your graphic notation piece must include dynamic contrasts.
- Your graphic notation piece must maintain tempo stability.
- Your graphic notation piece must show when the electronic sounds should sound alongside the acoustic sounds.

One of your group members will conduct/lead the performance of this piece, while the others will be performers alongside all others in class (and assign someone to manage the electronic aspect).

Make sure your electro-acoustic piece helps us understand your beliefs on what forgiveness and freedom sound like. Be prepared to support your composition with reasons for your decisions.

Appendix E

"A Better Place" by Playing for Change

Chords

F – Bb – F – C7
F – Bb – F – C7 – F
F – Bb – F – C7
F – Bb – F – Bb
F – Bb – F – Bb

Notes

1. https://www.un.org/en/about-us/un-charter/preamble.
2. Taken from: *The Bhagavad-Gita: Krishna's Counsel in Time of War*, translated by Eknath Easwaran. Tomales, California: Nilgiri Press, 2007, 48.
3. Kalhor, K. Quotation taken from liner notes to *Kronos Caravan*. Nonesuch 79490-2, 2000.
4. https://electrocd.com/en/oeuvre/37682/Hans_Tutschku/Issho_ni.
5. https://electrocd.com/en/oeuvre/37682/Hans_Tutschku/Issho_ni.
6. Moyo Rainos Mutamba, personal communication, June 4, 2021.
7. Maraire, D. Quotation taken from liner notes to *Pieces of Africa*. Elektra Nonesuch 79275-2, 1992.
8. Maraire, liner notes to *Pieces of Africa*.
9. https://playingforchange.com/videos/a-better-place/.
10. https://playingforchange.com/videos/redemption-song/.
11. All quotations taken from: *The Bhagavad-Gita: Krishna's Counsel in Time of War*, translated by Barbara Stoler Miller. New York: Bantam Books, 1986.
12. Quoted in Cressler, John D. *Reinventing Teenagers: The Gentle Art of Instilling Character in Our Young People*. Atlanta, Georgia: Xlibris, 2004, 170.
13. https://allpoetry.com/Look-To-This-Day.
14. Gandhi, M. *All Men Are Brothers: Life and Thoughts of Mahatma Gandhi*. New York: Continuum, 1990, 155.
15. King, M. L. *Strength to Love*. New York: Beacon Press, 1963/2019, 44.
16. Mother Teresa. *Love, a Fruit Always in Season: Daily Meditations from the Words of Mother Teresa of Calcutta*. San Francisco, California: Ignatius Press, 1987, 70.
17. Pope, A. "An Essay on Criticism," 1711, https://www.poetryfoundation.org/articles/69379/an-essay-on-criticism.
18. McLeod, M. "There's No Place to Go But Up"—bell hooks and Maya Angelou in conversation, January 1, 1998, https://www.lionsroar.com/theres-no-place-to-go-but-up/.
19. Tutu, D. *No Future Without Forgiveness*. New York: Image Doubleday, 2000, 273.

8

Epilogue

Creating Your Own Socially Just Music Lessons

This is something you can do! Although the complexity of the units in this book may seem daunting, there is no reason that your units must be complex; nor must they explore "as much" as illustrated in some of the units in this book. Instead, the units and lesson plans we've created serve merely as ideas for what you can do with your students, rather than as a blueprint to be copied. What we've supplied throughout this book can be understood as potential "jumping-off" points for your own brainstorming and planning. If you are feeling overwhelmed when considering planning your own social justice units, start slowly with two or three lessons as a unit. For example, this book divides units into several clusters of lessons; however, any one of those clusters could serve as the basis for an entire unit plan.

It is important to work with topics or issues that are timely, but more so, that are relevant to your students. When students find themselves fascinated with a topic, they invest in learning, music making, and social action that may evolve from a project. And if you are unsure "what" topics might interest your students most, ask them. They will likely feel much more involved if you involve them in curricular planning. Importantly, involving students in the curricular process is, in and of itself, a step toward recognizing ways to shift the "power dynamics" in a classroom. So, consult with your students as you plan, if and when you feel the time is right to do so.

Notably, social action is not always measured by, say, protest marches, sit-ins, or rallies. Social action means to make an issue public. Consider, for example, showcasing some of your students' work as part of a concert. Other ideas might include a classroom performance for parents, family, or younger students. Students could also display a video in the front hall that highlights their music making projects with some explanatory narrative about the topic: why this topic is important, and suggested solutions for change. In other words, your students' work is a means of educating others about something worth thinking about.

Finding a Topic or Issue

Topics can be political (e.g., "War" or "Protest in America"), conceptual (e.g., "Love" or "Peace"), or person-centered (e.g., "Beethoven Meets Spider-Man" or "Chavez"). In all accounts, the topic should be grounded in an issue of social justice. Such topics are usually best when they relate to students' lived experiences.

Music Lesson Plans for Social Justice. Lisa C. Delorenzo and Marissa Silverman, Oxford University Press. © Oxford University Press 2022.
DOI: 10.1093/oso/9780197581476.003.0008

At the time this book was written, schools were shuttered due to the COVID-19 pandemic. As a secondary general music teacher during this time, perhaps consider the following starter questions when planning units and/or topics for your classroom: "Why is this pandemic having a greater impact on people of color in America?" or "What freedoms have we lost (or gained) from complying with state regulations?" or "Is virtual learning equitable to in-person classroom learning?"

Inspiration for a topic can come from a song, a poem, a story, a news item, an invention, and more. In essence, stay attuned to issues that impact people and listen to what students talk about. Adolescence is a time when students are particularly sensitive to inequities, cultural identities, and social-emotional development. Teaching about issues of social justice through music has the impetus for empowering students and emphasizing the value of community for creating change.

Now What?

Creating lessons that have depth and breadth is a little like learning a challenging piece of music. As you become more familiar with the various "technical" layers (e.g., notes, fingerings, bowings), attention shifts to questions about how to make the music more meaningful: Where is the climax of the music? How does the structure of the piece lend itself to the overarching emotional scheme? What is the context of this music and how does that inform the meaning of the music, and therefore its performance?

In the same vein, a topic of social justice requires both knowing the context of the issue and asking questions that lead to information which may not have been apparent at first glance. You don't have to be an expert on the topic, but you do need to ask the kinds of questions that yield purposeful information from a variety of sources.

For example, when reflecting about, of, and through the unit "Climate Change," we knew only surface-level information about global warming. The more we read—internet-based resources, articles, newspaper provocations—the more questions emerged. What causes global warming? How does global warming affect humans and non-humans? What do we know about the damage of global warming over time? We soon realized that unusually hot summers were only the "tip of the iceberg." Indeed, as the axiom goes: The more we learn, the more we realize how little we know. Thus, more learning yielded more learning, and so it went. Additionally, the more we learned and were open to learning, the more we realized some of our assumptions were not true. At the start of this project, we thought of global warming as a simple rise in temperatures over time, never stopping to think about its egregious impact on human life, rising sea levels, animal/flora habitats, and more. Ironically, global warming persists due to human-created industries like factories, jet planes, and deforestation. This cyclical mess was the conceptual starting point for introductory lessons yielding a more refined sense of place and space.

Drowning in Information

If you take brief notes while unearthing information about a topic, keywords, themes, and ideas for lessons will begin to emerge. Your information, which once seemed like a spaghetti of facts, begins to fall into categories. At that point, it helps to design one or two "essential questions" that bring a variety of layers into clearer focus. Because of this, we created graphic organizers to systemize our information and visualize the scope of the unit. You may have a different way of working. Still, one good thing about a graphic organizer: it gives the principal or arts supervisor a comprehensive sketch of the purpose, materials, and contextual information that undergird the units of study and individual lesson plans.

How Do I Connect This to Music Learning?

The essence of teaching issues of social justice through music is the ability to balance the lessons so that music making remains at the forefront but serves to illuminate the social justice piece as well. Active music making prompts students to think like artists and creative people. The question, "How would (or how could) artists respond to inequities or trauma?" plays a key role in helping you plan lessons that connect a seemingly non-musical concept or event with a musical response. Consider these artistic practices: visual arts, poetry, music, theater, dance, and literature. In each case there are numerous examples of artists who express emotional responses with artistic clarity: for example, musicals such as *Rent*, paintings such as Edvard Munch's *The Scream*, literature such as *I Know Why the Caged Bird Sings*, or spoken word such as "The Hill We Climb" by Amanda Gorman at President Biden's 2021 inauguration ceremony. Existing artistic creations provide models and ideas for potential projects that are "arts intensive" while also speaking to matters of social justice.

Other Considerations

Each lesson should have some music making activity that challenges students to begin the abstract process of connecting social justice issues with musical responses. We like to work toward culminating projects, which take students a step beyond the musical activities they have experienced during each lesson. Often the musical activities in lessons are sequenced over time, and give students the tools they need for creating meaningful culminating projects. For this reason, it helps to envision a culminating project before planning the lessons. This gives the cluster of lessons direction and purpose.

Notably, too, culminating projects and musical activities in which the end result is open and co-constructed provide students with choice, ownership, responsibility, and flexibility. Too often in schools, students are not afforded opportunities to find themselves in what they do. Creative openings can be such instances where students not only find themselves, but find who they can be. And the more students are able to explore their own decision-making processes, creative problem-solving abilities, dispositions, and habits, as well as develop a willingness to try, fail, and try again, the more likely they will be able to understand the power and potency of choice.

We share the belief that good teaching includes a variety of musical genres from around the globe, especially popular musics. Moreover, any opportunity to bring in music of diverse cultures provides a way to expand the unit beyond the school community, be it local or national. Many issues of social justice have counter-responses in other countries. Sometimes a global view is important for experiencing the commonalities and differences in how people utilize and engage with the arts to make a statement. On the other hand, a telescopic dive into a case study (e.g., a first-person narrative of a refugee's flight from persecution) has a way of humanizing issues of social justice on a personal level.

Embrace Technology

Adolescents have rich musical minds that often lay untapped when many music teachers define music literacy solely as the ability to read music notation. Standard Western notation is particularly limiting, as it confines students' music making to what they can notate. Graphic notation and other forms of "non-traditional" notation, however, are extremely useful in coding complex musical ideas which may or may not be tonal, metrical, rhythmically sophisticated, or timbral in nature.

The use of technology allows students to compose at their musical levels without needing traditional, and often very particular, performance skills or notation-reading abilities. In this book, we have designed musical projects through GarageBand and iMovie with the understanding that other technologies and software (e.g., Soundtrap and other Digital Audio Workstations or DAWs, Audacity, or ChromeBooks) offer similar and/or enhanced tools for creating. We have tried to design technology-based projects that are accessible to students, knowing that the technology tools you use in your school community may be better suited to your students' needs.

In short, the use of music technology offers infinite possibilities for students in the music making process. Because there are so many choices, music technologies often help give students some options as starting points. The key in creative work is structuring musical tasks so as to give latitude without overwhelming your students. Too much latitude and students will spend most of the time trying to narrow down their choices. Not enough latitude confines student music making to simple sound bytes rather than meaningful artistic responses.

As always, the music teacher must "try out" the project first, not only to check its accessibility for students' diverse abilities, but also to become confident when facilitating creative technological work in the classroom. Consequently, you want to know the pitfalls and possibilities before launching a composition project via technology. That said, the use of technology has many entry points for different levels of musical thinking. Indeed, music technology tools are just like other more "traditional" musical instruments; there is a learning curve, and the tools possess limitless potential for compositional and creative processes.

Concluding Remarks

Like technology, the world is constantly changing. This dynamic, fluid process of change has an impact on social issues, popular and contemporary music, and the political climate. We hope, therefore, that music teachers will use this book with flexibility. Songs may go out of date, issues of social importance may be overshadowed by other issues of social urgency, and the schools themselves undergo change in leadership that may or may not be supportive of this approach to music education. However, across the country, schools are adjusting their mission to include social justice education. One of your many responsibilities is to advocate for the arts as an important vehicle for expressing meaningful connections with the world in which we live.

Teaching music in tandem with issues of social justice is a unique planning and teaching opportunity. Undoubtedly it requires more preparation than other kinds of lessons, but it is as stimulating and challenging for the teacher as it is for the students. Those of us who never tire of learning and who view life as a never-ending mystery are usually drawn to the magnitude and minutia of how the world works.

As *musicians*, we have an extraordinary medium for exploring and expressing our innermost feelings.

As *advocates* for social justice, we find social inequities unacceptable and look to the arts as a call for change.

And, as *music teachers* we continually seek ways to inspire artistry in our students, while also giving them the tools they need to advocate for a more equitable, peaceful society.

Index